SIDE by SIDE Plus

BOOK 3

Life Skills, Standards, & Test Prep

Steven J. Molinsky • Bill Bliss

Illustrated by Richard E. Hill

Dedicated to Tina Carver with gratitude for her inspiration and contribution to the development of the original *Side by Side* program.

Steven J. Molinsky
Bill Bliss

Side by Side Plus, Book 3

Pearson Education, 10 Bank Street, White Plains, NY 10606

Editorial director: *Pam Fishman*
Vice president, director of design and production: *Rhea Banker*
Director of electronic production: *Aliza Greenblatt*
Director of manufacturing: *Patrice Fraccio*
Senior manufacturing manager: *Edith Pullman*
Director of marketing: *Oliva Fernandez*
Production editor: *Diane Cipollone*
Senior digital layout specialists: *Wendy Wolf; Warren Fischbach; Lisa Ghiozzi*
Text design: *Wanda España, Wee Design Group; Wendy Wolf*
Cover design: *Wanda España, Wee Design Group; Warren Fischbach*
Realia creation: *Wendy Wolf; Warren Fischbach*
Image archivist: *Paula Williams*
Illustrations: *Richard E. Hill*
Principal photographer: *Paul I. Tañedo*
Contributing authors: *Laura English, Elizabeth Handley, Meredith Westfall*
Manager, visual research: *Beth Brenzel*
Image permission coordinator: *Angelique Sharps*
Photo researcher: *Teri Stratford*

Additional photos: p. 10a Burger/Photo Researchers, Inc.; p. 10b Wendy Wolf; p. 10c (*top*) Dennis O'Clair/Getty Images Inc./Stone Allstock, (*center*) Owen Franken/CORBIS, (*bottom*) William Manning/CORBIS; p. 20a (*middle, left*) Tony Freeman/PhotoEdit Inc., (*middle, center*) John Giustina/Getty Images, (*middle, right*) Jim Naughten/Getty Images, (*bottom, left*) John Lund/Drew elly/Getty Images, (*bottom, center*) iStockphoto, (*bottom, right*) JGI/Getty Images; p. 20c (*first*) Emanuel Gottlieb Leutze/Bettmann/CORBIS, (*second*) Joseph Sohm/Corbis/Bettmann, (*third*) John Trumbull/Bettmann/CORBIS, (*fourth*) The Granger Collection, New York; p. 20d (*top*) Corcoran Gallery of Art, painted by Gilbert Stuart/Corbis/Bettmann, (*middle*) Don Troiani, (*bottom*) painter Mathew Brady, photographer Alexander Gardner/Library of Congress; p. 20e (*top*) CORBIS-NY, (*bottom*) Bettmann/CORBIS; p. 33 (*top*) Alon Reininger/Contact Press Images Inc., (*bottom*) ©Underwood & Underwood/CORBIS; p. 34 (*top, left*) Naoki Okamoto/Black Star, (*top, center*) Michael Coyne/Black Star, (*top, right*) M. Granitsas/The Image Works, (*middle, left*) Rolf Hicker Photography/Alamy, (*middle, center*) Eye Ubiquitous/CORBIS, (*middle, right*) Stephen Ferry/Liaison Agency, Inc., (*bottom*) Michael Coyne/Black Star; p. 50a (*top*) Ilhan Ramic, (*bottom*) Tony Freeman/PhotoEdit Inc.; p. 50c Tanya Constantine/Getty Images; p. 65 (*top, right*) K. H. Photo/International Stock Photography Ltd., (*upper middle, right*) Spencer Grant/PhotoEdit, (*lower middle, right*) Ken Fisher/Stone, (*bottom, left*) Carrie E. Crane, (*bottom, center*) LookEngland/Alamy, (*bottom, right*) Carrie E. Crane; p. 66 (*top, left*) Paul Chesley/Stone, (*top, center*) Suzanne & Nick Geary/Stone, (*top, right*) Natalie Fobes/Stone, (*middle, left*) Greatstock Photographic Library/Alamy, (*middle, center*) Juan Carlos Ulate/Hulton/Archive, (*middle, right*) The Examiner, Mark Costantini/AP/Wide World Photos, (*bottom*) Monkey Business/Fotolia (*top*) Jeffrey Smith/iStockphoto, (*bottom*) Eric Fowke/PhotoEdit Inc.; p. 110d (*top*) Eric Fowke/PhotoEdit Inc., (*middle*) Will Hart; p.111 (*top*) Eric Risberg/AP/Wide World Photos, (*bottom, left*) ©The Walt Disney Company. All Rights Reserved./The Neal Peters Collection, (*bottom, right*) Mike Blake/Reuters/Liaison Agency, Inc.; p. 112 (*top, left*) ©Paul A. Souders/CORBIS, (*top, center*) Eye Ubiquitous/SuperStock, (*top, right*) Richard Lord/PhotoEdit, (*middle, left*) ©David & Peter Turnley/CORBIS, (*middle, center*) Corbis Bridge/Alamy, (*middle, right*) Yann Arthus-Bertrand/CORBIS, (*bottom*) Jupiterimages/SuperStock; p. 130b (*left, man in dress shirt*) SuperStock, Inc, (*left, woman in skirt*) Ryuichi Sato/Getty Images, (*left, sneakers*) Getty Images, Inc./Stockdisk, (*left, jeans*) Dorling Kindersley Media Library, (*left, tee shirts*) Raimund Koch/Getty Images, (*right, man in dress shirt*) Dorling Kindersley Media Library, (*right, jeans*) Peter Griffith/Getty Images, (*right, woman in skirt*) Ken Reid/Getty Images, (*right, sneakers*) Getty Images, Inc./Stockdisc, (*right, tee shirts*) Joerg Schwanke/SuperStock, Inc.; p. 144b, Radius Images/Glow Images; p. 145 Thomas Boehm/Alamy; p. 146 (*row 1, far left*) John Terence Turner/FPG International LLC, (*row 1, second from left*) T. Zuidema/The Image Works, (*row 1, second from right*) John Eastcott/Yva Momatiuk/Stock Boston, (*row 1, far right*) Topic Photo Agency/age footstock, (*row 2, far left*) Caroline Penn/CORBIS, (*row 2, second from left*) Massimo Pizzocaro/Alamy, (*row 2, second from right*) VCG/FPG International LLC, (*row 2, far right*) SuperStock, Inc., (*row 3, center*) Massimo Pizzocaro/Alamy, (*row 4, far left*) Jonathan Blair/CORBIS, (*row 4, second from left*) Spencer Grant/PhotoEdit, (*row 4, center*) Talby/CORBIS, (*row 4, second from right*) Fujifotos/The Image Works, (*row 4, far right*) Elyse Lewin/The Image Bank; p. 147 (*top, left*) Gary Buss/FPG International LLC, (*top, center*) Richard Lord/The Image Works, (*top, right*) SuperStock, (*bottom, far left*) SuperStock, Inc., (*bottom, second from left*) Gary A. Conner/PhotoEdit, (*bottom, second from right*) Myrleen Cate/PhotoEdit, (*bottom, far right*) Mart of Images/Alamy.

Library of Congress Cataloging-in-Publication Data

Molinsky, Steven J.
Side by side plus: life skills, standards & test prep / Steven J. Molinsky, Bill Bliss; illustrated by Richard E. Hill.— 3rd ed.
v. cm.
ISBN-13: 978-0-13-240256-9 (student book)
1. English language—Conversation and phrase books. 2. English language—Textbooks for foreign speakers. I. Bliss, Bill. II. Molinsky, Steven J. Side by side. III. Title.
PE1131.M584 2008
428.3'4—dc22
2007026849

Pearson Longman on the Web
PearsonLongman.com offers online resources for teachers and students.
Access our Companion Websites, our online catalog, and our local offices around the world.
Visit us at longman.com.

ISBN 978-0-13-240256-9; 0-13-240256-4

Printed in the United States of America
10 11 12 13 14 – V082 – 18 17 16 15 14 13

CONTENTS

Red type indicates new standards-based lessons.

Red type indicates new standards-based lessons.

Dear Friends,

Welcome to ***Side by Side Plus***—a special edition for adult learners that offers an integrated standards-based and grammar-based approach to language learning!

Flexible Language Proficiency *Plus* Life Skills

The core mission of *Side by Side Plus* is to build students' general language proficiency so they can use English flexibly to meet their varied needs, life circumstances, and goals. We strongly believe that language teachers need to preserve their role as true teachers of language even as we fill our lesson plans with required life-skill content and prepare students for standardized tests. Our program helps you accomplish this through a research-based grammatical sequence and communicative approach in which basic language lessons in each unit lead to standards-based lessons focused on students' life-skill roles in the community, family, school, and at work.

Keys to Promoting Student Persistence and Success

Student-Centered Learning The core methodology of *Side by Side Plus* is the guided conversation—a brief, structured dialog that students practice in pairs and then use as a framework to create new conversations. Through this practice, students work together to develop their language skills "side by side." They are not dependent on the teacher for all instruction, and they know how to learn from each other. This student-centered methodology and the text's easy-to-use format enable students to study outside of class with any speaking partner—a family member, a friend or neighbor, a tutor, or a co-worker, even if that person is also an English language learner. If students need to attend class intermittently or "stop out" for a while, they have the skills and text material to continue learning on their own.

Meaningful Instruction Relevant to Students' Lives Throughout the instructional program, civics topics and tasks connect students to their community, personalization questions apply lesson content to students' life situations, and critical-thinking activities build a community of learners who problem-solve together and share solutions.

Extending Learning Outside the Classroom The magazine-style Gazette sections in *Side by Side Plus* provide motivating material for students to use at home. Feature articles, vocabulary enrichment, and other activities reinforce classroom instruction through high-interest material that

students are motivated to use outside of class. A bonus Audio CD offers entertaining radio program-style recordings of key Gazette activities. (See the inside back cover for a description of other media materials and software designed to extend learning through self-study.)

Sufficient Practice + Frequent Assessment = Success Students need to experience success as language learners. While other programs "cover" many learning objectives, *Side by Side Plus* offers students carefully-sequenced intensive practice that promotes mastery and the successful application of language skills to daily life. Students can observe their achievement milestones through the program's frequent assessments, including check-up tests and skills checklists in the text and achievement tests in the accompanying workbook.

The "Fun Factor" We believe that language instruction is most powerful when it is joyful. There is magic in the power of humor, fun, games, and music to encourage students to take risks with their emerging language, to "play" with it, and to allow their personalities to shine through as their language skills increase. We incorporate these elements into our program to motivate students to persist in their language learning not only because they need it, but also because they enjoy it.

Multilevel Instruction *Side by Side Plus* provides exceptional resources to support multilevel instruction. The Teacher's Guide includes step-by-step instructions for preparing below-level and at-level students for each lesson and hundreds of multilevel activities for all students, including those above-level. The accompanying Multilevel Activity & Achievement Test Book and CD-ROM offer an array of reproducible multilevel worksheets and activities.

We hope your students enjoy using *Side by Side Plus*. We are confident that these resources will help them persist and succeed through a language learning experience that is effective . . . relevant to their lives . . . and fun!

Steven J. Molinsky
Bill Bliss

Guide to Life Skills, Standards, & Test Prep Features

Side by Side has helped over 25 million students worldwide persist and succeed as language learners. Now, in this special edition for adult learners in standards-based programs, ***Side by Side Plus*** builds students' general language proficiency *and* helps them apply these skills for success meeting the needs of daily life and work.

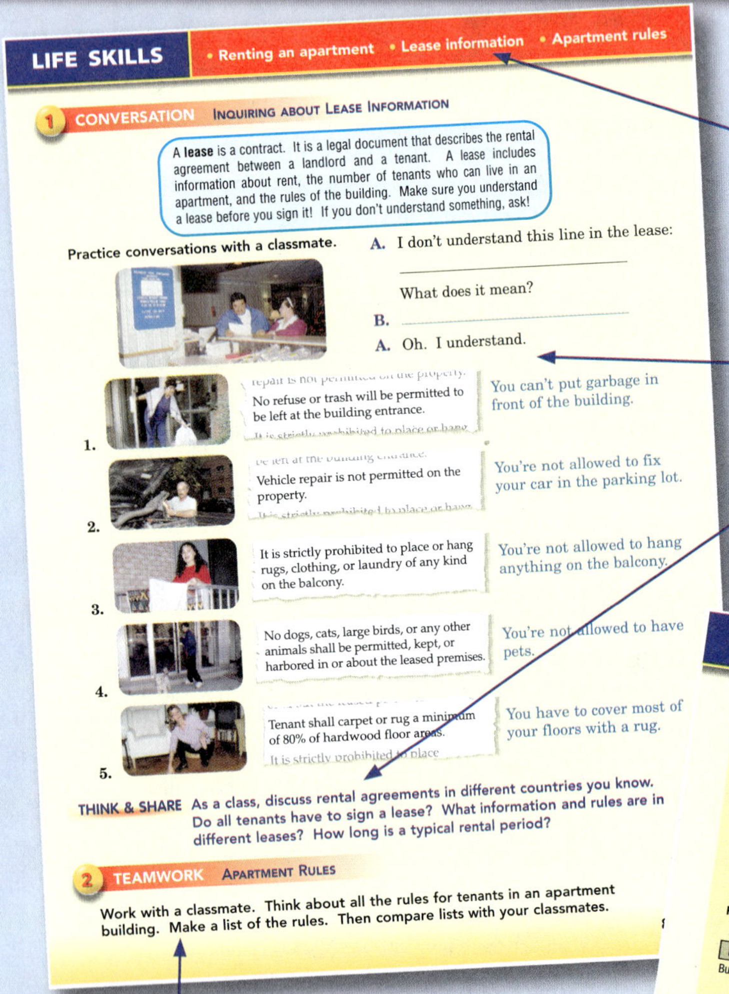

LIFE SKILLS • Renting an apartment • Lease information • Apartment rules

1 CONVERSATION INQUIRING ABOUT LEASE INFORMATION

A **lease** is a contract. It is a legal document that describes the rental agreement between a landlord and a tenant. A lease includes information about rent, the number of tenants who can live in an apartment, and the rules of the building. Make sure you understand a lease before you sign it! If you don't understand something, ask!

Practice conversations with a classmate.

A. I don't understand this line in the lease: ______ What does it mean?
B. ______
A. Oh. I understand.

1. No refuse or trash will be permitted to be left at the building entrance. — You can't put garbage in front of the building.
2. Vehicle repair is not permitted on the property. — You're not allowed to fix your car in the parking lot.
3. It is strictly prohibited to place or hang rugs, clothing, or laundry of any kind on the balcony. — You're not allowed to hang anything on the balcony.
4. No dogs, cats, large birds, or any other animals shall be permitted, kept, or harbored in or about the leased premises. — You're not allowed to have pets.
5. Tenant shall carpet or rug a minimum of 80% of hardwood floor areas. — You have to cover most of your floors with a rug.

THINK & SHARE As a class, discuss rental agreements in different countries you know. Do all tenants have to sign a lease? What information and rules are in different leases? How long is a typical rental period?

2 TEAMWORK APARTMENT RULES

Work with a classmate. Think about all the rules for tenants in an apartment building. Make a list of the rules. Then compare lists with your classmates.

Standards-based lessons at the end of every unit apply students' language learning to their life-skill roles in the community, family, school, and at work. Students develop the key competencies included in CASAS, BEST Plus, EFF, SCANS, Model Standards, and other major state and local curriculum frameworks and assessment systems.

Real-life conversation practice in authentic life-skill situations gets students talking through interactive pair work. **Extensive photographs and illustrations** provide clear contexts and support vocabulary learning.

Critical thinking and **problem-solving activities** help students focus on issues and problems and share ideas, experiences, and solutions.

Teamwork activities promote cooperative learning as students work together in pairs, groups, or as a class to share information and complete tasks.

Realia-based reading activities include yellow pages listings, maps, job applications, utility bills, workplace messages, medical appointment cards, store sale signs, advertisements, coupons, a health care poster, an accident report, a rental agreement, an apartment building notice, an employee manual, and a medical history form.

Life skills writing activities include lists, notes, personal information forms, employment application forms, a cover letter, and a resume.

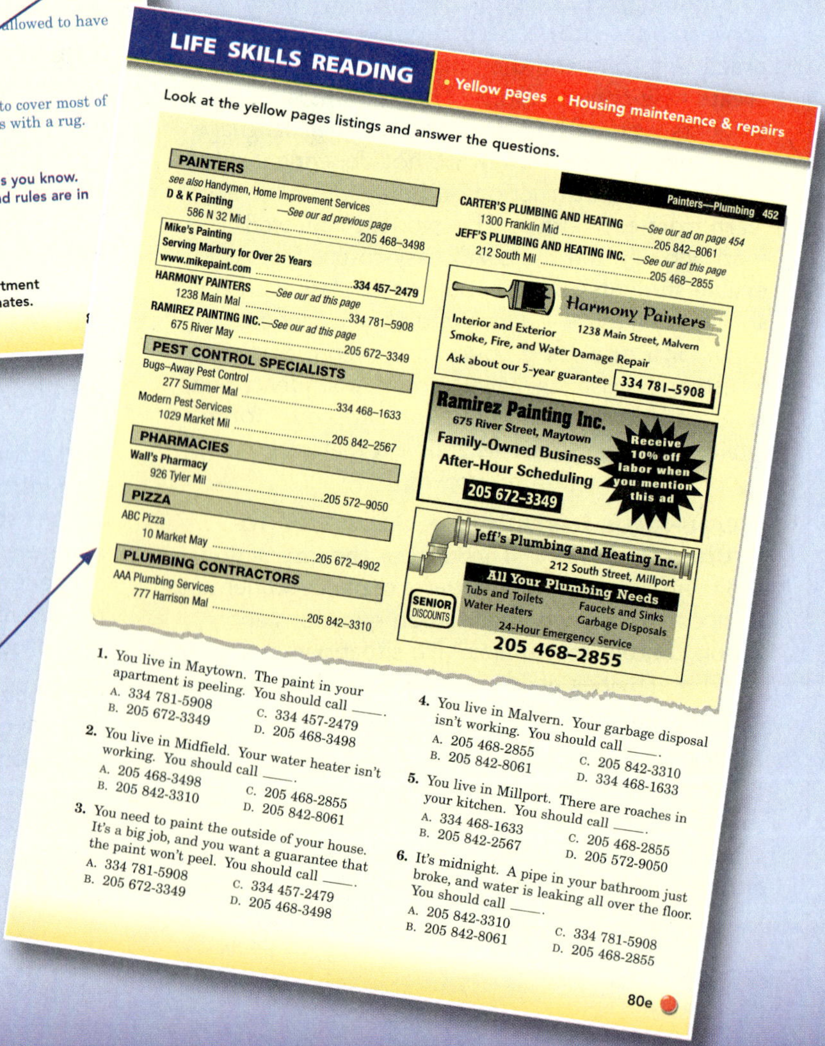

LIFE SKILLS READING • Yellow pages • Housing maintenance & repairs

Look at the yellow pages listings and answer the questions.

PAINTERS
see also Handymen, Home Improvement Services
D & K Painting 586 N 32 Mid —See our ad previous page 205 468-3498
Mike's Painting Serving Marbury for Over 25 Years www.mikepaint.com 334 457-2479
HARMONY PAINTERS 1238 Main Mal —See our ad this page 334 781-5908
RAMIREZ PAINTING INC. 675 River May —See our ad this page 205 672-3349

PEST CONTROL SPECIALISTS
Bugs-Away Pest Control 277 Summer Mal 334 468-1633
Modern Pest Services 1029 Market Mil 205 842-2567

PHARMACIES
Wall's Pharmacy 926 Tyler Mil 205 572-9050

PIZZA
ABC Pizza 10 Market May 205 672-4902

PLUMBING CONTRACTORS
AAA Plumbing Services 777 Harrison Mal 205 842-3310

Painters—Plumbing 452

CARTER'S PLUMBING AND HEATING 1300 Franklin Mid —See our ad on page 454 ....205 842-8061
JEFF'S PLUMBING AND HEATING INC. 212 South Mil —See our ad this page 205 468-2855

Harmony Painters
Interior and Exterior
1238 Main Street, Malvern
Smoke, Fire, and Water Damage Repair
Ask about our 5-year guarantee 334 781-5908

Ramirez Painting Inc.
675 River Street, Maytown
Family-Owned Business
After-Hour Scheduling
205 672-3349
Receive 10% off labor when you mention this ad

Jeff's Plumbing and Heating Inc.
212 South Street, Millport
All Your Plumbing Needs
Tubs and Toilets
Water Heaters
Faucets and Sinks
Garbage Disposals
SENIOR DISCOUNTS
24-Hour Emergency Service
205 468-2855

1. You live in Maytown. The paint in your apartment is peeling. You should call ____.
A. 334 781-5908 B. 205 672-3349 C. 334 457-2479 D. 205 468-3498

2. You live in Midfield. Your water heater isn't working. You should call ____.
A. 205 468-3498 B. 205 842-3310 C. 205 468-2855 D. 205 842-8061

3. You need to paint the outside of your house. It's a big job, and you want a guarantee that the paint won't peel. You should call ____.
A. 334 781-5908 B. 205 672-3349 C. 334 457-2479 D. 205 468-3498

4. You live in Malvern. Your garbage disposal isn't working. You should call ____.
A. 205 468-2855 B. 205 842-8061 C. 205 842-3310 D. 334 468-1633

5. You live in Millport. There are roaches in your kitchen. You should call ____.
A. 334 468-1633 B. 205 842-2567 C. 205 468-2855 D. 205 572-9050

6. It's midnight. A pipe in your bathroom just broke, and water is leaking all over the floor. You should call ____.
A. 205 842-3310 B. 205 842-8061 C. 334 781-5908 D. 205 468-2855

80e

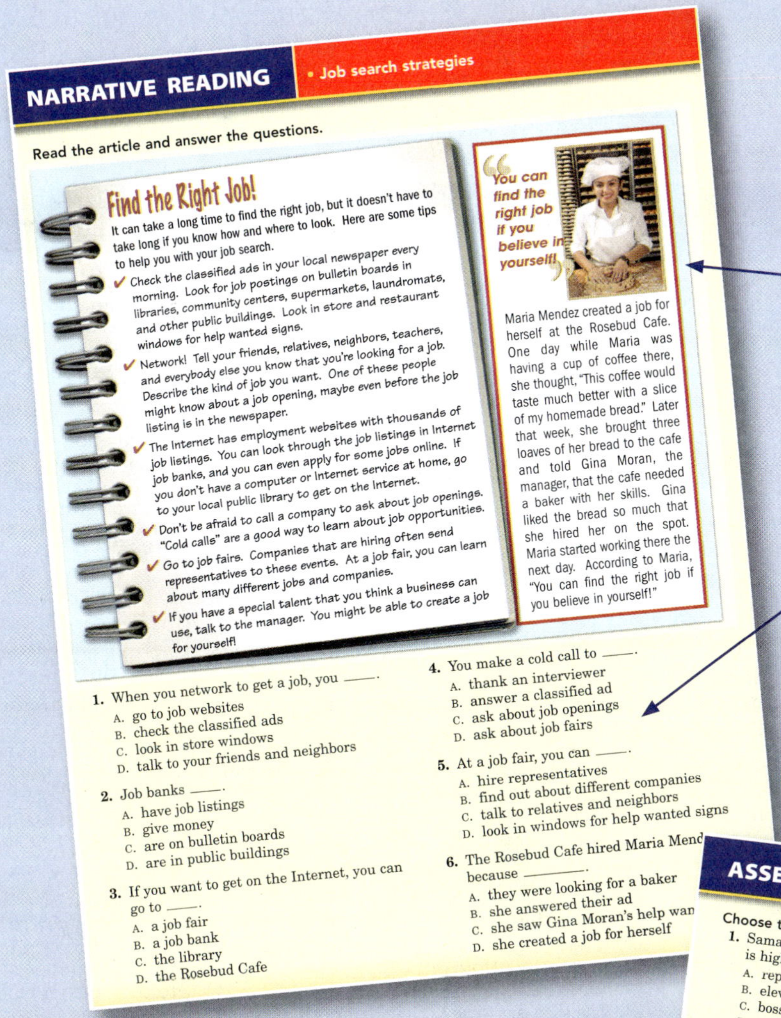
NARRATIVE READING • Job search strategies

Read the article and answer the questions.

Find the Right Job!

It can take a long time to find the right job, but it doesn't have to take long if you know how and where to look. Here are some tips to help you with your job search.

✓ Check the classified ads in your local newspaper every morning. Look for job postings on bulletin boards in libraries, community centers, supermarkets, laundromats, and other public buildings. Look in store and restaurant windows for help wanted signs.

✓ Network! Tell your friends, relatives, neighbors, teachers, and everybody else you know that you're looking for a job. Describe the kind of job you want. One of these people might know about a job opening, maybe even before the job listing is in the newspaper.

✓ The Internet has employment websites with thousands of job listings. You can look through the job listings in Internet job banks, and you can even apply for some jobs online. If you don't have a computer or Internet service at home, go to your local public library to get on the Internet.

✓ Don't be afraid to call a company to ask about job openings. "Cold calls" are a good way to learn about job opportunities.

✓ Go to job fairs. Companies that are hiring often send representatives to these events. At a job fair, you can learn about many different jobs and companies.

✓ If you have a special talent that you think a business can use, talk to the manager. You might be able to create a job for yourself!

"You can find the right job if you believe in yourself!"

Maria Mendez created a job for herself at the Rosebud Cafe. One day while Maria was having a cup of coffee there, she thought, "This coffee would taste much better with a slice of my homemade bread." Later that week, she brought three loaves of her bread to the cafe and told Gina Moran, the manager, that the cafe needed a baker with her skills. Gina liked the bread so much that she hired her on the spot. Maria started working there the next day. According to Maria, "You can find the right job if you believe in yourself!"

1. When you network to get a job, you ____.
   A. go to job websites
   B. check the classified ads
   C. look in store windows
   D. talk to your friends and neighbors
2. Job banks ____.
   A. have job listings
   B. give money
   C. are on bulletin boards
   D. are in public buildings
3. If you want to get on the Internet, you can go to ____.
   A. a job fair
   B. a job bank
   C. the library
   D. the Rosebud Cafe
4. You make a cold call to ____.
   A. thank an interviewer
   B. answer a classified ad
   C. ask about job openings
   D. ask about job fairs
5. At a job fair, you can ____.
   A. hire representatives
   B. find out about different companies
   C. talk to relatives and neighbors
   D. look in windows for help wanted signs
6. The Rosebud Cafe hired Maria Mend[...] because ____.
   A. they were looking for a baker
   B. she answered their ad
   C. she saw Gina Moran's help wan[...]
   D. she created a job for herself

Narrative reading passages offer practice with simple magazine articles on topics such as job search strategies, identity theft, small talk at work, and career advancement. **Academic lessons** in school textbook formats prepare students for success in continuing education through subject-matter content including government, history, and health.

Reading comprehension exercises in multiple-choice formats help students prepare for the reading section of standardized tests.

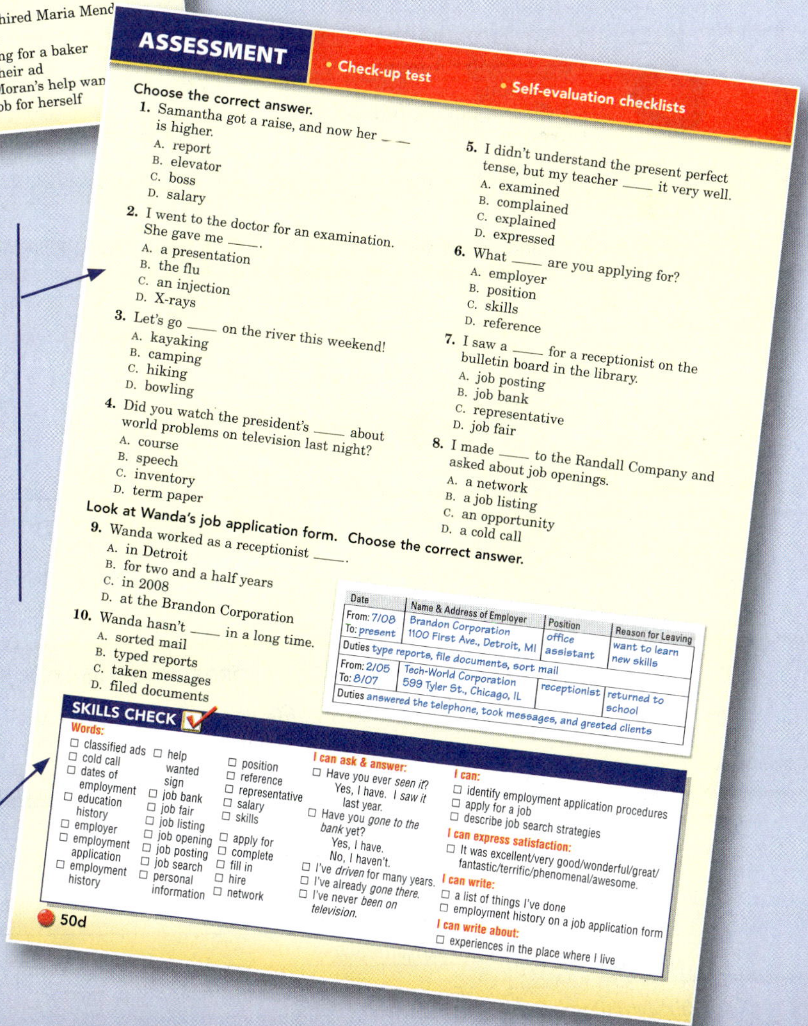
ASSESSMENT • Check-up test • Self-evaluation checklists

Choose the correct answer.

1. Samantha got a raise, and now her ____ is higher.
   A. report
   B. elevator
   C. boss
   D. salary
2. I went to the doctor for an examination. She gave me ____.
   A. a presentation
   B. the flu
   C. an injection
   D. X-rays
3. Let's go ____ on the river this weekend!
   A. kayaking
   B. camping
   C. hiking
   D. bowling
4. Did you watch the president's ____ about world problems on television last night?
   A. course
   B. speech
   C. inventory
   D. term paper
5. I didn't understand the present perfect tense, but my teacher ____ it very well.
   A. examined
   B. complained
   C. explained
   D. expressed
6. What ____ are you applying for?
   A. employer
   B. position
   C. skills
   D. reference
7. I saw a ____ for a receptionist on the bulletin board in the library.
   A. job posting
   B. job bank
   C. representative
   D. job fair
8. I made ____ to the Randall Company and asked about job openings.
   A. a network
   B. a job listing
   C. an opportunity
   D. a cold call

Look at Wanda's job application form. Choose the correct answer.

9. Wanda worked as a receptionist ____.
   A. in Detroit
   B. for two and a half years
   C. in 2008
   D. at the Brandon Corporation
10. Wanda hasn't ____ in a long time.
   A. sorted mail
   B. typed reports
   C. taken messages
   D. filed documents

Date	Name & Address of Employer	Position	Reason for Leaving
From: 7/08 To: present	Brandon Corporation 1100 First Ave., Detroit, MI	office assistant	want to learn new skills
Duties type reports, file documents, sort mail			
From: 2/05 To: 8/07	Tech-World Corporation 599 Tyler St., Chicago, IL	receptionist	returned to school
Duties answered the telephone, took messages, and greeted clients			

SKILLS CHECK ✓

Words:
- ☐ classified ads
- ☐ cold call
- ☐ dates of employment
- ☐ education history
- ☐ employer
- ☐ employment application
- ☐ employment history
- ☐ help wanted sign
- ☐ job bank
- ☐ job fair
- ☐ job listing
- ☐ job opening
- ☐ job posting
- ☐ job search
- ☐ personal information
- ☐ position
- ☐ reference
- ☐ representative
- ☐ salary
- ☐ skills
- ☐ apply for
- ☐ complete
- ☐ fill in
- ☐ hire
- ☐ network

I can ask & answer:
- ☐ Have you ever *seen* it? Yes, I have. I *saw* it last year.
- ☐ Have you *gone* to the bank yet? Yes, I have. No, I haven't.
- ☐ I've *driven* for many years.
- ☐ I've already *gone* there.
- ☐ I've never *been* on television.

I can:
- ☐ identify employment application procedures
- ☐ apply for a job
- ☐ describe job search strategies

I can express satisfaction:
- ☐ It was excellent/very good/wonderful/great/fantastic/terrific/phenomenal/awesome.

I can write:
- ☐ a list of things I've done
- ☐ employment history on a job application form

I can write about:
- ☐ experiences in the place where I live

50d

Check-up tests allow a quick assessment of student achievement and help prepare students for the kinds of test items found on standardized tests.

More complete **Achievement Tests** for each unit, including listening test items, are available as reproducible masters and printable disk files in the Teacher's Guide with Multilevel Activity & Achievement Test Book and CD-ROM. They are also available in the companion Activity & Test Prep Workbook.

Vocabulary checklists and **language skill checklists** help students review words they have learned, keep track of the skills they are developing, and identify vocabulary and skills they need to continue to work on. These lists promote student persistence as students assess their own skills and check off all the ways they are succeeding as language learners.

Scope and Sequence

All-Skills Communication: Listening, Speaking, Reading, Writing

Unit	Topics & Vocabulary	Grammar	Functional Communication	Listening & Pronunciation	Writing
1	• Describing habitual & ongoing activities • Telling about likes & dislikes • Describing frequency of actions • Telling about personal background & interests • Emergency room check-in • Preventing identity theft • Civics: U.S. government • Reading a social studies textbook lesson	Review: • Simple present tense • Present continuous tense • Subject & object pronouns • Possessive adjectives • Time expressions	• Engaging in small talk about self, family, interests, & leisure activities • Asking for & reacting to information • Giving personal information	• Listening for correct tense & person in information questions • Pronouncing reduced *are*	• Writing about studying English • Writing about yourself, your family, & your interests • Filling out a patient information form • Writing the names of current federal, state, & local government officials
2	• Reporting past activities • Mishaps • Difficult experiences • Describing a trip • Apologizing for lateness at work • Giving an excuse • Traffic accident report • Civics: U.S. history	Review: • Simple past tense (Regular & irregular verbs) • Past continuous tense	• Asking for & reporting information • Reacting to bad news • Apologizing • Giving excuses	• Listening for correct tense & meaning in information questions • Pronouncing *Did you*	• Writing about a trip you took • Filling out a traffic accident report • Creating a timeline
3	• Describing future plans & intentions • Telling about the future • Expressing time & duration • Talking on the telephone • Plans for the future • Asking a favor • Calling in sick at work • Calling school to report a child's absence • Writing a note to the teacher • Parent-school communication • Reading a campus map	Review: • Future: Going to • Future: Will • Future continuous tense • Time expressions • Possessive pronouns	• Asking & telling about future plans • Engaging in small talk about weekend plans • Making a telephone call to someone you know • Asking a favor • Asking to borrow an item	• Listening to conversations & making deductions about people's plans • Pronouncing *going to*	• Writing about something you're looking forward to • Writing a note to the teacher to explain a child's absence
Gazette	• Immigration around the world • Ellis Island • Interpreting a chart with population statistics • Culture concept: Immigrant neighborhoods around the world • Interview with an immigrant • Idioms	• Simple present tense • Simple past tense • Using present tense to express future • Future: Going to • Future: Will	• Describing neighborhoods • Describing personal history • Using idiomatic expressions	• Listening to messages on a telephone answering machine	• Writing an e-mail or instant message to tell about what you did last weekend & what you plan to do next weekend

CORRELATION and PLACEMENT KEY

Side by Side Plus 3 correlates with the following standards-based curriculum levels and assessment system score ranges:

NRS (National Reporting System) Educational Functioning Level	Low Intermediate
SPL (Student Performance Level)	4
CASAS (Comprehensive Adult Student Assessment System)	201–210
BEST Plus (Basic English Skills Test)	439–472
BEST Oral Interview	42–50
BEST Literacy	47–53

For correlation keys to other major state and local curriculum frameworks, please visit: www.pearsonlongman.com/sidebysideplus

Life Skills, Civics, Test Preparation, Curriculum Standards and Frameworks

Life Skills, Civics, & Test Preparation	EFF	SCANS/Employment Competencies	CASAS	LAUSD	Florida*
• Asking & answering personal information questions: name, address, telephone number, social security number, date of birth, place of birth, height, weight, marital status • Providing information about family members • Checking in at an emergency room • Interpreting a narrative reading about identity theft • Civics: Describing three branches of government, their functions, & their elected officials • Identifying current federal, state, & local government officials	• Interact in a way that is friendly • Identify family relationships • Develop & express sense of self • Work together • Keep pace with change • Provide for family members' safety	• Sociability • Self-esteem • Participate as a member of a team	0.2.1, 0.2.2, 0.2.4, 5.5.2, 5.5.3, 5.5.4, 5.5.8	1, 2, 3, 32	4.05.01, 4.05.02, 4.05.04, 4.12.03
• Apologizing & giving a reason for being late for work • Critical thinking: Good & bad excuses for being late for work • Interpreting & filling out traffic accident reports • Civics: U.S. history—major events, historical documents, key leaders • Study skill: Creating a history timeline	• Work together • Reflect & evaluate • Understand, interpret, & work with symbolic information	• Self-management: Assess self accurately • Responsibility • Participate as a member of a team • See things in the mind's eye (Interpret a diagram)	0.1.4, 1.9.7, 5.2.1, 5.2.2	4b, 23	4.02.02, 4.02.05, 4.12.04, 4.15.03
• Calling in sick at work • Calling school to report a child's absence • Parent-school communication • Interpreting a letter to parents from a school principal • Identifying U.S. school structure & grading system • Describing school expectations for students & parents • Interpreting a campus map to locate classrooms, offices, & other facilities	• Interact in a way that is friendly • Plan: Set a goal • Provide for family members' safety & physical needs • Understand, interpret, & work with symbolic information	• Sociability • Allocate time • Responsibility • Understand an organizational system (high school) • See things in the mind's eye (Interpret a chart & a map)	0.1.2, 0.1.3, 0.1.4, 0.2.4, 2.5.4, 2.5.5	3, 5a, 5b, 10, 11, 12b, 57	4.14.01, 4.14.02, 4.15.12
• Interpreting narrative readings about immigration & Ellis Island • Civics: U.S. immigration • Interpreting statistical facts in a table • Interpreting telephone messages on an answering machine	• Respect others & value diversity • Understand, interpret, & work with numerical information • Identify family relationships • Use technology	• Acquire & evaluate information • Work with cultural diversity • Identify goal-relevant activities • Work with technology	0.2.1, 0.2.3, 2.1.7, 2.7.2, 4.8.7, 7.2.4	1, 9, 18, 50	4.05.01, 4.06.02, 4.15.09, 4.15.12

EFF: Equipped for the Future (Content standards, Common activities, & Key activities for Citizen/Community Member, Worker, & Parent/Family role maps; EFF Communication and Reflection/Evaluation skills are covered in every unit)
SCANS: Secretary's Commission on Achieving Necessary Skills (U.S. Department of Labor)
CASAS: Comprehensive Adult Student Assessment System
LAUSD: Los Angeles Unified School District (ESL Intermediate Low content standards)
Florida: Adult ESOL High Beginning Standardized Syllabi

(*Florida benchmarks 4.15.0, 4.16.0, and 4.17.0 are covered in every unit.)

Scope and Sequence

All-Skills Communication: Listening, Speaking, Reading, Writing

Unit	Topics & Vocabulary	Grammar	Functional Communication	Listening & Pronunciation	Writing
4	• Describing skills • Describing actions that have occurred • Describing actions that haven't occurred yet • Making recommendations • Things to do where you live • Making lists • Employment application procedures • Job application forms • Employment history • Job search strategies	• Present perfect tense	• Expressing ability • Expressing jealousy • Engaging in small talk about experiences, movies, books, videos, and restaurants • Inquiring about & indicating completion of tasks • Expressing satisfaction	• Listening to narratives about tasks accomplished & indicating these tasks on a checklist • Pronouncing contractions with *is* & *has*	• Making a checklist of tasks done at school, at work, or at home • Writing about things you have done & haven't done in the place where you live • Filling out a job application form
5	• Discussing duration of activity • Medical symptoms & problems • Career advancement • Telling about family members • Job interview • Giving employment history • Cover letters & resumes • Employee manual: Workplace policies & expectations	• Present perfect vs. present tense • Present perfect vs. past tense • Since/For • Time expressions	• Asking for & reporting information • Engaging in small talk about interests & experiences • Reacting to information • Asking for clarification	• Listening for information about time & duration in conversations • Pronouncing reduced *have* & *has*	• Writing a story about your English teacher • Writing about your activities & interests • Writing a cover letter & a simple resume
Gazette	• "24/7" work schedules • Culture concept: Unique jobs around the world • Interview with a working couple about their work schedule • Interpreting a bar graph with information about vacation time in different countries • Idioms	• Present perfect tense • Simple present tense • Since/For	• Describing people's work schedules • Giving your opinion • Describing vacation time in different countries • Using idiomatic expressions	• Listening to voice-mail messages at work	• Writing an e-mail or instant message to tell about things you have done
6	• Discussing duration of activity • Reporting household repair problems • Describing tasks accomplished • Describing experiences • Job interviews • Renting an apartment • Lease information • Apartment rules • Utility bills • Housing maintenance & repairs • Yellow pages	• Present perfect continuous tense • Since/For • Time expressions	• Asking for & reporting information • Expressing surprise • Expressing nervousness • Reassuring someone • Asking about & telling about previous experiences	• Listening for particular forms of verbs in sentences • Listening & making deductions about who is speaking • Pronouncing reduced *for*	• Writing about places where you have lived, worked, & gone to school • Making a list of apartment building rules
7	• Discussing recreation preferences • Discussing things you dislike doing • Habits • Describing talents & skills • Telling about important decisions • Requests at work • Thanking someone • Borrow & lending • Workplace notes & messages • "Small talk" at work	• Gerunds • Infinitives • Review: Present perfect & present perfect continuous tenses	• Engaging in small talk about leisure activities • Introducing yourself • Attracting someone's attention • Offering & responding to advice • Expressing envy • Expressing appreciation • Sharing news about future plans • Congratulating	• Listening & making deductions about the context of conversations • Pronouncing reduced *to*	• Writing about an important decision • Making a list of topics for small talk

Life Skills, Civics, Test Preparation, Curriculum Standards and Frameworks

Life Skills, Civics, & Test Preparation	EFF	SCANS/Employment Competencies	CASAS	LAUSD	Florida*
• Job responsibilities • Following a sequence of employment application procedures • Describing employment history including employer, dates of employment, position, salary, supervisor, & reason for leaving • Identifying sources of job opportunities • Identifying job search strategies	• Interact in a way that is friendly • Create & pursue vision & goals • Work together • Plan: Develop an organized approach of activities & objectives	• Sociability • Self-management: Monitor progress • Decision-making • Allocate time • Understand an organizational system (workplace operations) • Identify goal-relevant activities • Self-management: Set personal goals • Participate as a member of a team • Identify human resources (occupations & work skills)	0.2.2, 0.2.4, 4.1.2, 4.1.3, 4.1.5, 4.6.1, 4.6.4	2, 3, 42, 43, 44, 45, 47b	4.01.01, 4.01.02, 4.01.04, 4.01.05, 4.01.06
• Describing medical symptoms & problems during an examination • Describing family members • Career advancement • Job interview • Describing work experience • Cover letters & resumes • Interpreting a new employee manual • Identifying workplace policies & expectations	• Identify problems • Identify a strong sense of family • Identify family relationships • Work together • Create & pursue vision & goals • Exercise rights & responsibilities	• Understand an organizational system (workplace) • Participate as a member of a team • Identify human resources (occupations & work skills)	0.1.6, 0.2.1, 0.2.3, 0.2.4, 4.1.2, 4.1.5, 4.2.1, 4.2.4	1, 3, 7, 9, 43, 44, 46	4.01.01, 4.01.02, 4.01.03, 4.01.05, 4.01.06, 4.01.07
• Interpreting a narrative reading about work schedules • Describing working parents' activities & responsibilities • Interpreting statistical information in a bar graph • Interpreting voice-mail messages at the workplace	• Keep pace with change • Respect others & value diversity • Identify a strong sense of family • Identify supportive family relationships • Provide for family members' safety & physical needs • Analyze & use information • Understand, interpret, & work with numbers • Use technology	• Work with cultural diversity • Acquire & evaluate information • See things in the mind's eye (Interpret a bar graph) • Work with technology	0.2.3, 2.1.7, 4.8.7, 6.7.2	9, 18, 50	4.01.01, 4.01.02, 4.02.01, 4.02.02, 4.06.02, 4.15.09, 4.15.12
• Reporting apartment maintenance & repair problems • Job interview • Job responsibilities • Inquiring about lease information when renting an apartment • Apartment building rules & regulations • Interpreting utility bills • Credit ratings • Interpreting an apartment building notice to tenants • Interpreting yellow pages listings	• Provide for family members' safety & physical needs • Develop & express sense of self • Work together • Manage resources • Analyze & use information	• Allocate time • Identify goal-relevant activities • Self-esteem • Understand a social system (apartment building rules & regulations) • Participate as a member of a team • Acquire & evaluate information	1.4.2, 1.5.3, 1.8.1, 1.8.2, 4.1.5	25, 26, 27, 43	4.01.06, 4.05.03, 4.06.04, 4.06.05, 4.08.03, 4.11.07, 4.11.08
• Making & responding to requests at work • Workplace tasks • Borrowing & lending items • Thanking someone • Workplace notes • Workplace e-mail messages • Making small talk at work • Understanding the importance of small talk • Interpreting paycheck & pay stub information	• Interact in a way that is friendly • Advocate & influence • Develop & express sense of self • Interact in a way that is courteous • Create & pursue vision & goals • Work together • Interact in a way that is tactful	• Sociability • Self-esteem • Identify goal-relevant activities • Self-management: Set personal goals • Participate as a member of a team • Understand an organizational system (workplace operations)	0.1.3, 0.1.4, 0.2.4, 4.6.4	3, 4a, 5a, 5b, 5e, 47d	4.01.02, 4.02.05, 4.02.06

Scope and Sequence

All-Skills Communication: Listening, Speaking, Reading, Writing

Unit	Topics & Vocabulary	Grammar	Functional Communication	Listening & Pronunciation	Writing
8	• Discussing things people had done • Discussing preparations for events • Describing consequences of being late • Describing accomplishments • Scheduling medical appointments • Medical appointment cards • Medical history forms • Preventive care recommendations • Public health information • Nutrition: The food pyramid • Reading a health textbook lesson	• Past perfect tense • Past perfect continuous tense	• Asking for & reporting information • Engaging in small talk about leisure activities • Sharing news about someone • Discussing feelings • Sharing experiences	• Listening to questions & choosing the correct response • Pronouncing reduced *had*	• Writing about plans that fell through • Writing about something you accomplished
Gazette	• The Jamaican bobsled team • Culture concept: Children & sports training around the world • Interview with an athlete • Interpreting a line graph with number facts • Idioms	• Gerunds • Infinitives	• Describing popular sports & children's sports training • Using idiomatic expressions	• Listening to sports broadcasts on the radio	• Writing an e-mail or instant message to tell about a favorite hobby
9	• Discussing when things are going to happen • Remembering & forgetting • Discussing obligations • Asking for & giving advice • School assignments • Making plans by telephone • Talking about important people in your life • Shopping for clothing • Identifying bargains • Returning & exchanging defective items • Advertisements • Store coupons	• Two-word verbs: Separable, Inseparable	• Asking for & reporting information about future events • Reminding someone • Remembering & forgetting • Making & responding to invitations • Expressing obligation • Asking for & offering advice	• Listening to determine subject matter of conversations • Pronouncing linked "t" between vowels	• Writing letters to offer advice • Writing about someone you admire
10	• Coincidences • Asking for & giving reasons • Describing people's backgrounds, interests, & personalities • Looking for a job • Referring people to someone else • Discussing opinions • Describing people's similarities & differences • Requesting help at work • Giving & following a sequence of instructions • Operating equipment • Career advancement • Continuing education • Developing a personal education plan	• Connectors: And . . . too And . . . either So, But, Neither	• Engaging in small talk • Giving excuses • Asking for & reporting information • Offering a suggestion • Describing family members	• Listening to determine subject matter of conversations • Pronouncing contrastive stress	• Writing about how you & another person are the same & different
Gazette	• Traditions, customs, modern life, & the ways people meet • Interpreting a bar graph with number facts about social behavior in different countries • Culture concept: Wedding customs & traditions around the world • Interviews with couples about how they met • Idioms	• Two-word verbs: Separable, Inseparable • Simple present tense • Simple past tense	• Describing customs & traditions • Describing how people met • Using idiomatic expressions	• Listening to answering machine messages to make deductions about people's likes & plans	• Writing an e-mail or instant message to tell about a best friend

Life Skills, Civics, Test Preparation, Curriculum Standards and Frameworks

Life Skills, Civics, & Test Preparation	EFF	SCANS/Employment Competencies	CASAS	LAUSD	Florida*
• Making, confirming, rescheduling, & canceling medical appointments • Interpreting medical appointment cards • Identifying public health clinics & other medical offices offering free or inexpensive medical care • Medical history forms • Preventive care recommendations • Immunizations • Medical screening tests available in the community • Public health information • Nutrition: The food pyramid	• Create & pursue vision & goals • Manage resources • Develop & express sense of self • Provide for family members' safety & physical needs • Identify community needs & resources • Analyze & use information	• Identify goal-relevant activities • Self-management: Set personal goals • Allocate resources • Acquire & evaluate information • See things in the mind's eye (Interpret a chart & a diagram)	0.2.4, 1.1.1, 1.1.7, 3.1.1, 3.2.1, 3.2.2	3, 31, 36, 37, 38, 39, 40, 41	4.05.03, 4.07.01, 4.07.03, 4.07.05, 4.07.06, 4.07.07, 4.07.08, 4.07.09
• Interpreting a narrative reading about international sports • Interpreting statistical facts in a line graph • Interpreting sports broadcasts on the radio	• Respect others & value diversity • Analyze & use information • Understand, interpret, & work with numbers	• Work with cultural diversity • Self-management: Set personal goals • Acquire & evaluate information • See things in the mind's eye (Interpret a line graph)	0.2.1, 0.2.3, 4.8.7, 6.7.1	1, 9, 50	4.05.01, 4.15.09, 4.15.12
• Family chores & responsibilities • Feedback on performance • Child-rearing • Offering assistance to a customer • Asking for clothing in a store • Describing clothing • Identifying sale prices & bargains • Returning & exchanging defective products • Interpreting store advertisements • Calculating sale prices • Comparing products & prices at different stores • Interpreting food product coupons	• Manage resources • Identify supportive family relationships • Meet family needs & responsibilities • Guide & support others • Work together • Gather, analyze, & use information	• Identify goal-relevant activities • Self-management: Assess self accurately • Responsibility • Participate as a member of a team • Allocate money • Acquire & evaluate information	1.2.1, 1.2.2, 1.2.3, 1.3.3, 1.3.5, 1.3.9	28, 29, 30	4.08.02, 4.11.01, 4.11.02, 4.11.04, 4.11.06, 4.11.10, 4.15.12
• Job interview • Requesting & offering help at work • Giving & following a sequence of instructions for operating equipment at work • Identifying skills, education, & positive job evaluations necessary for job retention & promotion • Identifying appropriate behavior, attire, attitudes, & social interactions for job retention & promotion • Identifying programs & classes available in adult & career education	• Interact in a way that is friendly • Develop & express sense of self • Guide & support others • Identify a strong sense of family • Seek & receive assistance • Give direction • Work together • Create & pursue vision & goals • Analyze & use information • Keep pace with change • Plan: Set a goal; Develop an organized approach of activities & objectives	• Sociability • Teach others new skills • Participate as a member of a team • Acquire & evaluate information • Identify goal-relevant activities • Self-management: Set personal goals	0.1.4, 0.2.1, 0.2.4, 2.5.5, 4.8.2, 7.1.1	1, 3, 4b, 13, 47b, 48, 53	4.03.01, 4.03.02, 4.03.03, 4.03.04, 4.05.01, 4.05.02, 4.05.04
• Interpreting statistical facts in a bar graph • Interpreting answering machine messages	• Respect others & value diversity • Identify the family system • Analyze & use information • Understand, interpret, & work with numbers • Use technology	• Work with cultural diversity • See things in the mind's eye (Interpret a bar graph) • Work with technology	0.2.1, 0.2.3, 4.8.7, 6.7.2	1, 9, 50	4.06.02, 4.15.09, 4.15.12

1

Review:
Simple Present Tense
Present Continuous Tense
Subject & Object Pronouns
Possessive Adjectives
Time Expressions

- Describing Habitual and Ongoing Activities
- Telling About Likes and Dislikes
- Describing Frequency of Actions
- Telling About Personal Background and Interests
- Emergency Room Check-In
- Preventing Identity Theft
- Civics: U.S. Government
- Reading a Social Studies Textbook Lesson

Vocabulary Preview

1 
2 
3 
4 
5 
6 
7 
8 
9 
10 
11 
12 

1. actor
2. dancer
3. driver
4. instructor
5. player
6. singer
7. skater
8. skier
9. swimmer
10. teacher
11. typist
12. violinist

They're Busy

Am	I	
Is	he she it	eating?
Are	we you they	

	I	am.
Yes,	he she it	is.
	we you they	are.

(I am)	I'm	eating.
(He is) (She is) (It is)	He's She's It's	
(We are) (You are) (They are)	We're You're They're	

A. Are you busy?

B. Yes, I am. I'm studying.

A. What are you studying?

B. I'm studying English.

1. Is Alan busy?
baking • cookies

2. Is Doris busy?
reading • the newspaper

3. Are your parents busy?
painting • the kitchen

4. Are you busy?
writing • a letter

5. Are you and Tom busy?
cooking • dinner

6. Is Ann busy?
knitting • a sweater

7. Is your brother busy?
ironing • his shirts

8. Are Mr. and Mrs. Garcia busy?
cleaning • their garage

9. Is Beethoven busy?
composing • a symphony

What Are They Doing?

Do	I / we / you / they	eat?
Does	he / she / it	

Yes,	I / we / you / they	do.
	he / she / it	does.

I / We / You / They	eat.
He / She / It	eats.

A. What are you doing?

B. I'm practicing the piano.

A. Do you practice the piano very often?

B. Yes, I do. I practice the piano whenever I can.

1. What's Carol doing?
watch the news

2. What's Edward doing?
swim

3. What are you doing?
study math

4. What are Mr. and Mrs. Park doing?
exercise

5. What are you and your friend doing?
play Scrabble

6. What's Mrs. Anderson doing?
read poetry

7. What's Daniel doing?
play baseball with his daughter

8. What are you doing?
chat online with my friends

9.

Do You Like to Ski?

No,	I / we / you / they	don't. (do not)
	he / she / it	doesn't. (does not)

I'm not . . .	
He / She / It	isn't . . . (is not)
We / You / They	aren't . . . (are not)

A. Do you like to ski?

B. No, I don't. I'm not a very good skier.

1. Does Richard like to sing?
singer

2. Does Brenda like to swim?
swimmer

3. Do Mr. and Mrs. Adams like to skate?
skaters

4. Does Arthur like to dance?
dancer

5. Do you like to type?
typist

6. Do you and your friend like to act?
actors

7. Does your grandmother like to drive?
driver

8. Do you like to play sports?
athlete

9. Does Howard like to cook?
cook

READING

PRACTICING

My sisters, my brother, and I are busy this afternoon. We're staying after school, and we're practicing different things.

I'm practicing soccer. I practice soccer every day after school. My soccer coach tells me I'm an excellent soccer player, and my friends tell me I play soccer better than anyone else in the school. I want to be a professional soccer player when I grow up. That's why I practice every day.

My sister Anita is practicing tennis. She practices tennis every day after school. Her tennis coach tells her she's an excellent tennis player, and her friends tell her she plays tennis better than anyone else in the school. Anita wants to be a professional tennis player when she grows up. That's why she practices every day.

My brother Hector is practicing the violin. He practices the violin every day after school. His music teacher tells him he's an excellent violinist, and his friends tell him he plays the violin better than anyone else in the school. Hector wants to be a professional violinist when he grows up. That's why he practices every day.

My sisters Jenny and Vanessa are practicing ballet. They practice ballet every day after school. Their ballet instructor tells them they're excellent ballet dancers, and their friends tell them they dance better than anyone else in the school. Jenny and Vanessa want to be professional ballet dancers when they grow up. That's why they practice every day.

READING *CHECK-UP*

Q & A

You're talking with the person who told the story on page 5. Using this model, create dialogs based on the story.

A. *What's your sister Anita* doing?
B. *She's* practicing *tennis.*
A. *Does she* practice very often?
B. Yes, *she does. She practices* every day after school.
A. *Is she a* good *tennis player?*
B. Yes, *she is. Her tennis instructor* says *she's* excellent, and *her* friends tell *her she plays tennis* better than anyone else in the school.

LISTENING

Listen and choose the correct answer.

1. a. I practice football.
   b. I'm practicing football.
2. a. Yes, I am.
   b. Yes, I do.
3. a. Yes, I am.
   b. Yes, I do.
4. a. She reads the newspaper.
   b. She's reading the newspaper.
5. a. My husband cooks.
   b. My husband is cooking.
6. a. No, they aren't.
   b. No, they don't.
7. a. Yes, when he grows up.
   b. Yes, when she grows up.
8. a. Yes, we do.
   b. Yes, you do.
9. a. Yes, they are.
   b. Yes, we are.
10. a. He's playing soccer.
    b. He wants to be a soccer player.

IN YOUR OWN WORDS

FOR WRITING AND DISCUSSION

Tell about studying English.

Do you go to English class? Where?
When do you go to class?
What's your teacher's name?

When do you practice English?
How do you practice?
Who do you practice with?

How Often?

I	my	me
he	his	him
she	her	her
it	its	it
we	our	us
you	your	you
they	their	them

Time Expressions

every day/week/weekend/month/year
every morning/afternoon/evening/night
every Sunday/Monday/Tuesday/. . .
every Sunday morning/afternoon/evening/night
every January/February/March/. . .

once a / twice a / three times a } day/week/month/year

all the time

A. Who are you calling?

B. **I'm** calling **my** sister in San Francisco.

A. How often do you call **her**?

B. I call **her** every Sunday evening.

A. What are George and Herman talking about?

B. **They're** talking about **their** grandchildren.

A. How often do they talk about **them**?

B. They talk about **them** all the time.

1. Who is Mr. Tanaka calling?
son in New York

2. Who is Mrs. Kramer writing to?
daughter in the army

3. What are the students talking about?
teachers

4. Who is Lenny arguing with?
landlord

5. Who is Martha sending an e-mail to?
granddaughter in Orlando

6. Who is Mr. Crabapple shouting at?
employees

7. What are your parents complaining about?
telephone bill

8. What is George watching?
favorite TV talk show

9. Who is Little Red Riding Hood visiting?
grandmother

10.

How to Say It!

Asking for and Reacting to Information

A. Tell me, *where are you from*?
B. *I'm from Madagascar.*
A. Oh. / Really? / Oh, really? / That's interesting.

Practice the interactions on this page, using expressions for asking for and reacting to information.

INTERACTIONS *Sharing Information*

Talking about yourself:

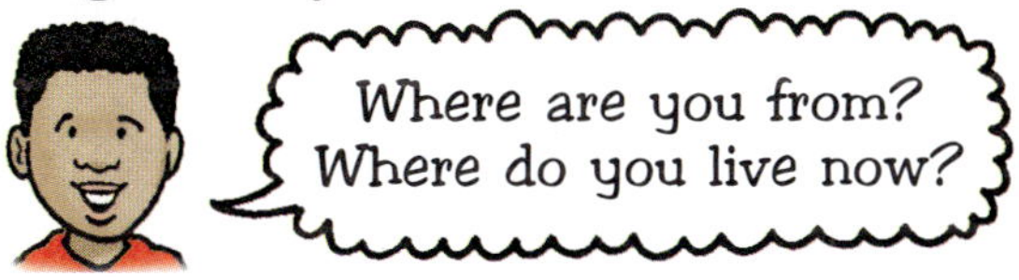

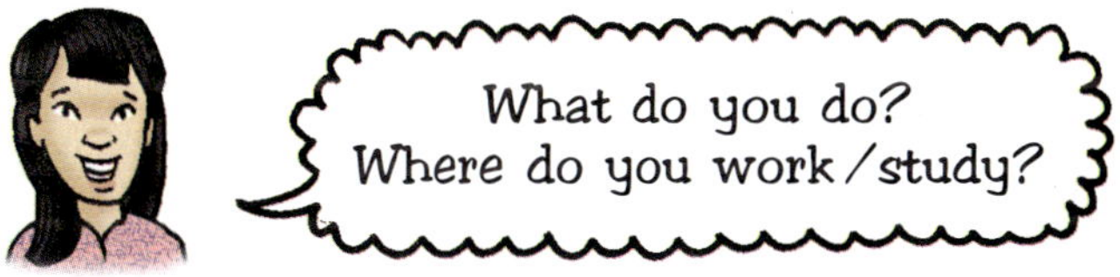

Talking about family:

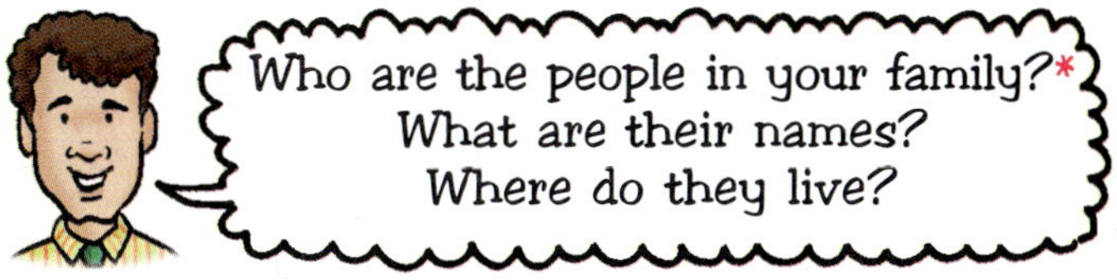

Talking about interests:

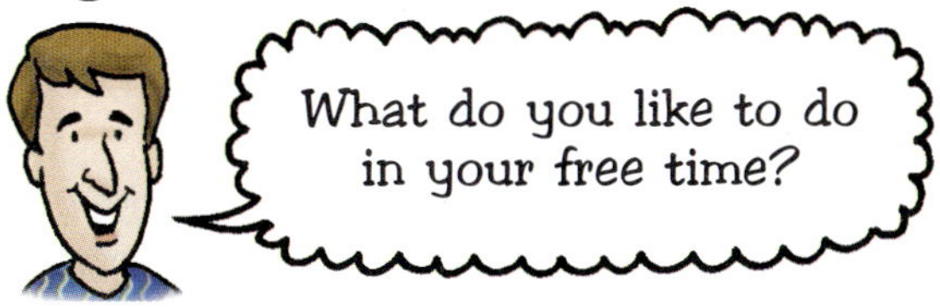

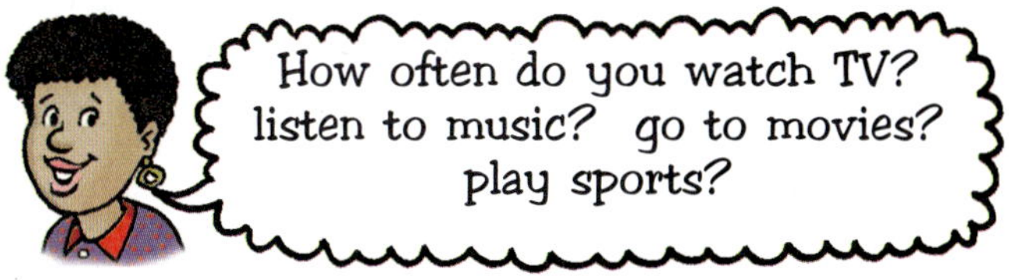

Practice conversations with other students. Get to know each other as you talk about yourselves, your families, and your interests.

* wife, husband, mother, father, daughter, son, sister, brother, grandmother, grandfather, granddaughter, grandson, aunt, uncle, cousin

Write in your journal about yourself, your family, and your interests.

PRONUNCIATION Reduced *are*

Listen. Then say it.

Who are you calling?

What are they talking about?

Where are you from?

What are you doing?

Say it. Then listen.

Who are you writing to?

What are they complaining about?

Where are they studying?

What are their names?

GRAMMAR FOCUS

Present Continuous Tense

(I am)	I'm	eating.
(He is) (She is) (It is)	He's She's It's	
(We are) (You are) (They are)	We're You're They're	

Am	I	eating?
Is	he she it	
Are	we you they	

To Be: Short Answers

Yes,	I	am.
	he she it	is.
	we you they	are.

No,	I'm	not.
	he she it	isn't.
	we you they	aren't.

Simple Present Tense

I We You They	eat.
He She It	eats.

Do	I we you they	eat?
Does	he she it	

Yes,	I we you they	do.
	he she it	does.

No,	I we you they	don't.
	he she it	doesn't.

Subject Pronouns	Possessive Adjectives	Object Pronouns
I	my	me
he	his	him
she	her	her
it	its	it
we	our	us
you	your	you
they	their	them

Choose the correct answer.

1. Mark is busy. (He irons He's ironing) his pants and shirts this morning.
2. My daughter (chats is chatting) online with her friends every day.
3. (We We're) watch (are our) favorite TV program every afternoon.
4. A. What (are our) Ann and Rita (do doing)?
   B. (They're Their) talking about (they're their) grandchildren.
5. Why (are do) your neighbors (argue arguing) with the landlord today?
6. (Is Does) your son (practice practicing) the piano every day?
7. (I'm calling I call) my cousins in Denver once a month.
8. A. (Is Does) your wife working today?
   B. No, she (is isn't). She (isn't doesn't) work on Saturday.

1 CONVERSATION Giving Personal Information

Look at the patient information form. Practice the conversation with a classmate.

Patient Information Form

NAME Rita (First) Sanchez (Last)

ADDRESS 84 Central Avenue (Number Street) 14G (Apartment)

Los Angeles (City) CA (State) 90034 (Zip Code)

TELEPHONE (213) 628-1367 SSN 236-84-7915

DATE OF BIRTH 4/16/81 PLACE OF BIRTH Mexico City

HEIGHT: 5 feet 3 inches WEIGHT: 162 pounds

MARITAL STATUS (check):

___ Single ✓ Married ___ Divorced ___ Widowed

FAMILY MEMBERS IN HOUSEHOLD (closest relatives):

Relationship:	Name:
husband	Roberto Sanchez
daughter	Jessica Sanchez

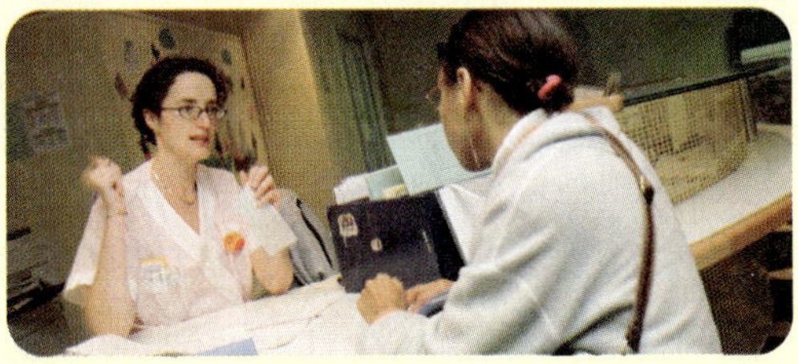

A. What's your name?
B. ________.
A. What's your address?
B. ________.
A. Home telephone number?
B. ________.
A. Your social security number?
B. ________.
A. What's your date of birth?
B. ________.
A. And your place of birth?
B. ________.
A. What's your height?
B. ________.
A. And your weight?
B. ________.
A. What's your marital status?
B. ________.
A. What family members live in your household?
B. ________.

2 TEAMWORK Checking In at an Emergency Room

Work with a classmate. You're checking in at an emergency room. Fill out the form and practice the conversation above. (Use any information you wish.)

Patient Information Form

NAME ________ (First) ________ (Last)

ADDRESS ________ (Number Street Apartment) ________ (City) ____ (State) ____ (Zip Code)

TELEPHONE ________ SSN ________ DATE OF BIRTH ________ PLACE OF BIRTH ________

HEIGHT: ___ feet ___ inches WEIGHT: ____ pounds

MARITAL STATUS (check):
___ Single ___ Married ___ Divorced ___ Widowed

FAMILY MEMBERS IN HOUSEHOLD (closest relatives):

Relationship:	Name:	Relationship:	Name:

Read the article and answer the questions.

Identity Theft

Every year nine million people are victims of identity theft. This common crime occurs when someone steals your personal information—for example, your social security number, your credit card and bank account numbers, or your driver's license. With this information, a thief can buy things with your credit card, withdraw money from your bank accounts, or open new credit card accounts in your name. A person can even buy a car with your credit information.

There are many ways thieves can get your personal information. Of course, they can steal your wallet or break into your house. They can also steal documents from your mailbox or from your trash. If you use your credit card at a restaurant or a store, they can steal your receipt, which has your credit card number and your signature. Some identity thieves get jobs in businesses so that they can steal information about customers and employees. Sometimes thieves bribe employees; they pay them for this information. They also use the telephone and the Internet to get your personal information.

Here are some things you can do to prevent identity theft. Carry only the forms of identification and the credit cards you need. Don't carry your Social Security card. Shred documents that have your personal information, such as pay stubs and account statements, before you throw them in the trash. (You can buy an inexpensive shredder that cuts these documents into very small pieces.) Get your mail from your mailbox every day. If you're going to be away from your home for several days, have a friend get your mail or ask the post office to hold it until your return. When you get money from a cash machine or pay with a credit card, put the receipt in your wallet. Don't throw it in the trash. Check your credit card and bank account statements each month to make sure that nobody else is using them. If a statement doesn't arrive when it should, call the company.

If you do all these things and you are still a victim of identity theft, report the crime to your credit card companies and the police. Close your credit card and bank accounts immediately and open new ones with new account numbers.

1. When someone steals your identity, that person steals your ____.
- A. car
- B. personal information
- C. mailbox
- D. cash

2. According to this article, you shouldn't ____.
- A. get money from a cash machine
- B. put credit card receipts in your wallet
- C. carry your Social Security card
- D. get your mail every day

3. According to this article, you should shred your ____.
- A. credit cards
- B. mail
- C. Social Security card
- D. account statements

4. You shouldn't throw your credit card receipt in the trash because ____.
- A. it has your Social Security number
- B. it has your bank account number
- C. it has your credit card number
- D. you need it to buy things

5. You should ____ every month to see if somebody is using your credit card.
- A. check your credit card statement
- B. call the Federal Trade Commission
- C. call the police
- D. get a new password

6. We can infer that an identity thief isn't going to steal your ____.
- A. passport
- B. tax information
- C. checkbook
- D. dictionary

CIVICS READING

• U.S. Government • Reading a textbook lesson

The Three Branches of Government

The United States government has three *branches* (parts)—the legislative branch, the executive branch, and the judicial branch.

The legislative branch, also called Congress, makes the laws of the United States and has the power to declare war. It has two parts—the Senate and the House of Representatives. There are one hundred senators, two from each state, and there are 435 representatives. The number of representatives from a state depends on how many people live there. States with very few people, such as Alaska and Wyoming, have only one representative, while states with large populations have more representatives. (California, for example, has 53.) Senators serve a six-year term. Representatives serve a two-year term.

The executive branch enforces the laws. The President, the Vice President, and the Cabinet are all part of this branch of government. The President is the chief executive of the United States and the Commander-in-Chief of the armed forces. When the President signs the bills that Congress writes, they become law. The members of the Cabinet give the President advice. The President appoints them.

Voters elect the President and the Vice President together for a four-year term. They must be thirty-five years old or more and natural-born citizens—they cannot come from another country. If the President dies, the Vice President becomes President. The President can serve two four-year terms.

The Supreme Court and other federal courts belong to the judicial branch of government. They *interpret* (explain) the law. The Supreme Court, the highest court in the land, is the last court to hear cases. Its decisions are final. The nine judges on the court are called Supreme Court justices. They serve for life. When a Supreme Court justice retires or dies, the President appoints a new justice. The Senate must approve this person.

Do you recognize each of these buildings? Who works there?

Did You Understand?

1. The _____ is part of the executive branch.

A. Supreme Court
B. Senate
C. Cabinet
D. House of Representatives

2. _____ serves a two-year term.

A. The President
B. The Vice President
C. A senator
D. A representative

3. _____ writes the bills that become laws.

A. The Supreme Court
B. The Cabinet
C. Congress
D. The President

4. The President does NOT _____.

A. appoint Supreme Court justices
B. change the Supreme Court's decisions
C. appoint Cabinet members
D. sign bills

5. In the United States, we do NOT elect _____.

A. the Vice President
B. our representatives
C. our senators
D. Supreme Court justices

6. Nevada has 3 representatives. We can infer that _____.

A. more people live in Nevada than in Alaska
B. Nevada has 3 senators
C. Nevada is bigger than Alaska
D. Wyoming's population is larger than Nevada's

CIVICS TODAY

Write your answers. Then discuss with the class.

Who is the President of the United States? Who is the Vice President?

Who is your representative in Congress? Who are your senators?

Who is the governor of your state? Who is the mayor or city manager of your city?

ASSESSMENT

• Check-up test • Self-evaluation checklists

Choose the correct answer.

1. My grandmother is knitting ____.
A. cookies
B. dinner
C. a sweater
D. her car

2. Roger is very talented. He composes ____.
A. paintings
B. music
C. the violin
D. computers

3. I'm ironing ____.
A. my bicycle
B. my son
C. the kitchen
D. these pants

4. My daughter ____ soccer every day after school.
A. practices
B. exercises
C. acts
D. goes

5. Marisa plays several sports. She's a very good ____.
A. artist
B. actress
C. athlete
D. driver

6. My height is ____.
A. 2/19/79
B. single
C. 173 pounds
D. 5 feet 4 inches

7. Unfortunately, identify theft is a common ____.
A. crime
B. document
C. receipt
D. information

8. If you don't want anyone to steal your identity, you should ____ your pay stubs.
A. steal
B. shred
C. bribe
D. report

9. There are three ____ of U.S. government.
A. courts
B. citizens
C. bills
D. branches

10. The executive branch of the government ____.
A. makes the laws
B. explains the laws
C. enforces the laws
D. writes the laws

SKILLS CHECK

Words:

☐ act
☐ argue
☐ bake
☐ call
☐ chat
☐ clean
☐ complain
☐ compose
☐ cook
☐ dance
☐ do
☐ drive
☐ exercise
☐ go
☐ iron
☐ knit
☐ live
☐ paint
☐ play
☐ practice
☐ read
☐ send
☐ shout
☐ sing
☐ ski
☐ skate
☐ study
☐ swim
☐ talk
☐ type
☐ visit
☐ watch
☐ work
☐ write

☐ actor
☐ dancer
☐ driver
☐ instructor
☐ player
☐ singer
☐ skater
☐ skier
☐ swimmer
☐ teacher
☐ typist
☐ violinist

I can ask & answer:

☐ Are you *busy*?
Yes, I am.
No, I'm not.

☐ Do you *work*?
Yes, I do.
No, I don't.

☐ What are you *cleaning*?
I'm *cleaning the floor*.

☐ I *work* very often.

I can ask for and react to information:

☐ Tell me, ____.
Oh./Really?/Oh, really?/That's Interesting.

I can:

☐ give personal information
☐ check in at an emergency room
☐ fill out a patient information form
☐ describe ways to prevent identity theft
☐ describe the three branches of government
☐ name federal, state, & local government officials

I can write about:

☐ myself, my family, and my interests

2

Review:
Simple Past Tense (Regular and Irregular Verbs)
Past Continuous Tense

- Reporting Past Activities
- Mishaps
- Difficult Experiences
- Describing a Trip
- Apologizing for Lateness at Work
- Giving an Excuse
- Traffic Accident Report
- Civics: U.S. History

Vocabulary Preview

1. break – broke
2. buy – bought
3. cut – cut
4. eat – ate
5. fall – fell
6. go – went
7. hurt – hurt
8. lose – lost
9. meet – met
10. ride – rode
11. sing – sang
12. speak – spoke
13. swim – swam
14. teach – taught
15. write – wrote

Did They Sleep Well Last Night?

What did { I / he / she / it / we / you / they } do?

{ I / He / She / It / We / You / They } worked.

{ I / He / She / It } was tired.

{ We / You / They } were tired.

A. Did Emma sleep well last night?

B. Yes, she did. She was VERY tired.

A. Why? What did she do yesterday?

B. She worked in her garden all day.

1. *you*
study English

2. *Rick*
paint his apartment

3. *you and your brother*
wash windows

4. *Ms. Taylor*
teach

5. *Henry*
deliver pizzas

6. *Sarah*
write letters

7. *Matthew*
ride his bicycle

8. *the president*
meet important people

9.

Did Robert Shout at His Dog?

Yes / No, { I / he / she / it / we / you / they } did / didn't.
(did not)

{ I / He / She / It } was / wasn't . . .
(was not)

{ We / You / They } were / weren't . . .
(were not)

A. Did Robert shout at his dog?

B. Yes, he did. He was angry.

A. Did Helen sleep well last night?

B. No, she didn't. She wasn't tired.

1. Did Howard fall asleep in class?
Yes, __________ . __________ *bored.*

2. Did Amy take the plane to Rio?
No, __________ . __________ *on time.*

3. Did you cry during the movie?
Yes, __________ . __________ *sad.*

4. Did Brad do well on his exam?
No, __________ . __________ *prepared.*

5. Did Frank and James forget their lines during the school play?
Yes, __________ . __________ *nervous.*

6. Did you and your sister cover your eyes during the science fiction movie?
No, __________ . __________ *scared.*

7. Did Abby finish her dinner?
Yes, __________ . __________ *hungry.*

8. Did Timmy drink all his milk?
No, __________ . __________ *thirsty.*

How Did Marty Break His Leg?

I He She It	was	working.
We You They	were	

A. How did Marty break his leg?

B. He broke it while he was snowboarding.

A. That's too bad!

1. How did Greta sprain her ankle?
play volleyball

2. How did Larry lose his wallet?
hike in the woods

3. How did Brian cut himself?
shave

4. How did Mr. and Mrs. Harper burn themselves?
prepare dinner

5. How did Stella rip her pants?
do her daily exercises

6. How did your grandfather trip and fall?
get off a bus

7. How did Peter poke himself in the eye?
talk on his cell phone

8. How did Marilyn cut herself?
chop onions

9. How did Timothy get a black eye?
fight with the kid across the street

10. How did Presto the Magician hurt himself?
practice a new magic trick

How to Say It!

Reacting to Bad News

Practice the conversations in this lesson again. React to the bad news in different ways.

DIFFICULT EXPERIENCES

Ms. Henderson usually teaches very well, but she didn't teach very well this morning. In fact, she taught very badly. While she was teaching, the school principal was sitting at the back of the room and watching her. It was a very difficult experience for Ms. Henderson. She realized she wasn't teaching very well, but she couldn't do anything about it. She was too nervous.

Stuart usually types very well, but he didn't type very well today. In fact, he typed very badly. While he was typing, his supervisor was standing behind him and looking over his shoulder. It was a difficult experience for Stuart. He realized he wasn't typing very well, but he couldn't do anything about it. He was too upset.

The Baxter Boys usually sing very well, but they didn't sing very well last night. In fact, they sang very badly. While they were singing, their parents were sitting in the audience and waving at them. It was a difficult experience for the Baxter Boys. They realized they weren't singing very well, but they couldn't do anything about it. They were too embarrassed.

The president usually speaks very well, but he didn't speak very well this afternoon. In fact, he spoke very badly. While he was speaking, several demonstrators were standing at the back of the room and shouting at him. It was a difficult experience for the president. He realized he wasn't speaking very well, but he couldn't do anything about it. He was too angry.

✓ READING *CHECK-UP*

Q & A

Ms. Henderson, Stuart, the Baxter Boys, and the president are talking with friends about their difficult experiences. Using this model, create dialogs based on the story on page 16.

A. You know . . . I didn't *teach* very well *this morning*.
B. You didn't?
A. No. In fact, I *taught* very badly.
B. That's strange. You usually *teach* VERY well. What happened?
A. While I was *teaching, the school principal was sitting at the back of the room and watching me*.
B. Oh. I bet that was a very difficult experience for you.
A. It was. I *was* very *nervous*.

MATCH

We often use colorful expressions to describe how we feel. Try to match the following expressions with the feelings they describe.

____ **1.**	"My stomach is growling."	a.	angry
____ **2.**	"I can't keep my eyes open."	b.	embarrassed
____ **3.**	"I'm jumping for joy!"	c.	tired
____ **4.**	"I'm seeing red!"	d.	nervous
____ **5.**	"I'm feeling blue."	e.	scared
____ **6.**	"I'm on pins and needles!"	f.	hungry
____ **7.**	"I'm shaking like a leaf!"	g.	sad
____ **8.**	"I'm ashamed to look at them straight in the eye."	h.	happy

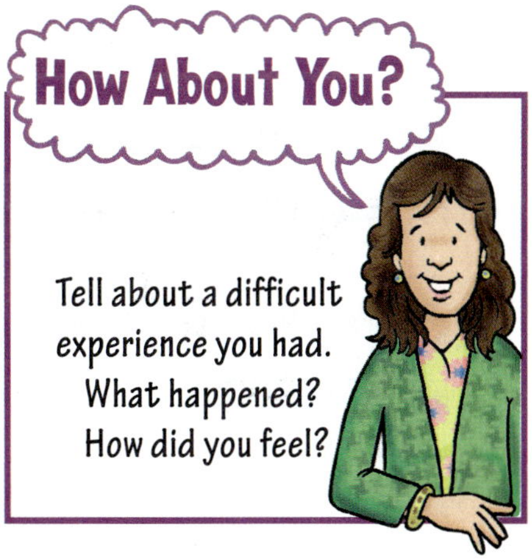

LISTENING

Listen and choose the correct answer.

1. a. Yes, I did.
b. Yes, I was.

2. a. Yes, they did.
b. Yes, they were.

3. a. He played soccer.
b. He was playing soccer.

4. a. No. I wasn't hungry.
b. Yes. I wasn't hungry.

5. a. He lost his wallet.
b. He was jogging in the park.

6. a. She was nervous.
b. She was looking over my shoulder.

7. a. Yes. I was prepared.
b. No. I was prepared.

8. a. I cut myself.
b. I was too upset.

Tell Me About Your Vacation

1. A. Did you go to Paris?
   B. No, __we didn't__.
   A. Where __did you go__?
   B. __We went__ to Rome.

2. A. Did you get there by boat?
   B. No, ________.
   A. How ________?
   B. ________ by plane.

3. A. Did you stay in a big hotel?
   B. No, ________.
   A. What kind of ________?
   B. ________ a small hotel.

4. A. Did you eat in fancy restaurants?
   B. No, ________.
   A. Where ________?
   B. ________ cheap restaurants.

5. A. Did you speak Italian?
   B. No, ________.
   A. What language ________?
   B. ________ English.

6. A. Did you take many pictures?
   B. No, ________.
   A. How many ________?
   B. ________ just a few pictures.

7. A. Did you buy any clothing?
B. No, ____________.
A. What ________________________?
B. ____________________ souvenirs.

8. A. Did you swim in the Mediterranean?
B. No, ____________.
A. Where ______________________?
B. _________ in the pool at our hotel.

9. A. Did you see the Colosseum?
B. No, ____________.
A. What ________________________?
B. ___________________ the Vatican.

10. A. Did you get around the city by taxi?
B. No, ____________.
A. How ________________________?
B. ________________________ by bus.

11. A. Did you meet a lot of Italians?
B. No, ____________.
A. Who ________________________?
B. ___________ a lot of other tourists.

12. A. Did you come home by plane?
B. No, ____________.
A. How ________________________?
B. _______________________ by boat.

Write in your journal about a trip you took. Where did you go? How did you get there? Where did you stay? What did you do there? How long were you there? Did you have a good time?

(If you have some photographs of your trip, bring them to class and talk about them with other students.)

PRONUNCIATION *Did you*

Listen. Then say it.

Did you go to Madrid?

Did you speak Spanish?

Where did you stay?

What did you do?

Say it. Then listen.

Did you meet a lot of people?

Did you have a good time?

How did you get there?

When did you get home?

GRAMMAR FOCUS

Simple Past Tense

What did	I he she it we you they	do?

I He She It We You They	worked.

Did	I he she it we you they	fall asleep?

Yes,	I he she it we you they	did.

No,	I he she it we you they	didn't.

I He She It	was	tired.
We You They	were	

I He She It	wasn't	tired.
We You They	weren't	

Past Continuous Tense

I He She It	was	working.
We You They	were	

Choose the correct answer.

1. A. What (do you did   did you do) last weekend?
   B. We (went   were going) to the beach.
2. A. Did you (ate   eat) all your dinner?
   B. No, we (did   didn't). We (wasn't   weren't) very hungry.
3. A. How (did they burn   they burned) themselves?
   B. They (were baking   were baked) cookies.
4. A. Did you (sleep   slept) well last night?
   B. Yes, I (did   didn't). I (were   was) very tired.
5. A. (Did he took   Did he take) the bus?
   B. No, he (wasn't   didn't). He (take   took) the train.
6. A. (How   How did) your grandmother (fall   fell)?
   B. She (was falling   fell) while (was she   she was) getting off a bus.

1 CONVERSATION APOLOGIZING FOR BEING LATE

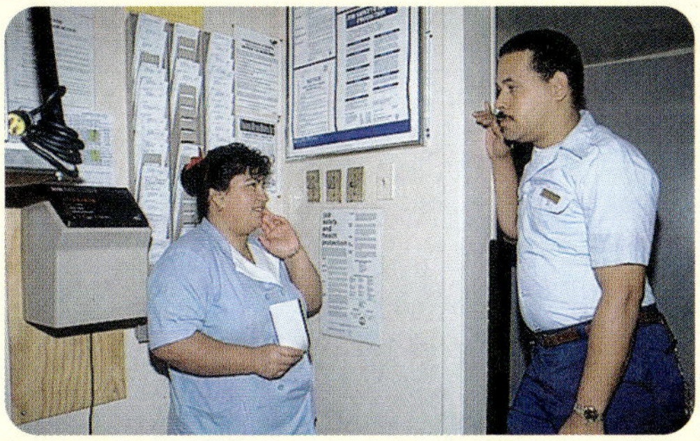

Practice conversations between an employee and a supervisor. Apologize for being late for work.

A. I'm sorry I'm late for work.
B. What happened?
A. ______________________
B. Oh. That's too bad.

1. I had a flat tire.

2. I missed the bus.

3. My car broke down.

4. The trains were running late.

5. Traffic was terrible. There was a bad accident.

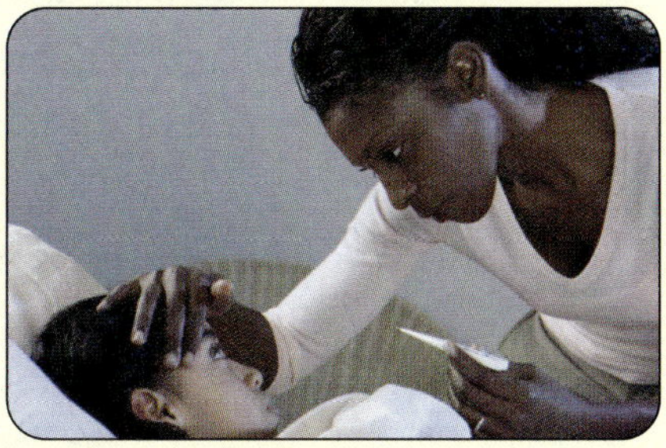

6. My daughter woke up with a high fever. I had to take her to the doctor.

2 TEAMWORK CRITICAL THINKING

Work with a classmate. What are some good excuses and bad excuses for being late for work? Make two lists. Practice new conversations with the good excuses. Then discuss your lists with your classmates.

Good Excuses	Bad Excuses
I had a flat tire.	I met an old friend on the street.

Look at the traffic accident report and answer the questions.

REPORT OF TRAFFIC ACCIDENT

9 - DIAGRAM

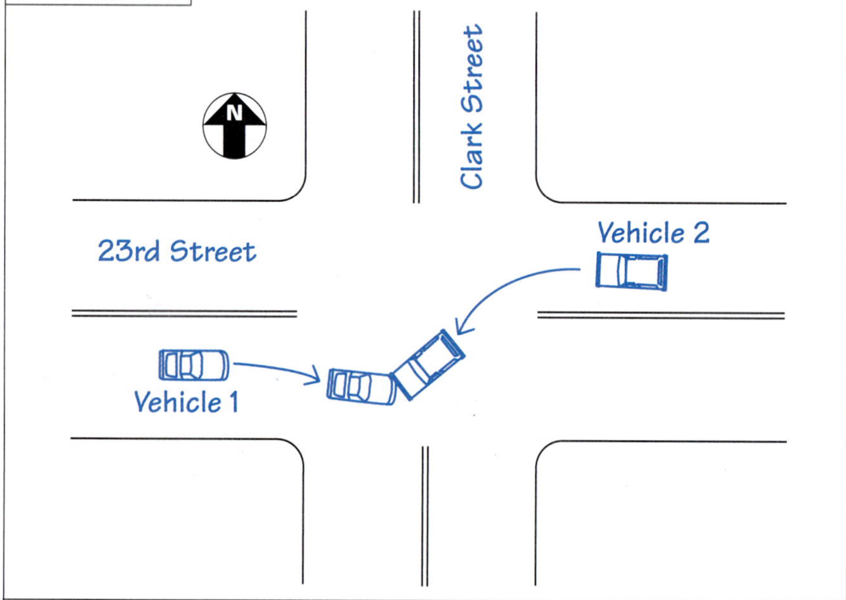

WEATHER CONDITIONS

01 Clear
02 Cloudy
03 Fog
04 Rain
05 Snow

04

ROAD SURFACE

01 Dry
02 Wet
03 Slippery
04 Icy

02

LIGHT CONDITIONS

01 Dawn
02 Daylight
03 Dusk
04 Dark

03

DESCRIBE WHAT HAPPENED:

I was driving east on 23rd Street. I stopped at a red light at the intersection of 23rd Street and Clark Street. When the light turned green, I entered the intersection. Vehicle 2 was going west on 23rd Street. The driver of Vehicle 2 was making a left turn onto Clark Street and didn't stop at the intersection. Vehicle 2 hit the front left side of my car while the driver was talking on his cell phone.

1. The driver of Vehicle 1 was ____.

A. driving north
B. driving west
C. driving east
D. making a turn

2. The driver of Vehicle 2 ____.

A. was making a right turn
B. hit the front right side of Vehicle 1
C. was driving east
D. was talking on a cell phone

3. The road was ____ when the accident occurred.

A. dry
B. wet
C. slippery
D. icy

4. The driver of Vehicle 2 was turning ____.

A. left onto 23rd Street
B. right onto 23rd Street
C. left onto Clark Street
D. right onto Clark Street

5. ____ when the accident occurred.

A. The traffic light was green
B. It was foggy
C. It was snowing
D. It was dark

6. The accident occurred at 6:30 P.M. We can infer that *dusk* means ____.

A. it was bright
B. it was sunny
C. it was starting to get light
D. it was starting to get dark

Read about the history of the United States and complete the sentences with these words.

began	described	ended	fought	lost	met	needed	sent	signed	wrote

The Revolutionary War

The Revolutionary War ________[1] in 1775 and ________[2] in 1783. The American colonies and England ________[3] for eight years because the colonies wanted to be independent from England. The English soldiers had more experience than the Americans, but England ________[4] the war.

In CONGRESS. July 4, 1776.
The unanimous Declaration of the ... States of America

The Declaration of Independence

In 1776, representatives from the thirteen colonies ________[5] at Independence Hall in Philadelphia. At the meeting, they decided to declare their independence. Thomas Jefferson was a great writer. He ________[6] the Declaration of Independence. This document says that the government must do what the people say and that all people have important rights.

July 4, 1776

On July 4, 1776, representatives of all thirteen colonies ________[7] the Declaration of Independence. John Hancock's signature is famous because it is larger than all the others. Today July 4th, Independence Day, is an important national holiday.

We the People
Article I

The Constitution

After the Revolutionary War, each state had its own laws. The central government was very weak. The thirteen states ________[8] a strong central government. In 1787, they ________[9] representatives to Philadelphia to write a Constitution for the new country. The Constitution ________[10] the powers of the national and state governments. It is the highest law in the United States.

became began bought fought grew led lost met served signed thought was

GEORGE WASHINGTON

Americans call George Washington "the father of our country." He was the leader of the Colonial Army during the Revolutionary War, and he was the leader of the representatives who ________[1] in Philadelphia in 1787 to write the Constitution. In 1789, George Washington ________[2] the first president of the United States. He ________[3] two terms.

THE CIVIL WAR

The Civil War was a war between the states in the North and the states in the South. It ________[4] in 1861 and ended in 1865. In the South, there were big farms called plantations where people ________[5] cotton. The workers on these plantations were slaves—people from Africa who had no rights or freedoms. The plantation owners ________[6] and sold them like furniture. People in the Northern states ________[7] slavery was wrong and wanted to free the slaves. In 1861, eleven Southern states formed the Confederacy and ________[8] against the Northern states (the Union). The Southern states ________[9] the war.

ABRAHAM LINCOLN

Abraham Lincoln ________[10] the sixteenth president. He ________[11] the Northern states during the Civil War and kept the nation together. In 1863, he ________[12] the Emancipation Proclamation, a document that freed the slaves. Five days after the Civil War ended, a man killed Lincoln. Americans remember Abraham Lincoln and George Washington on Presidents' Day, a national holiday on the third Monday in February.

came gave led made opened spoke was worked

IMMIGRATION

In the 1800s, many factories ________ (1) in American cities. These factories needed workers. Immigrants from many different countries ________ (2) to the United States and ________ (3) in the factories. In the 1900s, the government ________ (4) laws to stop immigration from many countries. The Immigration Act of 1965 changed this. It ________ (5) people from any country the right to apply to come to the United States.

THE CIVIL RIGHTS MOVEMENT

During the 1950s and 1960s, the civil rights movement worked to end discrimination against Blacks in the United States. Martin Luther King, Jr., the most famous civil rights leader, ________ (6) protests and demonstrations. He ________ (7) a great speaker. Hundreds of thousands of people heard him when he ________ (8) at the March on Washington in 1963. Americans remember Martin Luther King, Jr., on a national holiday on the third Monday in January.

HISTORY QUIZ

1. When did the Revolutionary War begin?
2. Who wrote the Declaration of Independence?
3. When is Independence Day?
4. What is the highest law in the United States?
5. Who is called "the father of our country"?
6. Who fought in the Civil War?
7. What document freed the slaves?
8. Who was the president during the Civil War?
9. What law made immigration easier?
10. Who was the most famous civil rights leader?

TEAMWORK U.S. HISTORY TIMELINE

Timelines are charts that show dates and events. Work with a classmate. Think about eight important events in U.S. history that occurred between 1770 and 1870. Make a timeline like the one below, and write each event and its year on the timeline.

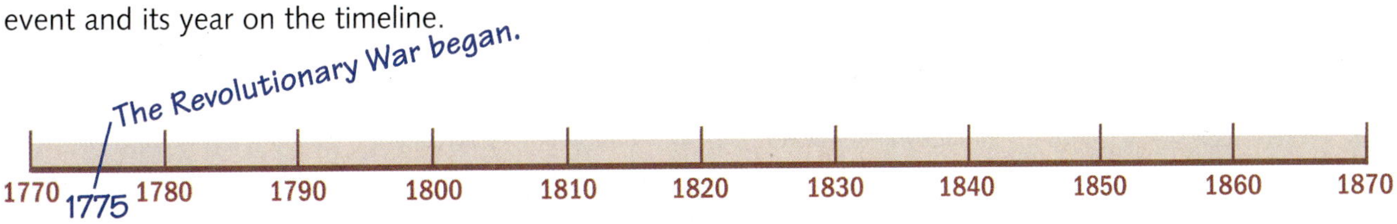

ASSESSMENT

• Check-up test • Self-evaluation checklists

Choose the correct answer.

1. He ____ and fell while he was getting out of a taxi.
- A. ripped
- B. tripped
- C. taught
- D. took

2. I sprained my ____ while I was jogging through the park.
- A. ankle
- B. uncle
- C. pants
- D. wallet

3. I'm really upset. I ____ my cell phone.
- A. met
- B. slept
- C. hiked
- D. lost

4. I fell asleep during the class because I was ____.
- A. prepared
- B. scared
- C. bored
- D. embarrassed

5. We ____ the city by taxi.
- A. got
- B. got around
- C. took
- D. went

6. My husband was in a terrible traffic ____.
- A. light
- B. vehicle
- C. report
- D. accident

7. When the light turned green, the car ____ the intersection.
- A. hit
- B. entered
- C. turned
- D. stopped

8. It was a long war. The two sides ____ against each other for five years.
- A. led
- B. lost
- C. fought
- D. declared

9. Americans remember Martin Luther King, Jr., on a national holiday in ____ every year.
- A. January
- B. February
- C. July
- D. September

10. I believe that all people should have the same ____.
- A. rights
- B. discrimination
- C. signature
- D. immigration

SKILLS CHECK

Words:

☐ burn
☐ chop
☐ cover
☐ cry
☐ deliver
☐ finish
☐ growl
☐ hike
☐ jump
☐ look
☐ paint
☐ play
☐ poke
☐ practice
☐ prepare
☐ realize
☐ rip
☐ shave
☐ shout
☐ snowboard
☐ sprain
☐ stay
☐ study
☐ talk
☐ trip
☐ type
☐ wash
☐ watch
☐ wave
☐ work

☐ become – became
☐ begin – began
☐ break – broke
☐ buy – bought
☐ come – came
☐ cut – cut
☐ do – did
☐ drink – drank
☐ eat – ate
☐ fall – fell
☐ feel – felt
☐ fight – fought
☐ forget – forgot
☐ get – got
☐ give – gave
☐ go – went
☐ grow – grew
☐ have – had
☐ hurt – hurt
☐ keep – kept
☐ lead – led
☐ lose – lost
☐ make – made
☐ meet – met
☐ ride – rode
☐ see – saw
☐ send – sent
☐ shake – shook
☐ sing – sang
☐ sit – sat
☐ sleep – slept
☐ speak – spoke
☐ stand – stood
☐ swim – swam
☐ take – took
☐ teach – taught
☐ tell – told
☐ think – thought
☐ wake – woke
☐ write – wrote

I can ask & answer:

☐ Did you *work*?
Yes, I did. / No, I didn't.
What did you do?
I *worked*.

☐ I was/wasn't *on time*.
☐ We were/weren't *on time*.

☐ I was *working*.
☐ We were *working*.

☐ Who/What/Where/How/How many/What kind of . . . did ____?

I can react to bad news:

☐ That's too bad!/That's a shame!/What a shame!/ What a pity!/I'm sorry to hear that.

I can:

☐ apologize for being late for work
☐ evaluate good and bad excuses for being late for work
☐ interpret a traffic accident report
☐ identify important events and people in U.S. history
☐ create a history timeline

I can write about:

☐ a trip I took

3

Review:
Future: Going to
Future: Will
Future Continuous Tense
Time Expressions
Possessive Pronouns

- Describing Future Plans and Intentions
- Telling About the Future
- Expressing Time and Duration
- Talking on the Telephone
- Asking a Favor
- Calling in Sick at Work
- Calling School to Report a Child's Absence
- Writing a Note to the Teacher
- Parent-School Communication
- Reading a Campus Map

VOCABULARY PREVIEW

yesterday | *today* | *tomorrow*

1. yesterday morning
2. this morning
3. tomorrow morning
4. yesterday afternoon
5. this afternoon
6. tomorrow afternoon
7. yesterday evening
8. this evening
9. tomorrow evening
10. last night
11. tonight
12. tomorrow night

What Are They Going to Do?

What	am	I	going to do?
	is	he / she / it	
	are	we / you / they	

(I am)	I'm	going to read.
(He is)	He's	
(She is)	She's	
(It is)	It's	
(We are)	We're	
(You are)	You're	
(They are)	They're	

Time Expressions

yesterday / this / tomorrow	morning / afternoon / evening	last night
		tonight
		tomorrow night
last / this / next	week / month / year / Sunday / Monday / . . .	
	spring / summer / . . .	
	January / February / . . .	

A. Are you going to buy a donut this morning?

B. No, I'm not. I bought a donut YESTERDAY morning.

A. What are you going to buy?

B. I'm going to buy a muffin.

1. Is Mr. Hopper going to have cake for dessert tonight?
ice cream

2. Is Valerie going to sing folk songs this evening?
Broadway show tunes

3. Are you and your family going to go to Europe this summer?
Hawaii

4. Is Gary going to wear his gray suit today?
his blue suit

5. Are your parents going to watch the movie on Channel 4 this Friday night?
the news program on Channel 7

6. Is Elizabeth going to go out with Jonathan this Saturday evening?
Bob

7. Is the chef going to make onion soup today?
pea soup

8. Is your sister going to take biology this semester?
astronomy

9. Are you and your brother going to play cards this afternoon?
chess

10. Are you going to be Superman this Halloween?
Batman

READING

PLANS FOR THE WEEKEND

It's Friday afternoon, and all the employees at the Liberty Insurance Company are thinking about their plans for the weekend. Milton is going to work in his garden. Diane is going to go hiking in the mountains. Carmen and Tom are going to play tennis. Jack is going to go water-skiing. Kate is going to build a tree house for her children. And Ray and his family are going to have a picnic.

Unfortunately, the employees at the Liberty Insurance Company are going to be very disappointed. According to the radio, it's going to "rain cats and dogs" all weekend.

✓ READING *CHECK-UP*

Q & A

The employees at the Liberty Insurance Company are talking with each other. Using this model, create dialogs based on the story.

A. Tell me, *Milton*, what are you going to do this weekend?
B. I'm going to *work in my garden*. How about you, *Diane*? What are YOU going to do?
A. I'm going to *go hiking in the mountains*.
B. Well, have a nice weekend.
A. You, too.

LISTENING

Listen to the conversation and choose the answer that is true.

1. a. He's going to wear his gray suit.
b. He's going to wear his brown suit.

2. a. They're going to have dinner at home.
b. They're going to have dinner at a restaurant.

3. a. They're going to watch Channel 5.
b. They're going to watch Channel 9.

4. a. He's going to call a mechanic.
b. He's going to call an electrician.

5. a. She's going to go to the supermarket tomorrow.
b. She's going to work in her garden tomorrow.

6. a. They're going to buy the computer.
b. They aren't going to buy the computer.

Will Ms. Martinez Return Soon?

(I will)	I'll	work.
(He will)	He'll	
(She will)	She'll	
(It will)	It'll	
(We will)	We'll	
(You will)	You'll	
(They will)	They'll	

I	won't work. (will not)
He	
She	
It	
We	
You	
They	

A. Will Ms. Martinez return soon?

B. Yes, she will. She'll return in a little while.

A. Will your sister return soon?

B. No, she won't. She won't return for a long time.

1. Will the play begin soon?
Yes, __________. __________ *at 7:30.*

2. Will the concert begin soon?
No, __________. __________ *until 8:00.*

3. Will Ken and Kim see each other again soon?
Yes, __________. __________ *this Saturday night.*

4. Will Larry and Lisa see each other again soon?
No, __________. __________ *until next year.*

5. Will the train arrive soon?
Yes, __________. __________ *in a few minutes.*

6. Will Flight 216 arrive soon?
No, __________. __________ *for several hours.*

7. Will David get out of the hospital soon?
Yes, __________. __________ *in a few days.*

8. Will Ralph get out of jail soon?
No, __________. __________ *for a few years.*

Will You Be Home This Evening?

I'll / He'll / She'll / It'll / We'll / You'll / They'll } be working.

A. Will you be home this evening?

B. Yes, I will. I'll be **watching videos**.

A. Will Nancy be home this evening?

B. No, she won't. She'll be **working overtime**.

1. *you*
pay bills

2. *Angela*
shop at the mall

3. *Mr. and Mrs. Chen*
paint their kitchen

4. *your sister*
attend a meeting

5. *you and your family*
ice skate

6. *Vincent*
browse the web

7. *you*
do research at the library

8. *Tess*
fill out her income tax form

9. *Mr. and Mrs. Silva*
work out at their health club

Can You Call Back a Little Later?

Create conversations based on the model above.

1. *do homework*

2. *iron*

3. *wash my windows*

4. *have dinner*

5. *give the kids a bath*

6.

Could You Do Me a Favor?

I	me	mine
he	him	his
she	her	hers
it	it	—
we	us	ours
you	you	yours
they	them	theirs

A. Could you do me a favor?

B. Sure. What is it?

A. I have to fix a flat tire, and I don't have a jack. Could I possibly borrow yours?

B. I'm sorry. I'm afraid I don't have one.

A. Oh. Do you know anybody who does?

B. Yes. You should call Joe. I'm sure he'll be happy to lend you his.

A. Thanks. I'll call him right away.

A. Could you do me a favor?

B. Sure. What is it?

A. I have to __________, and I don't have a __________. Could I possibly borrow yours?

B. I'm sorry. I'm afraid I don't have one.

A. Oh. Do you know anybody who does?

B. Yes. You should call __________. I'm sure ______'ll be happy to lend you ______ (his/hers/theirs).

A. Thanks. I'll call ______ (him/her/them) right away.

1. *fix my front steps*
   hammer

2. *assemble my new bookshelf*
   screwdriver

3. *write a composition*
   dictionary

4. *adjust my satellite dish*
   ladder

5. *go to a wedding*
   tuxedo

6.

How to Say It!

Asking for a Favor

A. Could you do me a favor? / Could you possibly do me a favor? / Could you do a favor for me? / Could I ask you a favor?

B. Sure. What is it?

Practice the conversations in this lesson again. Ask for a favor in different ways.

READING

SAYING GOOD-BYE

Mr. and Mrs. Karpov are at the Moscow airport. They're saying good-bye to their son Sasha and his family. It's a very emotional day. In a few minutes, Sasha and his family will get on a plane and fly to Canada. They won't be coming back. They're leaving Russia permanently, and Mr. and Mrs. Karpov won't be seeing them for a long, long time.

Sasha and his family are excited about their plans for the future. They're going to stay with his wife's relatives in Toronto. Sasha will work in the family's restaurant. His wife, Marina, will take any job she can find during the day, and she'll study English at night. The children will begin school in September.

Mr. and Mrs. Karpov are both happy and sad. They're happy because they know that their son will have a good life in his new home. However, they're sad because they know they're going to be very lonely. Their apartment will be quiet and empty, and they won't see their grandchildren grow up.

Some day Mr. and Mrs. Karpov will visit Toronto, or perhaps they'll even move there. But until then, they're going to miss their family very much. As you can imagine, it's very difficult for them to say good-bye.

READING *CHECK-UP*

TRUE OR FALSE?

1. Sasha and his family will be leaving Russia for a few minutes.
2. Marina's relatives live in Toronto.
3. Mr. Karpov is happy, and Mrs. Karpov is sad.
4. Mr. and Mrs. Karpov might move to Toronto.
5. Mr. and Mrs. Karpov are sad because they'll be at the Moscow airport until they visit Toronto or move there.

How About You?

- Tell about an emotional day in your life when you had to say good-bye.
- Tell about YOUR plans for the future.

ON YOUR OWN *Looking Forward*

Jerry is looking forward to this weekend. He isn't going to think about work. He's going to read a few magazines, work on his car, and relax at home with his family.

Amanda is looking forward to her birthday. Her sister is going to have a party for her, and all her co-workers and friends are going to be there.

Mr. and Mrs. Cook are looking forward to their summer vacation. They're going to go camping. They're going to hike several miles every day, take a lot of pictures, and forget about all their problems at home.

Mr. and Mrs. Lee are looking forward to their retirement. They're going to get up late every morning, visit friends every afternoon, and enjoy quiet evenings at home together.

What are YOU looking forward to? A birthday? a holiday? a day off? Talk about it with other students in your class.

Write in your journal about something you're looking forward to: What are you looking forward to? When is it going to happen? What are you going to do?

PRONUNCIATION *Going to*

going to = gonna

Listen. Then say it.

Are you going to buy bread today?

What are you going to eat?

I'm going to go camping.

Say it. Then listen.

Is she going to watch TV?

What's he going to wear?

They're going to make dinner.

GRAMMAR FOCUS

Future: Going to

What	am	I	going to do?
	is	he she it	
	are	we you they	

(I am)	I'm	going to read.
(He is) (She is) (It is)	He's She's It's	
(We are) (You are) (They are)	We're You're They're	

Possessive Pronouns

mine his hers — ours yours theirs

Future: Will

(I will) (He will) (She will) (It will) (We will) (You will) (They will)	I'll He'll She'll It'll We'll You'll They'll	work.

I He She It We You They	won't work.

Future Continuous Tense

(I will) (He will) (She will) (It will) (We will) (You will) (They will)	I'll He'll She'll It'll We'll You'll They'll	be working.

Complete the sentences.

1. A. What _____ you _____ _____ buy?
   B. _____ _____ _____ buy a new suit.
2. A. _____ Ms. Romero be back soon?
   B. Yes, _____ _____. _____ _____ back in an hour.
3. A. I don't have a ladder. Can I possibly borrow yours?
   B. I can't find _____. You should ask Mr. King. I'm sure _____ be happy to lend you _____.
4. A. Are you and your wife _____ _____ go to Canada for your vacation?
   B. No. I think _____ probably _____ to Mexico.
5. A. _____ the flight from Dallas arrive soon?
   B. No, _____ _____. _____ _____ _____ until after midnight.
6. A. _____ your parents be home this evening?
   B. Yes, _____ _____. _____ _____ watching their favorite TV program.

LIFE SKILLS

- Calling in sick at work
- Writing a note to the teacher
- Calling school to report a child's absence

1 CONVERSATION Calling in Sick at Work

Practice with a classmate.

A. Hello. This is ______(first & last name)______.
I won't be able to come to work today.
____

B. I'm sorry to hear that.

A. If I feel better tomorrow, I'll come to work.

B. Okay. Thank you for calling.

1. I have a bad stomachache.

2. I hurt my back.

3. I have a high fever.

4.

2 CONVERSATION Calling School to Report a Child's Absence

Practice with a classmate. Leave a message on the school voice-mail system.

A. This is the school attendance line. After the tone, please give your name, your child's name, and the reason for your child's absence. Thank you.

B. Hello. This is ______(first & last name)______.
My daughter/son ______(child's first name)______
won't be in school today.
____
Thank you.

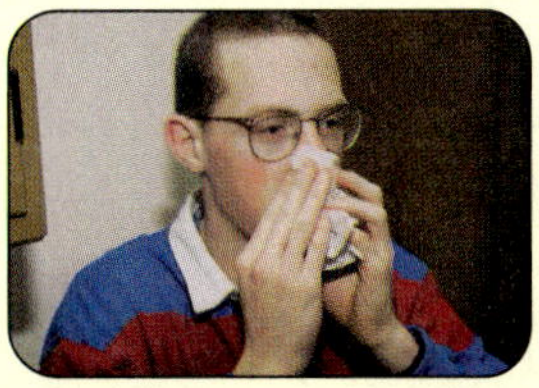

1. He has a bad cold.

2. She has a bad toothache.

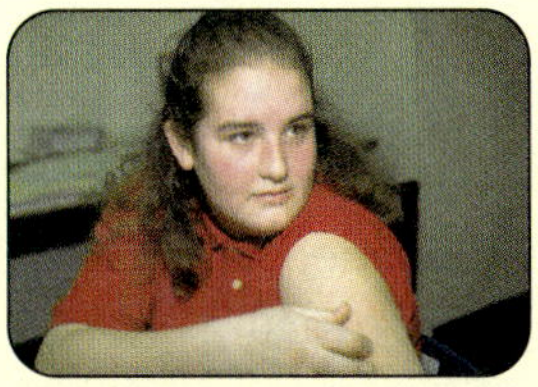

3. She has a bad rash.

4.

3 CLOZE READING & WRITING A Note to the Teacher

Complete the note.

going to
She'll
She's
will
won't

January 26

Dear Ms. Carter,

My daughter Yolanda ________1 be absent from school tomorrow. ________2 be in the hospital. She also ________3 be in school the next day. ________4 ________5 return to school next Monday.

Sincerely,
Anna Garcia

Your child will be absent from school tomorrow. Write a note to tell the teacher.

Jefferson High School
360 Grant Avenue, Pineland FL 33945

Dear Parents:

In a few weeks, your children will be entering our high school as our new ninth grade class. The next four years will be very exciting. Your children will be with us through their freshman, sophomore, junior, and senior years. This letter contains some important information for you.

Students at Jefferson High School must come to school every day unless they are sick, they have a medical or dental appointment, or they have another very good reason. Children who are absent very often cannot learn. Furthermore, education is *compulsory* for children between the ages of 6 and 16—they have to attend school.

If you know that your children are going to be absent, call the school's attendance line at 239-0922 on or before the day of the absence and leave a message explaining the reason for the absence. Although we want our students to be in school every day, they should not come to school if they have a high fever or if they might give an illness to another student.

Students bring home report cards four times a year. The chart to the right explains the grades that you will see on these report cards. We are proud that a large number of students at Jefferson High School are honor roll students who receive grades of A or B in all their classes.

Grade	Percent	Meaning
A	90% – 100%	excellent
B	80% – 89%	above average
C	70% – 79%	satisfactory
D	60% – 69%	needs improvement
F	0 – 59%	unsatisfactory

Homework is an important part of learning. It teaches students how to work independently and to manage their time. Your children will have about two hours of homework each day. Please make sure they have time to do their homework.

"Latch-key children" who come home to an empty house after school often get into trouble because there is nobody at home to supervise them. If your children attend an after-school program, you won't have to worry about their safety. Your children can participate in many interesting after-school activities. These include theater, photography, art, and sports.

We hope you attend school events and parent-teacher association meetings during the school year. If you have time, you can also volunteer to help at the school. We also hope to see you at our open house on October 26th, where you will have the opportunity to visit the school and meet your children's teachers.

Sincerely,

Eva Fernandez

Eva Fernandez, Principal

1. This letter is for the parents of ____.
- A. all students at this school
- B. students entering the ninth grade
- C. students with poor attendance
- D. honor students

2. Parents should NOT ____.
- A. supervise their children
- B. visit the school
- C. keep sick children at home
- D. send sick children to school

3. We can infer that the third year of high school is the ____ year.
- A. freshman
- B. sophomore
- C. junior
- D. senior

4. Honor students ____.
- A. need improvement
- B. get unsatisfactory grades
- C. are below average
- D. get high grades

5. According to this letter, homework teaches students to ____.
- A. work on their own
- B. work for freedom
- C. work with others
- D. work until late at night

6. The open house is ____.
- A. a parent-teacher association meeting
- B. a time to visit and meet the teachers
- C. at the principal's house
- D. for latch-key children

Look at the map of Clarksdale Community College and answer the questions.

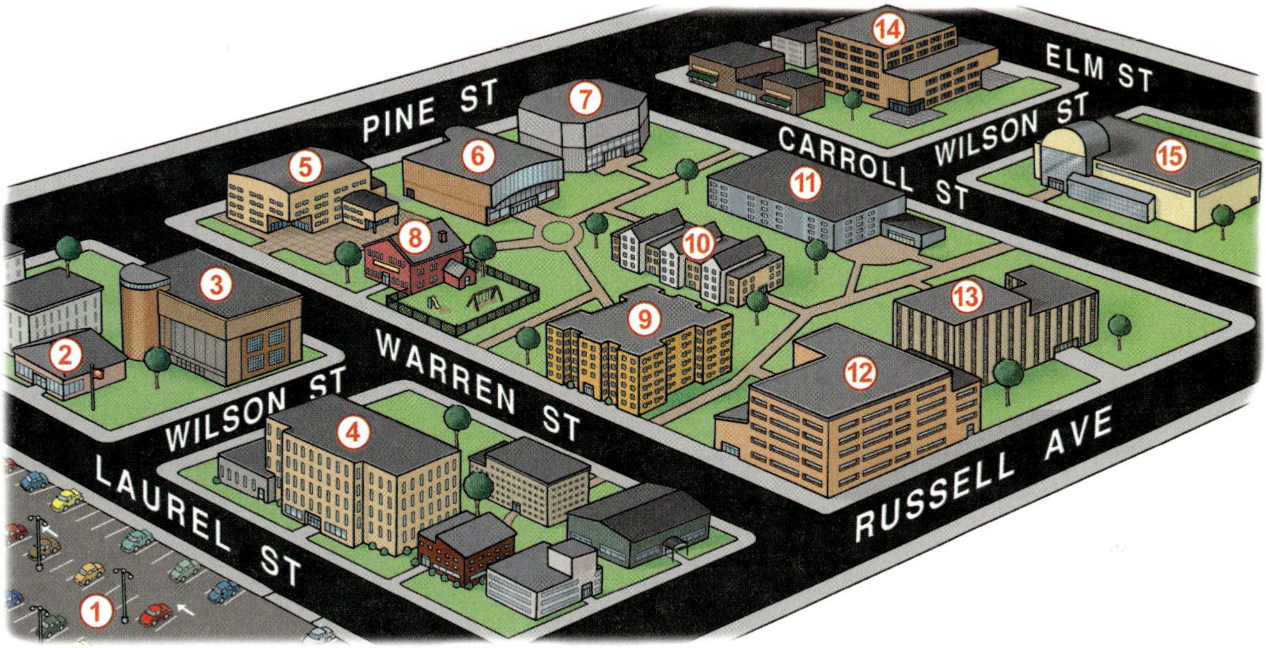

1 Parking Lot
2 Security/Safety
3 Burton Library
4 Baker Administration Building
5 Patterson Music Building
6 Espinosa Theater
7 Danson Art Museum
8 Williams Child-Care Center
9 Carter Hall
10 Lopez Hall
11 Tamworth Vocational Center
12 King Student Center/Bookstore
13 Rossi Hall
14 Fletcher Science Center
15 Rivera Gym

1. Carter Hall is on ____.
- A. Pine Street
- B. Warren Street
- C. Russell Avenue
- D. Wilson Street

2. Espinosa Theater is ____.
- A. across from Rossi Hall
- B. around the corner from the student center
- C. between the music building and the museum
- D. next to the vocational center

3. When you go from the student center to the gym, you pass ____.
- A. Danson Art Museum
- B. Patterson Music Building
- C. Fletcher Science Center
- D. Rossi Hall

4. You can buy books for your courses at ____.
- A. Baker Administration Building
- B. King Student Center
- C. Burton Library
- D. Carter Hall

5. The basketball court is in ____.
- A. Building 5
- B. Building 11
- C. Building 12
- D. Building 15

6. Susan is learning how to be a welder in ____.
- A. Building 2
- B. Building 4
- C. Building 11
- D. Building 14

7. The chemistry labs are in the building ____.
- A. on Elm Street
- B. on Laurel Street
- C. on Russell Avenue
- D. on Warren Street

8. Someone stole Amy's wallet. She should go to the building ____.
- A. on Pine Street
- B. on Warren Street
- C. on Laurel Street
- D. on Elm Street

Choose the correct answer.

1. Mrs. Wu is at a meeting. She'll _____ in a little while.
   A. return
   B. receive
   C. require
   D. realize

2. My wife and I will be _____ our income tax returns tonight.
   A. writing
   B. paying
   C. filling out
   D. working out

3. I'll be happy to _____ you my screwdriver.
   A. take
   B. browse
   C. borrow
   D. lend

4. My brother and I will be _____ a wedding in Cleveland this weekend.
   A. arriving
   B. attending
   C. assembling
   D. adjusting

5. I'm really _____ my vacation next month.
   A. looking for
   B. looking like
   C. looking forward to
   D. hoping

6. Oh, no! I have a flat tire, and I can't find my _____.
   A. lock
   B. ladder
   C. hammer
   D. jack

7. My daughter is a _____ in high school. She'll be going to college next year.
   A. sophomore
   B. senior
   C. junior
   D. freshman

8. This afternoon's meeting is _____ for all employees.
   A. compulsory
   B. capable
   C. independent
   D. absent

Look at the map of Fairview Community College and answer the questions.

9. Davis Library is _____.
   A. next to the science center
   B. across from the gym
   C. next to the theater
   D. between Ramirez Hall and De Costa Hall

10. To go from the parking lot to the theater, you pass _____.
   A. De Costa Hall
   B. the library
   C. the student center
   D. Ramirez Hall

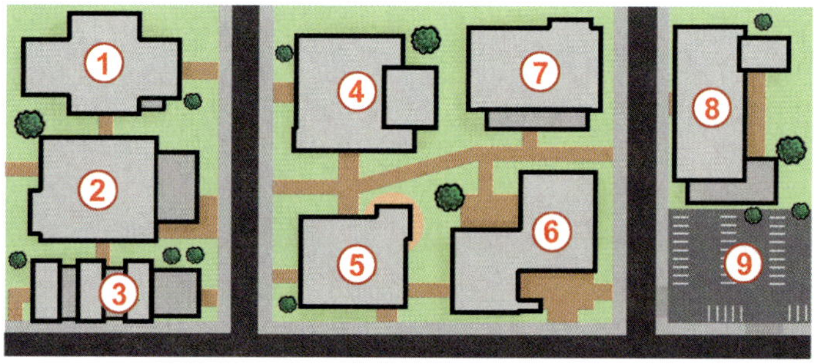

1 Ramirez Hall
2 Davis Library
3 De Costa Hall
4 Grant Administration Building
5 Henderson Theater
6 Jenkins Student Center
7 Chang Science Center
8 Delgado Gym
9 Parking Lot

SKILLS CHECK

Words:
- ☐ adjust
- ☐ assemble
- ☐ attend
- ☐ borrow
- ☐ browse
- ☐ call back
- ☐ come back
- ☐ do research
- ☐ fill out
- ☐ get out
- ☐ give *the kids* a bath
- ☐ go water-skiing
- ☐ hike
- ☐ ice skate
- ☐ imagine
- ☐ lend
- ☐ look forward to
- ☐ pay bills
- ☐ relax
- ☐ return
- ☐ stay with
- ☐ work on
- ☐ work out

I can ask & answer:
- ☐ What are you going to *do*? I'm going to *read*.
- ☐ Will you *be home this evening*? Yes, I will./No, I won't.
- ☐ I'll *work*.
- ☐ I won't *work*.
- ☐ I'll be *working*.
- ☐ How much longer will you be *ironing*?
- ☐ I'll be *ironing* for *another 10 minutes*.

I can:
- ☐ call in sick at work
- ☐ call school to report a child's absence
- ☐ interpret a high school grading system
- ☐ describe school procedures
- ☐ identify parent responsibilities
- ☐ interpret a college campus map

I can ask a favor:
- ☐ Could you do me a favor?
- ☐ Could you possibly do me a favor?
- ☐ Could you do a favor for me?
- ☐ Could I ask you a favor?

I can write:
- ☐ a note to my child's teacher

I can write about:
- ☐ something I'm looking forward to

Feature Article
Fact File
Around the World
Interview
We've Got Mail!

SIDE by SIDE Gazette

Global Exchange
Listening
Fun with Idioms
What Are They Saying?

Volume 3 Number 1

Immigration Around the World

Where do immigrants move, and why?

More than 145 million immigrants live outside their native countries. Immigrants move to other countries for different reasons. Some people move because of war, political or economic problems, or natural disasters such as earthquakes and floods. Some immigrants move to be with family members, to marry, or to find better living conditions.

Where are immigrants moving from? And what countries are they moving to? One of the largest immigration flows is from Latin America and Asia to the United States. Another immigrant flow is from Eastern Europe, the former Soviet republics, and North Africa to Western Europe. Many immigrants also move from Africa and Asia to the Middle East. In countries such as Saudi Arabia, 90% of the total population is now foreign born.

When immigrants arrive in a new country, they often live in urban neighborhoods. As a result of immigration, many city neighborhoods change. Immigrants open new stores, restaurants, and other businesses. For example, the historic Esquilino neighborhood in Rome is now the home of a large number of Chinese immigrants. There are also many new immigrants from Albania, Moldova, Bulgaria, and Ukraine. In some schools in Athens, 50% of the children are foreign born. Los Angeles and New York are two cities in the United States with very large immigrant populations. In Los Angeles, 37% of the population is foreign born, and children in the public schools speak 82 different languages. In New York, 40% of the population is foreign born, and children speak 140 different languages in the schools.

Immigrants arriving in their new country

Ellis Island

Ellis Island was an immigration center on an island in the harbor of New York City. Between 1892 and 1954, 12 million immigrants passed through Ellis Island. At Ellis Island, immigration officials checked immigrants' documents, gave them medical examinations, and decided if the immigrants could stay in the United States. Most immigrants came from Italy, Russia, Hungary, Austria, Austria-Hungary, Germany, England, and Ireland. More than 40% of all Americans today have a present or past relative who came through Ellis Island.

Ellis Island registration hall

FACT FILE

Countries with Large Numbers of Immigrants

Country	Immigrant Population (in millions)
United States	28.4
Germany	7.5
Saudi Arabia	6
Canada	4.9
Australia	4.4
France	4.3

Around the World

Immigrant Neighborhoods

There are many interesting immigrant neighborhoods around the world. In these neighborhoods, immigrants can often speak their native languages, buy products from their countries, and eat in restaurants that serve their favorite foods.

a Cuban neighborhood in Miami, Florida

Vietnamese immigrants in Sydney, Australia

Turkish immigrants in Berlin, Germany

Chinatown in Toronto, Canada

Japanese immigrants in Sao Paulo, Brazil

a Russian neighborhood in Brooklyn, New York

What are different immigrant neighborhoods you know?

Interview

*A **Side by Side Gazette** reporter recently visited Mr. Tran Nguyen, a Vietnamese immigrant in Australia. Mr. Nguyen lives and works in a Vietnamese and Chinese neighborhood in the suburbs of Melbourne.*

Q: When did you immigrate to Australia, and why?

A: Well, my brother left Vietnam in 1983 and came here to Australia. Seven years later, his wife and children joined him. I came here three years ago with my wife and children to be with my brother and his family.

Q: Do you work?

A: Yes. I work seven days a week in my brother's restaurant, and I go to English classes at night.

Q: What did you do in Vietnam?

A: I was a teacher. I taught mathematics. I want to be a teacher here someday, but first I want to send my children to college.

Q: What do you miss most about Vietnam?

A: I miss my community and my friends. In Vietnam, people took care of each other. It's not the same here. Everyone here works very hard. People are very busy. They don't have much time to spend with friends.

Q: What do you like about your life here?

A: We have many opportunities. My wife and I both have good jobs, and my son and daughter will go to college someday. I think we will have a very good future here, and we're very grateful.

We've Got Mail!

Dear Side by Side,

I have a question about tenses in English. Sometimes I hear people use the present tense when they are talking about the future. For example, I was watching a TV program in English yesterday, and I heard a man say, "I'm flying to London tomorrow. My plane leaves at 9:30." But if a man is talking about tomorrow, shouldn't he use the future tense? I think the correct way to say this is: "I'm going to fly to London tomorrow. My plane will leave at 9:30." Did the man on the TV program make a mistake?

Sincerely,
"Tense About the Future"

Dear "Tense About the Future,"

Your question is a very good one. No, the man on the TV program didn't make a mistake. We often use the present tense to talk about events in the future or about definite plans that we have. For example, you can say:

My brother's wedding is next Saturday.
I'm having a party tomorrow.
They're going to the beach this weekend.
The plumber is coming tomorrow morning.

We can also use the present tense to talk about future events that happen at a definite time or on a regular schedule. For example, you can say:

The movie begins at 7:30 tonight.
The office opens tomorrow morning at 9 A.M.
The train arrives at 6:15.
The store closes tonight at 10 P.M.

So, you don't need to be "tense" about the future! You can use both the present and the future tenses to talk about future time.

We hope this answers your question. Thanks for your letter, and good luck with your English!

Sincerely,
Side by Side

Global Exchange

NickyG: Hi. It's Sunday night here, and I just finished my biology homework. Before I turn off my computer, I want to tell you about my weekend. It was really great. I went camping with some of my friends. We left early Saturday morning and drove to the mountains. We hiked for several hours to a beautiful lake. We went swimming, we cooked over a campfire, and we slept outside. We told stories and sang songs until after midnight. In the morning, we made a big breakfast, we swam again, and then we packed up our things, hiked back to the car, and came home. How about you? How was your weekend? Write back soon. Okay?

Smile9: Hi. It's Monday morning here. I'm sitting in the computer lab at my school, and your message just arrived! I'm happy to hear from you again. My weekend wasn't as exciting as yours. I have final exams in all my courses this week, so I stayed home and studied all weekend. But I'm really looking forward to next weekend. Our family is going to travel to the place where my parents grew up. We're having a big family reunion on Saturday. All my relatives will be there. We don't see them very often, so it will be a very special time. I'll tell you about it when I return. Oh. Here comes my teacher! I've got to go! Talk to you soon.

Send a message to a keypal. Tell about what you did last weekend. Tell about your plans for next weekend.

LISTENING

You Have Five Messages!

_e_	1 Sarah	a.	will be visiting his parents.
___	2 Bob	b.	will be studying.
___	3 Paula	c.	will be attending a wedding.
___	4 Joe	d.	will go to the party.
___	5 Carla	e.	will be taking her uncle to the hospital.

FUN with IDIOMS

Do You Know These Expressions?

_e_	1. It's raining cats and dogs!	a.	I'll call you.
____	2. What's cooking?	b.	It was difficult.
____	3. I'm tied up right now.	c.	It was easy.
____	4. I'll give you a ring tomorrow.	d.	What's new?
____	5. The English test was a piece of cake!	e.	It's raining very hard.
____	6. The English test was no picnic!	f.	I'm busy.

What Are They Saying?

4

Present Perfect Tense

- Describing Skills
- Describing Actions That Have Occurred
- Describing Actions That Haven't Occurred Yet
- Making Recommendations
- Things To Do Where You Live
- Making Lists
- Employment Application Procedures
- Job Application Forms
- Employment History
- Job Search Strategies

VOCABULARY PREVIEW

Things to Do Today

1 

❑ go to the bank

2 

❑ do the laundry

3 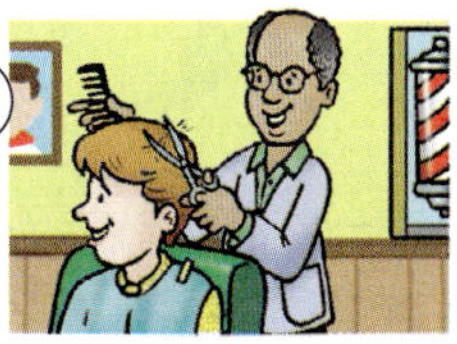

❑ get a haircut

4 

❑ write to Grandma

5 

❑ take the dog for a walk

6 

❑ give the dog a bath

7 

❑ speak to the landlord

8 

❑ drive the kids to their dance lesson

9 

❑ eat lunch

10 

❑ ride my exercise bike

11 

❑ swim

12 

❑ see a movie

Things I've Done Today: I've . . .

☑ **1.** gone to the bank
☑ **2.** done the laundry
☑ **3.** gotten a haircut
☑ **4.** written to Grandma
☑ **5.** taken the dog for a walk
☑ **6.** given the dog a bath
☑ **7.** spoken to the landlord
☑ **8.** driven the kids to their dance lesson
☑ **9.** eaten lunch
☑ **10.** ridden my exercise bike
☑ **11.** swum
☑ **12.** seen a movie

I've Driven Trucks for Many Years

A. Do you know how to **drive** trucks?

B. Yes. I've **driven** trucks for many years.

1. *write reports*
written

2. *fly airplanes*
flown

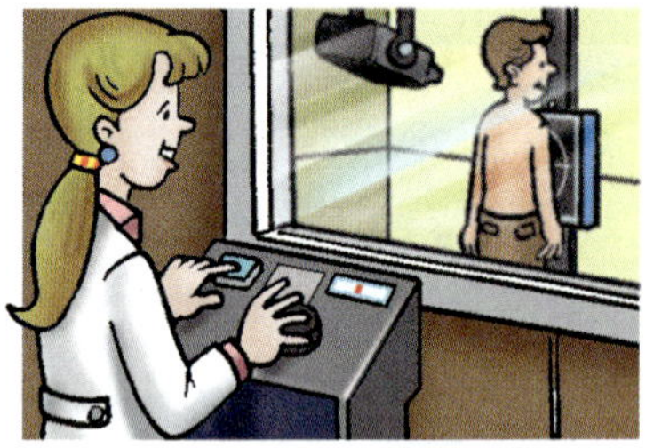

3. *take X-rays*
taken

4. *speak Swahili*
spoken

5. *eat with chopsticks*
eaten

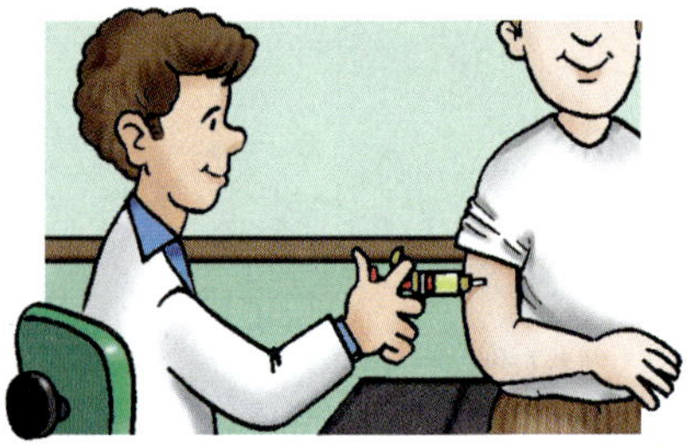

6. *give injections*
given

7. *draw cartoons*
drawn

8. *do yoga*
done

9. *ride horses*
ridden

I've Never Eaten Lunch with the Boss

A. I'm going to **eat** lunch with the boss tomorrow.

B. I'm jealous. I've never **eaten** lunch with the boss.

1. *fly in a helicopter*
flown

2. *see a Broadway show*
seen

3. *go on a cruise*
gone

4. *sing at the White House*
sung

5. *swim at the Ritz Hotel*
swum

6. *get a raise*
gotten

7. *be on television*
been

8. *take a ride in a hot-air balloon*
taken

9. *ride in a limousine*
ridden

Have You Ever Seen a Rainbow?

see
saw
seen

A. Have you ever **seen** a rainbow?

B. Yes, I have. I **saw** a rainbow last year.

go
went
gone

1. *go scuba diving*

give
gave
given

2. *give a speech*

wear
wore
worn

3. *wear a kimono*

eat
ate
eaten

4. *eat cotton candy*

take
took
taken

5. *take a first-aid course*

fall
fell
fallen

6. *fall asleep in class*

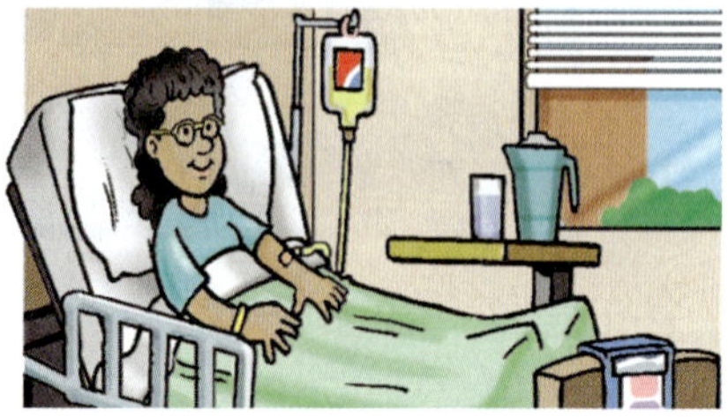

be
was
been

7. *be in the hospital*

get
got
gotten

8. *get stuck in an elevator*

Have You Written the Report Yet?

Have	I / we / you / they	eaten?
Has	he / she / it	

Yes,	I / we / you / they	have.
	he / she / it	has.

write
wrote
written

A. Have you **written** the report yet?

B. Yes, I have. I **wrote** the report a little while ago.

go
went
gone

A. Has David **gone** to the bank yet?

B. Yes, he has. He **went** to the bank a little while ago.

drive
drove
driven

1. *you*
drive the new van

give
gave
given

2. *Nancy*
give her presentation

get
got
gotten

3. *the employees*
get their paychecks

take
took
taken

4. *you and Robert*
take inventory

meet
met
met

5. *George*
meet the new boss

explain
explained
explained

6. *I*
explain the present perfect tense

He's Already Gone Bowling This Week

(I have)	I've	eaten.
(We have)	We've	
(You have)	You've	
(They have)	They've	
(He has)	He's	
(She has)	She's	
(It has)	It's	

go
went
gone

A. Why isn't Charlie going to **go** bowling tonight?

B. He's already **gone** bowling this week.

A. Really? When?

B. He **went** bowling yesterday.

see
saw
seen

1. Why isn't Vicky going to see a movie this evening?

eat
ate
eaten

2. Why aren't Mr. and Mrs. Kendall going to eat at a restaurant tonight?

get
got
gotten

3. Why isn't Roy going to get a haircut today?

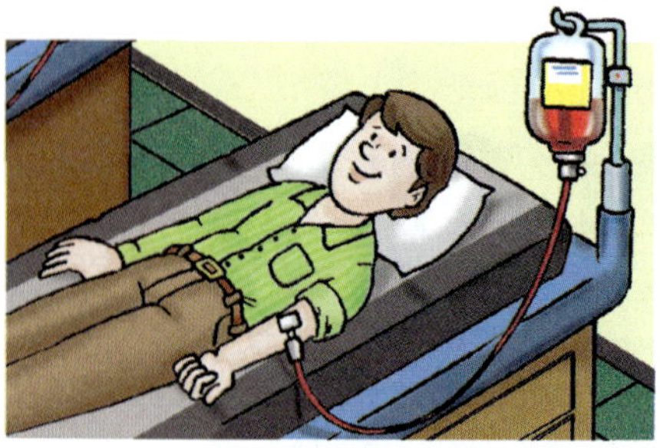

give
gave
given

4. Why aren't you going to give blood today?

take
took
taken

5. Why isn't Shirley going to take her children to the zoo this afternoon?

wear
wore
worn

6. Why isn't Fred going to wear his purple tie today?

drive
drove
driven

7. Why aren't you and your family going to drive to the mountains today?

write
wrote
written

8. Why isn't Julie going to write to her best friend today?

do
did
done

9. Why isn't Gary going to do his laundry today?

swim
swam
swum

10. Why aren't your parents going to swim at the health club today?

buy
bought
bought

11. Why aren't you going to buy bananas today?

have
had
had

12. Why aren't Mr. and Mrs. Davis going to have spaghetti for dinner tonight?

wash
washed
washed

13. Why isn't Jim going to wash his car this morning?

play
played
played

14. Why isn't your grandmother going to play Bingo today?

READING

WE CAN'T DECIDE

My friends and I can't decide what to do tonight. I don't want to see a movie. I've already seen a movie this week. Maggie doesn't want to go bowling. She has already gone bowling this week. Mark doesn't want to eat at a restaurant. He has already eaten at a restaurant this week. Betty and Mike don't want to play cards. They have already played cards this week. And NOBODY wants to go dancing. We have all gone dancing this week.

It's already 9 P.M., and we still haven't decided what we're going to do tonight.

ROLE PLAY

You and other students are the people in the story above. Create a role play based on the situation. Use these lines to start your conversation.

A. Look! It's already 9 P.M., and we still haven't decided what we're going to do tonight. Does anybody have any ideas?
B. I don't know.
C. Do you want to see a movie?
D. No, not me. I've already . . .
E. Does anybody want to . . . ?
F. I don't. I've already . . .
G. I have an idea. Let's . . .
H. No, I don't want to do that. I've already . . .

COMPLETE THE STORY

Fill in the correct words to complete the story.

Alvin has a very bad cold. He has been sick all week. He has tried very hard to get rid of his cold, but nothing he has done has helped. At the beginning of the week, he went to a clinic and saw a doctor. He followed the doctor's advice all week. He stayed home, took aspirin, drank* orange juice, ate chicken soup, and rested in bed.

At this point, Alvin is extremely frustrated. Even though he has ________1 to a clinic and ________2 a doctor, ________3 home, ________4 aspirin, ________5 orange juice, ________6 chicken soup, and ________7 in bed, he STILL has a very bad cold. Nothing he has ________8 has helped.

* drink – drank – drunk

They Haven't Had the Time

I / We / You / They	haven't (have not)	eaten.*
He / She / It	hasn't (has not)	

A. Do you like to **swim**?

B. Yes, but I haven't **swum** in a long time.

A. Why not?

B. I haven't had the time.

A. Does Rita like to **draw**?

B. Yes, but she hasn't **drawn** in a long time.

A. Why not?

B. She hasn't had the time.

1. Do you like to ride your bicycle?

2. Does Arthur like to write poetry?

3. Does Kathy like to go kayaking?

4. Do you and your brother like to play Monopoly?

5. Does Laura like to make her own clothes?

6. Do you like to see your old friends?

7. Do Mr. and Mrs. Bell like to take dance lessons?

8. Does Grandpa like to do magic tricks?

9.

* In the present perfect tense, the word after **have** or **has** is a past participle. Some past participles are the same as the past tense (for example, **played**, **washed**, **made**). Other past participles are different from the past tense (for example, **swum**, **drawn**, **ridden**). We will tell you when the past participles are different. A list of these words is in the Appendix at the end of the book.

Has Timmy Gone to Bed Yet?

Have	I we you they	eaten?
Has	he she it	

No,	I we you they	haven't.
	he she it	hasn't.

A. Has Timmy gone to bed yet?

B. No, he hasn't. He has to go to bed now.

1. *Amanda*
do her homework

2. *you*
take your medicine

3. *James*
get up

4. *Debbie and Danny*
leave for school

5. *Jennifer*
call her supervisor

6. *you*
write your term paper

7. *you and your sister*
feed the dog

8. *you*
speak to your landlord

9. *Harry*
pay his electric bill

READING

WORKING OVERTIME

I'm an employee of the Goodwell Computer Company. This is a typical Friday afternoon at our office. All the employees are working overtime. We haven't gone home because we haven't finished our work yet. Friday is always a very busy day.

The secretary still hasn't typed two important letters. The bookkeeper hasn't written all the paychecks. The office clerks haven't delivered all the mail. And the boss still hasn't spoken to three important people who are waiting to see her.

As for me, I'm the custodian, and I haven't finished my work yet either. I still haven't cleaned all the offices because my co-workers haven't gone home yet! I'm not really surprised. Friday is always a very busy day at our office.

✓ READING *CHECK-UP*

Q & A

The custodian at the Goodwell Computer Company is talking with the employees on a typical Friday afternoon. Using this model, create dialogs based on the story.

A. I see you haven't gone home yet.
B. No, I haven't. I still haven't *typed two important letters*.
A. Well, have a good weekend.
B. You, too.

WHAT'S THE WORD?

1. A. Have you (see) ______ the letter from the Lexon Company?
B. Yes. I ______ it on your desk.

2. A. Have you (eat) ______ lunch yet?
B. Yes. I ______ a few minutes ago.

3. A. Has the bookkeeper (go) ______ to the bank yet?
B. Yes, she ______. She ______ there this morning.

4. A. Have you (speak) ______ to the boss about your vacation?
B. Yes, I ______. I ______ to her about it yesterday.

5. A. Have you (make) ______ plans for my trip to Chicago yet?
B. Yes. I ______ them yesterday.

6. A. Has anybody (read) ______ today's *New York Times*?
B. Yes. I ______ it on my way to work.

7. A. Has the office clerk (take) ______ the mail to the post office yet?
B. No, he ______. He ______ it to the mail room, but ______ ______ ______ it to the post office yet.

8. A. Has John (finish) ______ his work?
B. Yes, he ______. He's already (go) ______ home.

Have You Seen Any Good Movies Recently?

A. Have you seen any good movies recently?

B. Yes, I have. I saw a very good movie last week.

A. Really? What movie did you see?

B. I saw *The Wedding Dancer*.

A. Oh. How was it?

B. It was excellent. It's one of the best movies I've ever seen.

A. Have you ________ any good ________s recently?

B. Yes, I have. I ________ a very good ________ last week.

A. Really? What ________ did you ________?

B. I ________ "______________________."

A. Oh. How was it?

B. It was excellent. It's one of the best ________s I've ever ________.

1. *read • book*

2. *rent • video*

3. *go to • restaurant*

How to Say It!

Expressing Satisfaction

A. How was it?

B.
- It was excellent.
- It was very good.
- It was wonderful.
- It was great.
- It was fantastic.
- It was terrific.
- It was phenomenal.
- It was awesome.

Practice the conversations in this lesson again. Express satisfaction in different ways.

READING

LINDA LIKES NEW YORK

Linda has lived in New York for a long time. She has done a lot of things in New York. She has gone to the top of the Empire State Building, she has visited the Statue of Liberty, she has taken a tour of the United Nations, and she has seen several Broadway shows.

However, there are a lot of things she hasn't done yet. She hasn't gone to any museums, she hasn't seen Ellis Island, and she hasn't been in Times Square on New Year's Eve.

Linda likes New York. She has done a lot of things, and there are still a lot more things to do.

LISTENING

Linda is on vacation in San Francisco. This is her list of things to do. Check the things on the list Linda has already done.

- ___ see the Golden Gate Bridge
- ___ visit Golden Gate Park
- ___ take a tour of Alcatraz prison
- ___ go to Chinatown
- ___ ride a cable car
- ___ eat at Fisherman's Wharf
- ___ buy souvenirs

Alan is a secretary in a very busy office. This is his list of things to do before 5 P.M. on Friday. Check the things on the list Alan has already done.

- ___ call Mrs. Porter
- ___ type the letter to the Mervis Company
- ___ take the mail to the post office
- ___ go to the bank
- ___ send an e-mail to the company's office in Denver
- ___ speak to the boss about my salary

It's Saturday, and Judy and Paul Johnson are doing lots of things around the house. This is the list of things they have to do today. Check the things on the list they've already done.

- ___ do the laundry
- ___ wash the kitchen windows
- ___ pay the bills
- ___ give the dog a bath
- ___ clean the garage
- ___ fix the bathroom sink
- ___ repair the fence
- ___ vacuum the living room rug

Make a list of things you usually do at school, at work, or at home. Then check the things you've already done this week. Share your list with other students. Tell about what you've done and what you haven't done.

PRONUNCIATION Contractions with *is* & *has*

he is = he's he has = he's	she is = she's she has = she's

Listen. Then say it.

He is a good painter.

He has painted for a long time.

She is a good teacher.

She has taught for a long time.

Say it. Then listen.

He is a taxi driver.

He has driven a taxi for a long time.

She is an actress.

She has acted for a long time.

Think about your experiences in the place where you live. What have you done? What haven't you done yet? Write about it in your journal.

GRAMMAR FOCUS

Present Perfect Tense

(I have) I've (We have) We've (You have) You've (They have) They've		eaten.
(He has) He's (She has) She's (It has) It's		

I We You They	haven't	eaten.
He She It	hasn't	

Have	I we you they	eaten?
Has	he she it	

Yes,	I we you they	have.
	he she it	has.

No,	I we you they	haven't.
	he she it	hasn't.

Irregular Verbs

be – was/were – been
do – did – done
draw – drew – drawn
drink – drank – drunk
drive – drove – driven
eat – ate – eaten
fall – fell – fallen
fly – flew – flown
get – got – gotten
give – gave – given
go – went – gone
ride – rode – ridden
see – saw – seen
sing – sang – sung
speak – spoke – spoken
swim – swam – swum
take – took – taken
wear – wore – worn
write – wrote – written

Complete the sentences with the correct forms of these verbs.

be draw go ride see sing take wear

1. I love to draw. _____ _____ for many years.
2. _____ you ever _____ a rainbow?
3. My parents _____ never _____ dance lessons.
4. _____ already _____ that song. We _____ it a little while ago.
5. My grandson _____ _____ his bicycle in a long time.
6. _____ you ever _____ on TV? Yes, I _____.
7. Joe _____ already _____ that tie this week. He _____ it yesterday.
8. _____ Marta _____ to sleep yet? Yes, _____ _____. She _____ to sleep an hour ago.

1 READING How to Fill Out an Employment Application

It's important to fill out an employment application form completely and correctly. Read the suggestions for completing this company's form.

Steps for Completing Your Job Application Form

1. Fill in all your personal information.
2. State the position you are applying for.
3. Complete your education history, including high school, college, and vocational school.
4. List your current and former jobs.
5. Write your dates of employment for each position.
6. Write each employer's name and address.
7. Give the reason for leaving each position.
8. Give the names and addresses of three references.
9. Describe your skills, including languages you speak.
10. Check the application to make sure all information is correct and complete.

2 CONVERSATION Applying for a Job

Practice with a classmate. Ask about all the steps for completing a job application form.

A. Have you completed your application form?
B. Yes, I have.
A. Have you filled in all your personal information?[1]
B. Yes, I have.
A. Have you ______________?[2]
B. Yes, I have.
A. Have you ______________?[3–10]
B. Yes, I have.

3 TEAMWORK Application Forms

Find job application forms in the community and bring them to class. Fill out a form. Then exchange forms with a classmate and check each other's work. As a class, compare all the different application forms that students find.

Look at the job application form and answer the questions.

NAME	Lessard (Last)	Daniel (First)	Louis (Middle)	DATE	9/01/08
				SOCIAL SECURITY NUMBER	749-10-2792
ADDRESS	895 North West 15th Street Miami, FL 33132			TELEPHONE NUMBER	(305) 579-3457

EMPLOYMENT HISTORY (LIST MOST RECENT OR PRESENT EXPERIENCE FIRST)

Date	Name & Address of Employer	Position	Salary	Name of Supervisor	Reason for Leaving
From: 3/08 To: present	Miami Family Physicians 9952 Center Ave., Miami, FL	medical assistant	$29,000/yr	Dr. Omar Hasan	want to learn new skills
Duties schedule appointments, measure height and weight, take blood pressure, do lab tests, change dressings					
From: 1/05 To: 2/08	High Street Medical Associates 1750 High St., Miami, FL	medical assistant	$26,500/yr	Dr. Susan McCann	left for a better job
Duties filed medical records, greeted patients, measured their height and weight, and took their blood pressure					
From: 5/01 To: 5/03	Diamond Health Club 1900 Grand St., Miami, FL	office assistant	$25,500/yr	Debby Lewis	returned to school
Duties answered the telephone, sorted mail, filed information, and typed memos					
From: 3/00 To: 4/01	CompuTech Corporation 1273 Washington Ave., Miami, FL	receptionist	$25,000/yr	Nina Marino	company closed
Duties greeted clients, answered the telephone, and took messages					
From: 1/96 To: 2/00	Dependable Hardware 632 Shore Blvd., Tampa, FL	salesperson	$10.00/hr	Fernando Nuñez	moved to Miami
Duties recommended tools and other hardware to customers, took inventory, and operated a cash register					
From: 3/95 To: 12/95	Buy Low Supermarket 468 West Orange Ave., Tampa, FL	cashier	$7.50/hr	Jeff Carson	left for a better job
Duties operated a cash register					

1. Daniel worked as ____ for two years.
   A. an office assistant
   B. a receptionist
   C. a salesperson
   D. a cashier

2. After CompuTech Corporation closed, Daniel ____.
   A. returned to school
   B. moved to Miami
   C. answered the telephone and sorted mail
   D. recommended tools and other hardware

3. Daniel is filling out this application on September 1, 2008. He has worked at Miami Family Physicians for ____.
   A. half a year
   B. a year
   C. a year and a half
   D. nine months

4. Daniel hasn't ____ in a long time.
   A. taken blood pressure
   B. changed dressings
   C. operated a cash register
   D. done lab tests

5. Daniel has ____ in two different jobs.
   A. taken inventory
   B. answered the telephone
   C. scheduled appointments
   D. typed memos

6. We can infer that Daniel attended school ____.
   A. in 2000 and 2001
   B. in 2001 and 2002
   C. in 2002 and 2003
   D. in 2003 and 2004

Read the article and answer the questions.

Find the Right Job!

It can take a long time to find the right job, but it doesn't have to take long if you know how and where to look. Here are some tips to help you with your job search.

- ✔ Check the classified ads in your local newspaper every morning. Look for job postings on bulletin boards in libraries, community centers, supermarkets, laundromats, and other public buildings. Look in store and restaurant windows for help wanted signs.
- ✔ Network! Tell your friends, relatives, neighbors, teachers, and everybody else you know that you're looking for a job. Describe the kind of job you want. One of these people might know about a job opening, maybe even before the job listing is in the newspaper.
- ✔ The Internet has employment websites with thousands of job listings. You can look through the job listings in Internet job banks, and you can even apply for some jobs online. If you don't have a computer or Internet service at home, go to your local public library to get on the Internet.
- ✔ Don't be afraid to call a company to ask about job openings. "Cold calls" are a good way to learn about job opportunities.
- ✔ Go to job fairs. Companies that are hiring often send representatives to these events. At a job fair, you can learn about many different jobs and companies.
- ✔ If you have a special talent that you think a business can use, talk to the manager. You might be able to create a job for yourself!

"You can find the right job if you believe in yourself!"

Maria Mendez created a job for herself at the Rosebud Cafe. One day while Maria was having a cup of coffee there, she thought, "This coffee would taste much better with a slice of my homemade bread." Later that week, she brought three loaves of her bread to the cafe and told Gina Moran, the manager, that the cafe needed a baker with her skills. Gina liked the bread so much that she hired her on the spot. Maria started working there the next day. According to Maria, "You can find the right job if you believe in yourself!"

1. When you network to get a job, you ____.
A. go to job websites
B. check the classified ads
C. look in store windows
D. talk to your friends and neighbors

2. Job banks ____.
A. have job listings
B. give money
C. are on bulletin boards
D. are in public buildings

3. If you want to get on the Internet, you can go to ____.
A. a job fair
B. a job bank
C. the library
D. the Rosebud Cafe

4. You make a cold call to ____.
A. thank an interviewer
B. answer a classified ad
C. ask about job openings
D. ask about job fairs

5. At a job fair, you can ____.
A. hire representatives
B. find out about different companies
C. talk to relatives and neighbors
D. look in windows for help wanted signs

6. The Rosebud Cafe hired Maria Mendez because ____.
A. they were looking for a baker
B. she answered their ad
C. she saw Gina Moran's help wanted sign
D. she created a job for herself

ASSESSMENT

• Check-up test • Self-evaluation checklists

Choose the correct answer.

1. Samantha got a raise, and now her _____ is higher.
   A. report
   B. elevator
   C. boss
   D. salary

2. I went to the doctor for an examination. She gave me _____.
   A. a presentation
   B. the flu
   C. an injection
   D. X-rays

3. Let's go _____ on the river this weekend!
   A. kayaking
   B. camping
   C. hiking
   D. bowling

4. Did you watch the president's _____ about world problems on television last night?
   A. course
   B. speech
   C. inventory
   D. term paper

5. I didn't understand the present perfect tense, but my teacher _____ it very well.
   A. examined
   B. complained
   C. explained
   D. expressed

6. What _____ are you applying for?
   A. employer
   B. position
   C. skills
   D. reference

7. I saw a _____ for a receptionist on the bulletin board in the library.
   A. job posting
   B. job bank
   C. representative
   D. job fair

8. I made _____ to the Randall Company and asked about job openings.
   A. a network
   B. a job listing
   C. an opportunity
   D. a cold call

Look at Wanda's job application form. Choose the correct answer.

9. Wanda worked as a receptionist _____.
   A. in Detroit
   B. for two and a half years
   C. in 2008
   D. at the Brandon Corporation

10. Wanda hasn't _____ in a long time.
   A. sorted mail
   B. typed reports
   C. taken messages
   D. filed documents

Date	Name & Address of Employer	Position	Reason for Leaving
From: 7/08 To: present	Brandon Corporation 1100 First Ave., Detroit, MI	office assistant	want to learn new skills
Duties type reports, file documents, sort mail			
From: 2/05 To: 8/07	Tech-World Corporation 599 Tyler St., Chicago, IL	receptionist	returned to school
Duties answered the telephone, took messages, and greeted clients			

SKILLS CHECK

Words:

- ☐ classified ads
- ☐ cold call
- ☐ dates of employment
- ☐ education history
- ☐ employer
- ☐ employment application
- ☐ employment history
- ☐ help wanted sign
- ☐ job bank
- ☐ job fair
- ☐ job listing
- ☐ job opening
- ☐ job posting
- ☐ job search
- ☐ personal information
- ☐ position
- ☐ reference
- ☐ representative
- ☐ salary
- ☐ skills
- ☐ apply for
- ☐ complete
- ☐ fill in
- ☐ hire
- ☐ network

I can ask & answer:

- ☐ Have you ever *seen it*?
  Yes, I have. I *saw it* last year.
- ☐ Have you *gone to the bank* yet?
  Yes, I have.
  No, I haven't.
- ☐ I've *driven* for many years.
- ☐ I've already *gone there*.
- ☐ I've never *been on television*.

I can:

- ☐ identify employment application procedures
- ☐ apply for a job
- ☐ describe job search strategies

I can express satisfaction:

- ☐ It was excellent/very good/wonderful/great/fantastic/terrific/phenomenal/awesome.

I can write:

- ☐ a list of things I've done
- ☐ employment history on a job application form

I can write about:

- ☐ experiences in the place where I live

5

Present Perfect vs. Present Tense
Present Perfect vs. Past Tense
Since / For

- Discussing Duration of Activity
- Medical Symptoms and Problems
- Career Advancement
- Telling About Family Members
- Job Interview
- Giving Employment History
- Cover Letters and Resumes
- Employee Manual: Workplace Policies and Expectations

VOCABULARY PREVIEW

1. astronaut
2. cashier
3. clerk
4. computer programmer
5. doctor/physician
6. guidance counselor
7. guitarist
8. journalist
9. manager
10. musician
11. police officer
12. president
13. salesperson
14. taxi driver
15. vice president

How Long?

for	since
three hours	three o'clock
two days	yesterday afternoon
a week	last week
a long time	2000
.	.
.	.
.	.

A. How long have you known* each other?

B. We've known each other **for three years**.

*know – knew – known

A. How long have you been sick?

B. I've been sick **since last Friday**.

1. How long have Tom and Janet known each other?
two years

2. How long have Mr. and Mrs. Garcia been married?
1995

3. How long have you had a stomachache?
ten o'clock this morning

4. How long has Melanie had the measles?
five days

5. How long has Ms. Bennett been a guidance counselor?
nineteen years

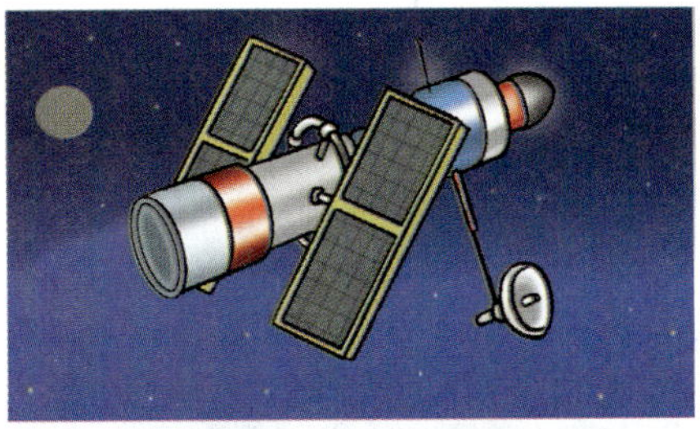

6. How long have there been satellites in space?
1957

7. How long have you owned this car?
three and a half years

8. How long has Bob owned his own house?
1999

9. How long have you been interested in astronomy?
many years

10. How long has Glen been interested in photography?
a long time

11. How long have you been here?
1979

12. How long has your son had blue hair?
a week

READING

A VERY DEDICATED DOCTOR

Dr. Fernando's waiting room is very full today. A lot of people are waiting to see him, and they're hoping that the doctor can help them. George's neck has been stiff for more than a week. Martha has had a bad headache since yesterday, and Lenny has felt dizzy since early this morning. Carol has had a high fever for two days, Bob's knee has been swollen for three weeks, Bill's arm has been black and blue since last weekend, and Tommy and Julie have had little red spots all over their bodies for the past twenty-four hours.

Dr. Fernando has been in the office since early this morning. He has already seen a lot of patients, and he will certainly see many more before the day is over. Dr. Fernando's patients don't know it, but he also isn't feeling well. He has had a pain in his back since last Thursday, but he hasn't taken any time to stay at home and rest. He has had a lot of patients this week, and he's a very dedicated doctor.

READING *CHECK-UP*

Q & A

Dr. Fernando's patients are talking to him about their problems. Using this model, create dialogs based on the story.

A. So how are you feeling today, *George*?
B. Not very well, Dr. Fernando.
A. What seems to be the problem?
B. *My neck is stiff.*
A. I see. Tell me, how long *has your neck been stiff?*
B. *For more than a week.*

CHOOSE

1. They've known each other since _____.
   a. 2000
   b. three years
2. I've been interested in astronomy for _____.
   a. last year
   b. one year
3. She has been a doctor for _____.
   a. two years ago
   b. two years
4. He has had a toothache since _____.
   a. yesterday
   b. two days
5. We've been here for _____.
   a. one hour
   b. one o'clock
6. There have been two robberies in our neighborhood since _____.
   a. one month
   b. last month
7. My grandparents have owned this house for _____.
   a. a long time
   b. many years ago
8. They've been in love since _____.
   a. last spring
   b. three months

CHOOSE

1. My right arm has been very _____.
   a. dizzy
   b. stiff
2. My son has a high _____.
   a. fever
   b. pain
3. Tell me, how long has your knee been _____?
   a. nauseous
   b. swollen
4. Ted's leg has been black and _____.
   a. blue
   b. red
5. Dr. Fernando, there are several patients in the _____.
   a. past 24 hours
   b. waiting room
6. Look! I have spots all over my _____!
   a. measles
   b. body

Since I Was a Little Girl

A. Do you know how to ski?

B. Yes. I've known how to ski **since I was a little girl**.

A. Are you two engaged?

B. Yes. We've been engaged **since we finished college**.

1. Does your sister Jennifer play the cello?
since she was eight years old

2. Is your friend Michael a professional musician?
since he graduated from music school

3. Do you have a personal computer?
since I started high school

4. Are you interested in modern art?
since I read about Picasso

5. Is Paul interested in Russian history?
since he visited Moscow

6. Does Timmy know how to count to ten?
since he was two years old

7. Do you like jazz?
since I was a teenager

8. Do you own your own business?
since I got out of the army

9. Do you know Mr. Wilson?
since I was a little boy

10. Do you have termites?
since we bought the house

11. Are you afraid of boats?
since I saw "Titanic"

12. Do your children know about "the birds and the bees"?*
since they were nine years old

*the facts of life

Have You Always Taught History?

A. Have you always taught history?

B. No. **I've taught** history for the past three years. Before that, **I taught** geography.

A. Has Victor always been a taxi driver?

B. No. **He's been** a taxi driver since he immigrated to this country. Before that, **he was** an engineer.

1. Have you always liked classical music?
the past five years

2. Has Carlos always been the store manager?
last January

3. Has Kimberly always had short hair?
she started her new job

4. Has your son always wanted to be an astronaut?
the past five or six years

5. Has Ron always spoken with a southern accent?
he moved to Georgia

6. Have you and your wife always had a dog?
the last six months

7. Have you always drunk skim milk?
I went on a diet

8. Has Carol always owned a sports car?
she won the lottery

How to Say It!

Reacting to Information

Practice the conversations in this lesson again. React to information in different ways.

How About You?

What is your present address? How long have you lived there?
What was your last address? How long did you live there?

Who is the leader of your country? How long has he/she been the leader?
Who was the last leader of your country? How long was he/she the leader?

Who is your English teacher now? How long has he/she been your teacher?
Who was your last English teacher? How long was he/she your teacher?

READING

A WONDERFUL FAMILY

Mr. and Mrs. Patterson are very proud of their family. Their daughter, Ruth, is a very successful engineer. She has been an engineer since she finished college. Her husband's name is Pablo. They have been happily married for thirty-five years. Pablo is a professional guitarist. He has known how to play the guitar since he was four years old.

Ruth and Pablo have two children. Their son, David, is a computer programmer. He has been interested in computers since he was a teenager. Their daughter, Rita, is a physician. She has been a physician since she finished medical school in 1997.

Mr. and Mrs. Patterson also have a son, Herbert. Herbert is single. He has been a bachelor all his life. He's a famous journalist. They haven't seen him since he moved to Singapore several years ago.

Mr. and Mrs. Patterson feel fortunate to have such wonderful children and grandchildren. They're very proud of them.

✓ READING *CHECK-UP*

TRUE OR FALSE?

1. Ruth got married thirty-five years ago.
2. Ruth's husband is a professional violinist.
3. Ruth and Pablo have two teenagers.
4. The Pattersons' grandson is interested in computers.
5. Rita has been in medical school since 1997.
6. Herbert has never been married.
7. Herbert hasn't seen his parents since they moved to Singapore several years ago.

LISTENING

Listen to the conversation and choose the answer that is true.

1. a. She doesn't have a backache now.
   b. She still has a backache.
2. a. His father is an engineer.
   b. His father isn't an engineer.
3. a. Her knee isn't swollen now.
   b. Her knee is still swollen.
4. a. He isn't a teenager.
   b. He's a teenager.
5. a. She has lived in Tokyo for five years.
   b. She lived in Tokyo for five years.
6. a. Roger lives in Cairo.
   b. Roger has lived in Cairo.
7. a. Amy went home two days ago.
   b. Amy hasn't been home for two days.
8. a. He has lived in Toronto for three years.
   b. He lived in Toronto for three years.

READING

WORKING THEIR WAY UP TO THE TOP

Louis is very successful. For the past six years, he has been the manager of the Big Value Supermarket on Grant Street. Louis has worked very hard to get where he is today. First, he was a clerk for two years. Then, he was a cashier for three years. After that, he was an assistant manager for five years. Finally, six years ago, he became the manager of the store. Everybody at the Big Value Supermarket is very proud of Louis. He started at the bottom, and he has worked his way up to the top.

Kate is very successful. For the past two years, she has been the president of the Marcy Company. Kate has worked very hard to get where she is today. She started her career at the Marcy Department Store in Dallas, Texas. First, she was a salesperson for three years. Then, she was the manager of the Women's Clothing Department for ten years. Then, she was the store manager for eight years. After that, she moved to New York and became a vice president. Finally, two years ago, she became the president. Everybody at the Marcy Company is very proud of Kate. She started at the bottom, and she has worked her way up to the top.

✓ READING *CHECK-UP*

TRUE, FALSE, OR MAYBE?

Answer True, False, or Maybe (if the answer isn't in the story).

1. Louis started as a cashier at the Big Value Supermarket.
2. He has worked there for sixteen years.
3. All employees at the Big Value Supermarket start at the bottom.
4. Kate has been the manager of the Women's Clothing Department in Dallas for ten years.
5. The Women's Clothing Department was on the bottom floor of the store.
6. Kate hasn't been a vice president for two years.

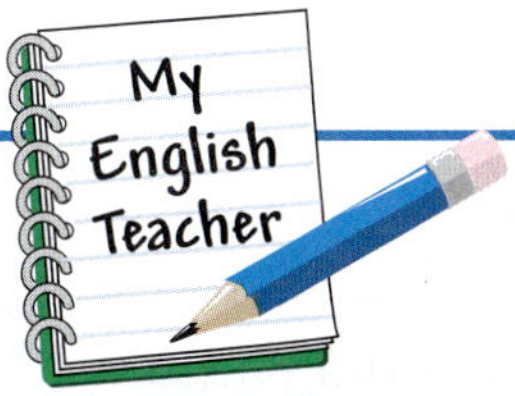

Writing

Write a story about your English teacher.

How long have you known him/her?
How long has he/she been an English teacher?
What did he/she do before that? How long?

Where does he/she live?
How long has he/she lived there?
Has he/she lived anywhere else? Where? How long?

Besides teaching English, what is your English teacher interested in?
How long has he/she been interested in that?

ROLE PLAY *It's Been a Long Time*

A. George!

B. Tony! I can't believe it's you! I haven't seen you in years.

A. That's right, George. It's been a long time. How have you been?

B. Fine. And how about YOU?

A. Everything's fine with me, too.

B. Tell me, Tony, do you still live on Main Street?

A. No. I haven't lived on Main Street for several years. I live on River Road now. And how about YOU? Do you still live on Central Avenue?

B. No. I haven't lived on Central Avenue since 1995. I live on Park Boulevard now.

A. Tell me, George, are you still a barber?

B. No. I haven't been a barber for several years. I'm a computer programmer now. And how about YOU? Are you still a painter?

A. No. I haven't been a painter for a long time. I'm a carpenter now.

B. Tell me, Tony, do you still play the saxophone?

A. No. I haven't played the saxophone for many years. And how about YOU? Do you still go fishing on Saturday mornings?

B. No. I haven't gone fishing on Saturday mornings since I got married.

A. Well, George, I'm afraid I have to go now. We should get together soon.

B. Good idea, Tony. It's been a long time.

Pretend that it's ten years from now. You're walking along the street and suddenly you meet a student who was in your English class. Try this conversation. Remember, you haven't seen this person for ten years.

A. ____________!

B. ____________! I can't believe it's you! I haven't seen you in years.

A. That's right, ____________. It's been a long time. How have you been?

B. Fine. And how about YOU?

A. Everything's fine with me, too.

B. Tell me, ____________, do you still live on ____________?

A. No. I haven't lived on ____________ (for/since) ____________. I live on ____________ now. And how about YOU? Do you still live on ____________?

B. No. I haven't lived on ____________ (for/since) ____________. I live on ____________ now.

A. Tell me, ____________, are you still (a/an) ____________?

B. No. I haven't been (a/an) ____________ (for/since) ____________. I'm (a/an) ____________ now. And how about YOU? Are you still (a/an) ____________?

A. No. I haven't been (a/an) ____________ (for/since) ____________. I'm (a/an) ____________ now.

B. Tell me, ____________, do you still ____________?

A. No. I haven't ____________ (for/since) ____________. And how about YOU? Do you still ____________?

B. No. I haven't ____________ (for/since) ____________.

A. Well, ____________, I'm afraid I have to go now. We should get together soon.

B. Good idea, ____________. It's been a long time.

PRONUNCIATION Reduced *have* & *has*

Listen. Then say it.

How long have you been sick?

How long has Ms. Bennett been a teacher?

Bob has been the manager for six months.

Say it. Then listen.

How long have you known each other?

How long has Mr. Perkins had a stomachache?

Kate has been the president for the past two years.

Write in your journal about your activities and interests. What sport or musical instrument do you play? How long have you known how to play it? Why do you like it? What other things are you interested in? How long have you been interested in those things? Why do you like them?

GRAMMAR FOCUS

SINCE/FOR

We've known each other	since	three o'clock. yesterday afternoon. last week. 2000. we were in high school.
	for	three hours. two days. a week. a long time.

PRESENT PERFECT VS. PRESENT TENSE

I **know** how to ski.

I**'ve known** how to ski since I was a little girl.

PRESENT PERFECT VS. PAST TENSE

Victor **was** an engineer.

He**'s been** a taxi driver since he immigrated.

Choose the correct word.

1. My wife and I (knew have known) each other (since for) 1989.
2. My daughter (is sick has been sick) (since for) several days.
3. How long (have you had do you have) a stomachache?
4. (Are you Have you been) interested in photography now?
5. (We've owned We own) our own business (since for) several years.
6. (She's had She had) a cat (since for) last year. Before that, (she's had she had) a dog.
7. Alexander (was has been) a taxi driver (since for) he came to this country. Before that, (he was he's been) an engineer.
8. I (didn't see haven't seen) you in a long time. How (are have) you been?
9. I (haven't lived didn't live) on Oak Street for many years. (I've lived I live) on Pine Street now.

1 CONVERSATION Describing Work Experience

Look at the job application forms. Practice conversations with your classmates.

A. Where do you work now?
B. I work at ___(employer)___.
A. How long have you worked there?
B. I've worked there since ___(month)___ ___(year)___.
A. Where did you work before that?
B. I worked at ___(employer)___.
A. How long did you work there?
B. I worked there for ___(number of years/months)___.

1.

DATE	EMPLOYER
From: 6/07 To: present	Zenith Computer Company
From: 5/05 To: 5/07	Carter Insurance

2.

DATE	EMPLOYER
From: 1/08 To: present	The Hamilton Hotel
From: 12/06 To: 12/07	The Bayside Inn

3.

DATE	EMPLOYER
From: 9/06 To: present	Save-Mart Department Store
From: 1/06 To: 8/06	Super Price Discount Store

Now practice conversations using your own employment information. (If you aren't working now, talk about going to school.)

2 CONVERSATION Asking for Clarification

A. Have you ever been ________?
B. I'm sorry. I don't understand what "________" means.
A. Have you ever been ________?
B. I understand. No, I haven't.

Practice with a classmate.

1. terminated
   fired from a job
2. incarcerated
   in jail

TEAMWORK Work with a classmate. What are other questions people have asked you that you didn't understand? Make a list. Then share as a class. Discuss what each question means.

LIFE SKILLS READING • A cover letter and resume

Read the cover letter and resume and answer the questions.

568 East 34th Street
Sunrise, FL 33304

January 15, 2009

Ms. Monica Jordan
Seaside Restaurant Company
1200 Marine Avenue
Seaside, FL 33308

Dear Ms. Jordan:

I would like to apply for the position of manager of the Seaside Restaurant. I saw your advertisement in the *Sunrise Times*. As you can see from my resume, I have the experience and skills to manage a successful restaurant. Under my management, the Garden Restaurant has become the most popular family restaurant in the Sunrise area. The number of people we serve has grown from 200 to 300 customers each night.

I look forward to hearing from you to arrange an interview.

Sincerely,
Linda Palermo
Linda Palermo

Linda Palermo Tel 954-589-4312
568 East 34th Street, Sunrise, FL 33304

Work Experience:

2006–present	**Manager**, Garden Restaurant, Sunrise, FL Hire, train, and supervise a staff of 15 dining room and kitchen workers. Order supplies. Plan menus. Handle customer complaints.
2002–2005	**Chef**, Ocean House, Miami, FL Prepared fish, seafood, and vegetable dishes. Created exciting new recipes.
2000–2001	**Prep Cook**, Health Food Markets, North Miami, FL Worked as part of a kitchen team to prepare takeout food. Peeled, sliced, and chopped ingredients. Kept kitchen area clean.
1999–2000	**Deli Counter Clerk**, Health Foods Markets, North Miami, FL Weighed and packaged food. Made sandwiches. Prepared salad plates. Recommended food. Gave excellent customer service.

1. Linda has been the manager of a restaurant _____.
- A. for one year
- B. since 2002
- C. since 2006
- D. since she left Health Foods Market

2. Linda was _____ for four years.
- A. a deli counter clerk
- B. a chef
- C. a prep cook
- D. a manager

3. Linda worked at Health Food Markets _____.
- A. for one year
- B. for two years
- C. for three years
- D. for five years

4. In her present job, Linda does NOT _____.
- A. prepare food
- B. hire cooks and prep cooks
- C. supervise waiters and waitresses
- D. listen to customers when they complain

5. Linda learned about this job from _____.
- A. a friend
- B. the Internet
- C. a help wanted sign
- D. the newspaper

6. Before Linda became manager, the Garden Restaurant _____.
- A. was the most popular restaurant in Sunrise
- B. had 200 customers every night
- C. had 300 customers every night
- D. had more than 200 customers every night

WRITING You're applying for a job. Write a cover letter and a resume.

Read the manual for new employees and answer the questions.

The Brayburn Company

Hours of Work—Full-time employees work a 40-hour week—8:00 AM to 5:00 PM, Monday to Friday. Full-time employees get a one-hour lunch break and two fifteen-minute breaks each day.

Time Clocks and Time Sheets—Employees either punch a time clock (with a time card) or fill out a time sheet to record the hours they work. If you use the time clock, you must punch in when you start work, punch out for lunch, punch in when you return to work, and punch out at the end of the day. Never punch in for another worker. If you use a time sheet, you must fill out the form each day to record the hours you have worked. At the end of each week, all employees must sign their time cards or time sheets and get their supervisors' signatures. Time cards and time sheets are due in the payroll office every Monday at 9:00 AM.

Payment Schedule—Employees get paid each week on Friday. You can either receive your paycheck from your supervisor at 4 PM on Friday or sign up for direct deposit. When you sign up for direct deposit, we deposit your pay into your bank account each Friday.

Sick Time—Full-time employees get one paid sick day each month for a total of twelve sick days a year. Employees can take unused sick days from previous years when necessary.

Vacation Time—Full-time employees get two weeks of vacation with pay during each of their first ten years of employment. After ten years, they get three weeks of vacation per year. Employees cannot save up their vacation days to use in future years.

Absence and Tardiness—It's important to have good attendance and to be on time. Use sick leave as little as possible (for medical reasons only), but stay home when you have a fever and can infect others. If you can't come to work, call your supervisor no later than one hour after your work shift starts. Employees who are often absent or late can lose their jobs.

1. Full-time employees at the Brayburn Company do NOT ____.
- A. work five days a week
- B. work forty hours a week
- C. have a thirty-minute lunch break
- D. get paid once a week

2. Workers punch out when they ____.
- A. go to lunch
- B. arrive at work
- C. return to work
- D. receive their paychecks

3. When you sign up for direct deposit of your paycheck, ____.
- A. you receive your paycheck at 4 PM
- B. you save up your vacation days
- C. your supervisor signs your paycheck
- D. you don't get your paycheck at work

4. Lee has worked for fifteen months. She has taken nine sick days. She hasn't used ____.
- A. three sick days
- B. six sick days
- C. twelve sick days
- D. fifteen sick days

5. It's Don's eleventh year at work. He can ____.
- A. take one week of vacation this year
- B. take two weeks of vacation this year
- C. take three weeks of vacation this year
- D. take four weeks of vacation this year

6. If your work shift starts at 8:00 AM and you're going to miss work, ____.
- A. call your supervisor before 8:00 AM
- B. call your supervisor before 9:00 AM
- C. call your supervisor before 10:00 AM
- D. ask another worker to punch in for you

Choose the correct answer.

1. Ahmed called his doctor because he felt ____.
   A. engaged
   B. busy
   C. dizzy
   D. full
2. We're upset because our house has ____.
   A. termites
   B. satellites
   C. measles
   D. a high fever
3. When did your parents immigrate to this ____?
   A. store
   B. business
   C. house
   D. country
4. Someday I want to ____ my own business.
   A. know
   B. own
   C. count
   D. wait for
5. Ben comes to work early and leaves very late. He's a very dedicated ____.
   A. store manager
   B. teenager
   C. patient
   D. bachelor
6. Dolores is a professional ____. She plays the cello.
   A. physician
   B. musician
   C. engineer
   D. journalist
7. I've decided to sign up for ____.
   A. a sick day
   B. a timesheet
   C. my supervisor's signature
   D. direct deposit of my paycheck
8. All of our employees get ____ with pay.
   A. good attendance
   B. a time clock
   C. two weeks of vacation
   D. signatures

Look at Michael Rivera's work experience. Choose the correct answer.

9. Michael has ____ since 2008.
   A. waited on customers
   B. trained sales clerks
   C. inspected items
   D. hired sales clerks
10. Michael hasn't ____ for many years.
    A. worked in Philadelphia
    B. unpacked boxes
    C. managed a store
    D. supervised employees

Work Experience:

2008–present	**Store Manager**, Regency Department Store, Philadelphia, PA Manage the store. Hire and supervise a staff of 75 employees.
2004–2007	**Assistant Manager**, Regency Department Store, Philadelphia, PA Helped the store manager. Trained sales clerks.
1998–2003	**Sales Clerk**, Wilkins Department Store, Atlanta, GA Waited on customers. Used a cash register.
1996–1997	**Stock Clerk**, Wilkins Department Store, Atlanta, GA Unpacked boxes. Inspected items. Put prices on items.

SKILLS CHECK

Words:

- ☐ astronaut
- ☐ barber
- ☐ carpenter
- ☐ cashier
- ☐ clerk
- ☐ computer programmer
- ☐ doctor/physician
- ☐ engineer
- ☐ guidance counselor
- ☐ guitarist
- ☐ journalist
- ☐ manager
- ☐ musician
- ☐ painter
- ☐ police officer
- ☐ president
- ☐ salesperson
- ☐ taxi driver
- ☐ vice president
- ☐ black and blue
- ☐ dizzy
- ☐ fever
- ☐ measles
- ☐ pain
- ☐ patient
- ☐ stiff
- ☐ swollen
- ☐ absence
- ☐ attendance
- ☐ direct deposit
- ☐ lunch break
- ☐ paycheck
- ☐ payment schedule
- ☐ payroll office
- ☐ shift
- ☐ sick day
- ☐ tardiness
- ☐ time clock
- ☐ time sheet
- ☐ punch in
- ☐ punch out

I can ask & answer:

- ☐ How long have you *been here*?
  I've *been here* for *two years*.
  I've *been here* since *2005*.
- ☐ I've been *the manager* for *two years*/since *2007*.
  Before that, I was *a cashier*.
- ☐ Where do you work now?
- ☐ How long have you worked there?
- ☐ Where did you work before that?
- ☐ How long did you work there?

I can:

- ☐ describe my work experience
- ☐ ask for clarification
- ☐ interpret a new employee manual
- ☐ describe workplace rules and policies

I can react to information:

- ☐ Oh. I didn't know that.
- ☐ Oh. I didn't realize that.
- ☐ Oh. I wasn't aware of that.

I can write:

- ☐ a cover letter
- ☐ a simple resume

I can write about:

- ☐ my English teacher
- ☐ my activities and interests

Feature Article
Fact File
Around the World
Interview
We've Got Mail!

SIDE by SIDE Gazette

Global Exchange
Listening
Fun with Idioms
What Are They Saying?

Volume 3 | Number 2

"24/7"
24 Hours a Day/7 Days a Week

Work schedules are changing all over the world

More and more companies around the world are operating twenty-four hours a day, seven days a week. Many of these companies do business with companies in other time zones around the world. Other companies sell products to customers worldwide. In an age of instant communication by telephone, by fax, and over the Internet, many businesses must stay open all the time to serve their customers. International banks, computer companies, manufacturing companies, and businesses that sell their products over the World Wide Web are examples of such companies.

Employees of these "24/7" companies have seen changes in their work schedules in recent years. About twenty percent of employees don't work on a traditional "9 to 5" daytime schedule anymore. Their companies have switched them to other shifts, such as 3:00 P.M. to 11:00 P.M., or 11:00 P.M. to 7:00 A.M. In the past, many factory workers, doctors and nurses, police, firefighters, and others had these shifts, but now many office workers have also started to work during these hours.

Many local businesses have adjusted their hours to serve the employees of these companies. More and more supermarkets are open 24 hours a day. Restaurants and coffee shops close later and open earlier. And businesses such as photocopy centers, health clubs, laundromats, and even some child-care centers are always open.

Describe the work schedules of people you know. Are there any "24/7" businesses in your area? What's your opinion about these businesses and their employees' work schedules?

A sign of the times

The night shift

A typical night at the office

A health club that's open 24 hours a day

A coffee shop that never closes

Late-night shopper at the supermarket

AROUND THE WORLD

Unique Jobs

Some jobs are unique. They exist only in certain countries.

a subway pusher in Japan

a tulip farmer in Holland

a reindeer herder in Siberia

a safari guide in Africa

a coffee plantation worker in Colombia

a dog day-care worker in California

What unique jobs do you know? In what countries do these jobs exist?

Interview

Mr. and Mrs. Roberto Souza have two children, ages two and four. Mr. Souza works the day shift at a manufacturing company, and Mrs. Souza works at night in an office. Their lives are certainly busy!

Q: Mr. Souza, can you describe your typical day?

A: I get up at 5:30 A.M. I take a shower, eat breakfast, and make my lunch. Sometimes I do some laundry before I go to work. I leave the house at 6:30 A.M.

Q: Is anyone in your house awake when you leave?

A: No. Everyone is still asleep. I work from 7:00 A.M. until 3:00 P.M. After work, I pick up my kids at their grandmother's apartment. Usually we go food shopping and then we go home to make dinner. My wife has already left for work. I play with the kids, we eat dinner, and then I put the kids to bed. I'm normally asleep by 10:00 P.M.

Q: And Mrs. Souza, what about your day?

A: The kids and I get up at 7:00. We eat breakfast, and then they play while I do some housework. Sometimes we go to the park or we visit family or friends. Other times we go shopping. I take the kids to my mother's apartment at 2:00 P.M., and I'm at work by 3:00 P.M. I come home at 11:30 P.M. That's my day!

Q: It sounds exhausting! When do you have time to see your husband?

A: Sometimes he waits for me to come home, but usually he has already gone to bed. Believe it or not, we really see each other only on the weekends.

Q: Mr. Souza, what's the most difficult thing about your work schedule?

A: Communication. We leave each other notes and messages about bills, shopping, doctor's appointments, and everything else.

Q: And tell me, Mrs. Souza, is there anything good about these work schedules?

A: Yes. The children are always with a parent or a grandparent. They don't have to go to daycare, which is expensive. We know these schedules won't last forever. When the children are both in school, maybe we can each have a daytime job. I hope so!

FACT FILE

Vacation Time in Different Countries

Employees in different countries have different amounts of vacation time. What's the typical amount of vacation time employees receive in different countries you know? How do people usually spend their vacation time?

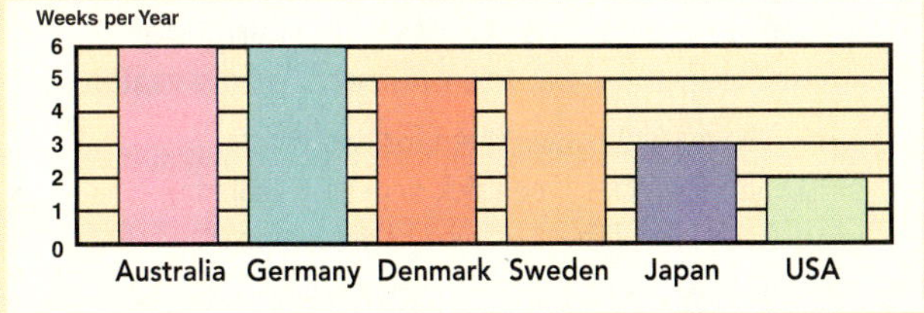

LISTENING

Office Voice Mail

Has Sam . . .

		Yes	No
1	written a note to Mrs. Wilson?	___	___
2	called Mr. Chen?	___	___
3	sent an e-mail about the meeting?	___	___
4	spoken to the custodian?	___	___
5	made a list of the employees?	___	___
6	given the list to Ms. Baxter?	___	___
7	taken the package to the post office?	___	___

FUN with IDIOMS

Do You Know These Expressions?

d	1.	My new co-worker is a real peach.	a.	He's funny.
____	2.	She's the top banana in our company.	b.	He's afraid.
____	3.	He's a real ham at office parties.	c.	She's intelligent.
____	4.	He's a couch potato.	d.	He's nice.
____	5.	She's a smart cookie.	e.	He's lazy.
____	6.	He wants to ask for a raise, but he's chicken.	f.	She's the boss.

We've Got Mail!

Dear Side by Side,

We are students in Mr. Smith's class at the English Language Center, and we are very confused! We just don't understand the present perfect tense. We don't have this tense in our languages. We don't know when to use it, and we really don't like all these past participles, such as "given" and "driven." Why do we need this tense anyway? Why can't we just use the tenses we already know?

Sincerely,
"Perfectly Happy with the Present and the Past"

Dear "Perfectly Happy,"

The present perfect tense has always been difficult for learners of English. We'll try to explain it to you with some examples.

We use the present perfect tense to talk about:

- things that happened (or didn't happen) sometime in the past, but the exact time isn't important. For example:

  I have (I've) already seen that movie.*
  He has (He's) never ridden a motorcycle.
  She hasn't gone to the bank yet.

- things that happened many times in the past. For example:

  I have (I've) driven trucks for many years.
  We have (We've) eaten lunch there many times.

- things that happened in the past and are still happening in the present. For example:

  I have (I've) known them for two years.
  She has (She's) been sick since last Thursday.
  They have (They've) lived here for a year.

It's interesting how different languages express time in different ways, and we can understand why this tense is difficult for you. In your languages, you might say:

✗ I live here since last year.
✗ I am living here since last year.
✗ I lived here since last year.

In English, these are all wrong. Sorry! The correct way to say this is:

✓ I have (I've) lived here since last year.

This means "I lived here before, and I still live here now."

So that's why we need the present perfect tense in English. Thanks for your question, and good luck!

Sincerely,
Side by Side

PEARSON EDUCATION Level 3 Side by Side

* If the exact time IS important, we use the past tense: "I saw a movie yesterday."

Global Exchange

Alex32: I'm sorry I haven't written for a while. I've been very busy. I've taken four exams this week, and I have to take one more tomorrow. This weekend I'm going to relax. I'm going to see the new Julia Richards movie. (My sister saw it last week, and she says it's one of the best movies she's ever seen.) I'm also going to eat dinner with my family at a new Indian restaurant. I'm looking forward to it. We haven't been to a restaurant in a long time, and I've never eaten Indian food. And I'm going to visit our city's modern art museum. Believe it or not, I've lived here all my life, and I've never gone there! So, how have you been? Have you seen any movies recently? Have you eaten at any restaurants? Have you gone to any interesting places?

Tell a keypal about some things you've done recently.

What Are They Saying?

6

Present Perfect Continuous Tense

- Discussing Duration of Activity
- Reporting Household Repair Problems
- Describing Tasks Accomplished
- Reassuring Someone
- Describing Experiences
- Job Interviews
- Renting an Apartment
- Lease Information
- Apartment Rules
- Utility Bills
- Housing Maintenance and Repairs
- Yellow Pages

VOCABULARY PREVIEW

1. ask for a raise
2. complain
3. date
4. direct traffic
5. do sit-ups
6. leak
7. look for
8. mend
9. peel
10. pick apples
11. ring
12. stand in line

How Long Have You Been Waiting?

(I have)	I've	been working.
(We have)	We've	
(You have)	You've	
(They have)	They've	
(He has)	He's	
(She has)	She's	
(It has)	It's	

A. How long have you been waiting?

B. I've been waiting **for two hours**.

A. How long has your neighbor's dog been barking?

B. It's been barking **since this morning**.

1. How long has Yasmin been studying English?
eight months

2. How long have Mr. and Mrs. Green been living on School Street?
1994

3. How long has the phone been ringing?
two minutes

4. How long have you been feeling bad?
yesterday morning

5. How long have we been driving?
five hours

6. How long has it been snowing?
late last night

7. How long has Ted been having problems with his back?
high school

8. How long have you been practicing the piano?
half an hour

9. How long have Barry and Susan been dating?
three and a half years

10. How long has your baby son been crying?
early this morning

11. How long have I been running?
twenty minutes

12. How long have we been jogging?
about an hour

They've Been Arguing All Day

Have	I we you they		
		been working?	
Has	he she it		

A. What are your neighbors doing?

B. They're arguing.

A. Have they been arguing for a long time?

B. Yes, they have. They've been arguing all day.*

*Or: all morning / all afternoon / all evening / all night

1. *you*
   studying

2. *Gary*
   exercising

3. *Brenda*
   waiting for the bus

4. *your parents*
   watching the news

5. *your car*
   making strange noises

6. *Officer Lopez*
   directing traffic

7. *Jim*
   looking for his keys

8. *you and your friends*
   standing in line for concert tickets

9.

READING

APARTMENT PROBLEMS

Mr. and Mrs. Banks have been having a lot of problems in their apartment recently. For several weeks their bedroom ceiling has been leaking, their refrigerator hasn't been working, and the paint in their hallway has been peeling. In addition, they have been taking cold showers since last week because their water heater hasn't been working, and they haven't been sleeping at night because the heating system has been making strange noises.

Mr. and Mrs. Banks are furious. They have been calling the manager of their apartment building every day and complaining about their problems. He has been promising to help them, but they have been waiting for more than a week, and he still hasn't fixed anything at all.

✔ READING *CHECK-UP*

Q & A

Mr. and Mrs. Banks are calling the manager of their apartment building for the first time about each of the problems in their apartment. Using this model, create dialogs based on the story.

A. Hello.
B. Hello. This is *Mrs.* Banks.
A. Yes, *Mrs.* Banks. What can I do for you?
B. We're having a problem with *our bedroom ceiling.*
A. Oh? What's the problem?
B. *It's leaking.*
A. I see. Tell me, how long *has it been leaking?*
B. *It's been leaking for about an hour.*
A. All right, *Mrs.* Banks. I'll take care of it as soon as I can.
B. Thank you.

How About You?

Have you been having problems in your apartment or house recently? Tell about some problems you've been having.

No Wonder They're Tired!

A. You look tired. What have you been doing?

B. I've been writing letters since nine o'clock this morning.

A. Really? How many letters have you written?

B. Believe it or not, I've already written fifteen letters.

A. You're kidding! Fifteen letters?! NO WONDER you're tired!

A. Anthony looks tired. What has he been doing?

B. He's been making pizzas since ten o'clock this morning.

A. Really? How many pizzas has he made?

B. Believe it or not, he's already made seventy-five pizzas.

A. You're kidding! Seventy-five pizzas?! NO WONDER he's tired!

1. *you*
   plant flowers

2. *Ms. Perkins*
   give piano lessons

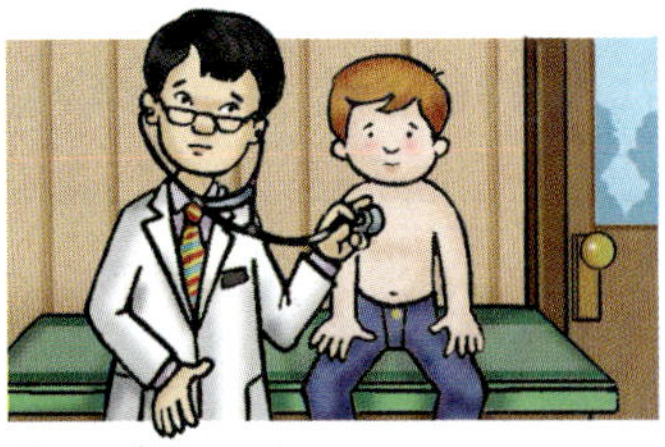

3. *Dr. Chen*
   see patients

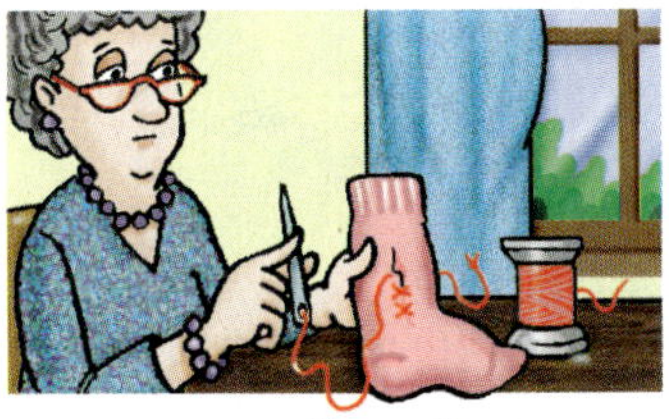

4. *your grandmother*
   mend socks

5. *you*
   pick apples

6. *Tom and Sally*
   write thank-you notes

7. *Chester*
   take photographs

8. *Thelma*
   draw pictures

9. *you*
   go to job interviews

10. *Jackie*
    clean cages

11. *Rick*
    do sit-ups

12. *Dr. Harris*
    deliver babies

How to Say It!

Expressing Surprise

Practice the conversations in this lesson again. Express surprise in different ways.

There's Nothing to Be Nervous About!

A. I'm nervous.

B. Why?

A. I'm going to **fly in an airplane** tomorrow, and I've never **flown in an airplane** before.

B. Don't worry! I've been **flying in airplanes** for years. And believe me, there's nothing to be nervous about!

1. *drive downtown*

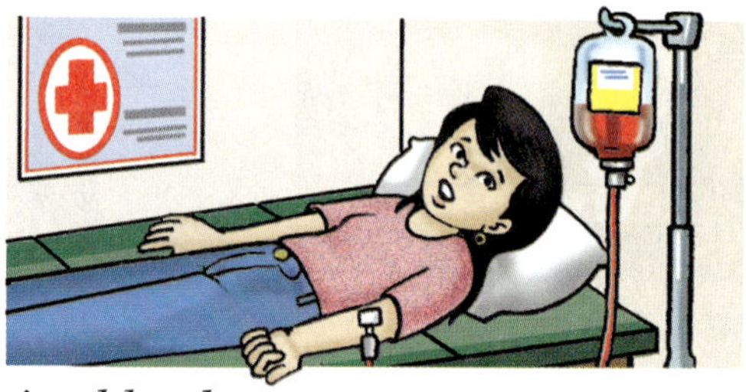

2. *give blood*

3. *buy a used car*

4. *do a chemistry experiment*

5. *run* in a marathon*

6. *go to a job interview*

*run – ran – run

7. *speak at a meeting*

8. *sing in front of an audience*

9. *take a karate lesson*

10. *ask for a raise*

11. *go out on a date*

12.

INTERVIEW *Have You Ever . . . ?*

Interview other students in your class about experiences they have had. Ask these questions and make up your own questions. Then tell the class about these experiences.

Have you ever met a famous person?
(Who did you meet?)

Have you ever spoken at a meeting?
(Where did you speak? What did you say?)

Have you ever been in the hospital?
(Why were you there?)

Have you ever lost something important or valuable?
(What did you lose?)

Have you ever been very embarrassed?
(What happened?)

Have you ever been in an accident?
(What happened?)

ROLE PLAY *At a Job Interview*

Complete this conversation and act it out with another student.

A. Tell me, (Mr./Ms./Mrs./Miss ____________), how long have you been living in ____________?

B. I've been living in ____________ (for/since) ____________.

A. And where else have you lived?

B. I've also lived in ____________.

A. Oh. How long did you live there?

B. I lived there for ____________.

A. Okay. I see here on your resume that you're studying ____________.

B. That's correct.

A. How long have you been studying ____________?

B. (For/Since) ____________.

A. Where?

B. At ____________.

A. Tell me about your work experience. Where do you work now?

B. I work at ____________.

A. How long have you been working there?

B. I've been working there (for/since) __________.

A. And what do you do there?

B. I ________________.

A. And where did you work before that?

B. I worked at ____________.

A. How long did you work there?

B. For ____________.

A. What did you do?

B. I ________________.

A. Well, I don't have any more questions.

B. I appreciate the opportunity to meet with you. Thank you very much.

A. It's been a pleasure. We'll call you soon.

READING

IT'S BEEN A LONG DAY

Frank has been assembling cameras since 7 A.M., and he's very tired. He has assembled 19 cameras today, and he has NEVER assembled that many cameras in one day before! He has to assemble only one more camera, and then he can go home. He's really glad. It's been a long day.

Julie has been typing letters since 9 A.M., and she's very tired. She has typed 25 letters today, and she has NEVER typed that many letters in one day before! She has to type only one more letter, and then she can go home. She's really glad. It's been a very long day.

Officer Jackson has been writing parking tickets since 8 A.M., and he's exhausted! He has written 211 parking tickets today, and he has NEVER written that many parking tickets in one day before! He has to write only one more parking ticket, and then he can go home. He's really glad. It's been an extremely long day.

✓ READING *CHECK-UP*

Q & A

Co-workers are talking with Frank, Julie, and Officer Jackson. Using this model, create dialogs based on the story.

A. *Frank*, you look tired.
B. I am. I've been *assembling cameras* since *7* A.M.
A. Really? How many *cameras* have you *assembled*?
B. Believe it or not, I've already *assembled 19 cameras* today.
A. That's a lot of *cameras*!
B. I know. I've never *assembled* that many *cameras* in one day before!

LISTENING

WHICH WORD DO YOU HEAR?

Listen and choose the correct answer.

1. a. gone — b. going
2. a. written — b. writing
3. a. seen — b. seeing
4. a. taken — b. taking
5. a. given — b. giving
6. a. driven — b. driving

WHO IS SPEAKING?

Listen and decide who is speaking.

1. a. a landlord — b. a boss
2. a. a student — b. a teacher
3. a. a singer — b. a dentist
4. a. a window washer — b. a baby-sitter
5. a. a doctor — b. a bookkeeper
6. a. a movie theater cashier — b. a police officer

PRONUNCIATION Reduced *for*

Listen. Then say it.

I've been working for two hours.

She's been waiting for the bus.

Have you been studying for a long time?

Say it. Then listen.

He's been jogging for thirty minutes.

We've been looking for our keys.

Has she been exercising for a long time?

Write in your journal about places where you have lived, worked, and gone to school.

Where do you live now? How long have you been living there? Where else have you lived? How long did you live there?

Where do you work or go to school now? How long have you been working or going to school there? Where else have you worked or gone to school? How long did you work or study there? What did you do? What did you study?

GRAMMAR FOCUS

PRESENT PERFECT CONTINUOUS TENSE

(I have) (We have) (You have) (They have)	I've We've You've They've	been working.
(He has) (She has) (It has)	He's She's It's	

Have	I we you they	been working?
Has	he she it	

Yes,	I we you they	have.
	he she it	has.

Complete the sentences with *since* or *for* and the correct forms of these verbs.

live	practice	stand	take	write

1. A. How long _____ you and your husband _____ _________ in Los Angeles?
   B. _____ _____ _________ in Los Angeles (since for) three years.
2. A. How long _____ your daughter _____ _________ the piano?
   B. _____ _____ _________ the piano (since for) 9:00 A.M.
3. A. _____ your friends _____ _________ in line for a long time?
   B. Yes, _____ _____. _____ _____ _________ in line (since for) about an hour.
4. Ms. Lee _____ _____ _________ photographs (since for) early this morning.
   _____ already _________ more than fifty photographs!
5. I'm very busy. _____ _____ _________ letters (for since) five hours.
   _____ already _________ twenty letters!

1 CONVERSATION INQUIRING ABOUT LEASE INFORMATION

A **lease** is a contract. It is a legal document that describes the rental agreement between a landlord and a tenant. A lease includes information about rent, the number of tenants who can live in an apartment, and the rules of the building. Make sure you understand a lease before you sign it! If you don't understand something, ask!

Practice conversations with a classmate.

A. I don't understand this line in the lease:

____

What does it mean?

B. ______________________

A. Oh. I understand.

1. 

No refuse or trash will be permitted to be left at the building entrance.

You can't put garbage in front of the building.

2. 

Vehicle repair is not permitted on the property.

You're not allowed to fix your car in the parking lot.

3. 

It is strictly prohibited to place or hang rugs, clothing, or laundry of any kind on the balcony.

You're not allowed to hang anything on the balcony.

4. 

No dogs, cats, large birds, or any other animals shall be permitted, kept, or harbored in or about the leased premises.

You're not allowed to have pets.

5. 

Tenant shall carpet or rug a minimum of 80% of hardwood floor areas.

It is strictly prohibited to place

You have to cover most of your floors with a rug.

THINK & SHARE As a class, discuss rental agreements in different countries you know. Do all tenants have to sign a lease? What information and rules are in different leases? How long is a typical rental period?

2 TEAMWORK APARTMENT RULES

Work with a classmate. Think about all the rules for tenants in an apartment building. Make a list of the rules. Then compare lists with your classmates.

Read the utility bills and answer the questions.

California Power and Light
P.O. Box 3566
Los Angeles, CA 90016
Web address: www.cpl.com

Customer assistance line
1-800-555-7600
To report a power outage
1-800-555-3000

Account Number **235-12-55-78304**
Hector Nieves
15 Park Drive
Los Angeles, CA 90020

Billing Date: 10/15/10
Payment Due: 11/10/10
Next Meter Read Date: 11/14/10

Billing Summary

Amount of Previous Statement 9/15/10	$ 94.32
Payment Received— 10/08/10 Thank You	94.32
Balance Before Current Charges	0.00
Current Charges	89.91
Your Total Balance Due	$ 89.91

Your current energy usage

Meter Number	From	To	Usage
AB910731	9/14/10	10/14/10	
	50719	51291	572 kilowatt hours

Reminder — a 9% late payment will be added to the total unpaid balance of your account if a full payment is not received by the due date on this bill.

SE Southern Energy P.O. Box 2569 Miami, FL 33101 Visit us at www.senergy.com

Samira Mohammed
23 McDonald Street
Miami FL 33121

Statement Date
8/23/10
Past Due After
9/12/10
Account #456-382-09

Meter Number
H564364

Service Address
23 McDonald Street
Miami, FL

Billing Period:
From 7/23/10 to 8/23/10

Days in Billing Period: 31

Total Gas Used: 35 Therms

Next Meter Reading: 9/23/10

Account Activity

BALANCE LAST STATEMENT	$ 45.19
Credits and Adjustments	
GAS PAYMENT 9/04/10	45.19-
Current Charges	
PAST DUE LAST STATEMENT	0.00
GAS CHARGE	38.63
Balance Information	
TOTAL AMOUNT DUE	$ 38.63
GAS BALANCE	$ 38.63
SERVICE BALANCE	$ 0.00

To avoid a late payment charge of 2%, please pay the total amount by 9/12/10.
Billing questions? Call 1-800-327-3270
24-hour customer service 1-800-327-5000

July 14 — August 13 2010 | **Bell Telephone Statement** | Account Number **5792104857**

Lena James | Customer Service 1-800-666-2901

146 Grove Street
Long Beach, CA 90802

Summary of Charges

Total charges from your last bill	$ 87.32
Payments through 8/13	0.00
Remaining balance	87.32
Current charges	
Local Services	37.55
Long Distance Services	3.60
Total Current Charges	41.15
Late Payment Charge	2.75
Total Amount Due by 9/7/10	**$ 131.22**

Send payment to:
Bell Telephone
P.O Box 5683
Long Beach, CA 90745

If paid after 9/7/10, the amount due will be $141.22

Long Distance Calls

Date	Number called	Where	Time	Rate	Mins.	Amount
7/29	212-873-9854	NYC, NY	8:20 p.m.	night	40	2.50
8/06	307-760-4782	Lar, WY	5:00 p.m.	eve	20	1.10

1. Hector has to pay his electric bill on or before ____.
- A. September 14
- B. October 15
- C. November 10
- D. November 14

2. Hector will pay ____ for the electricity he used from 9/14 to 10/14.
- A. $0.00
- B. $89.91
- C. $94.32
- D. $184.23

3. Samira has to pay the gas bill ____.
- A. on August 23
- B. on September 4
- C. after September 12
- D. before September 13

4. If Samira smells gas in her apartment, she should ____.
- A. call 1-800-327-5000
- B. call 1-800-327-3270
- C. write to Southern Energy
- D. visit www.senergy.com

5. The past balance on Lena's telephone bill is ____.
- A. $0.00
- B. $2.75
- C. $37.55
- D. $87.32

6. The total new charges for the current month on Lena's telephone bill are ____.
- A. $3.60
- B. $37.55
- C. $41.15
- D. $131.22

7. If Lena pays her bill after the due date, her late payment charge next month will be ____.
- A. $2.75
- B. $3.60
- C. $10.00
- D. $131.22

8. We can infer that utility company meters measure ____.
- A. due dates
- B. amounts of gas or electricity you use
- C. total amount due
- D. days in a billing period

Consumer Tip If you want to rent an apartment or borrow money, you need a good **credit rating**. A credit rating is a grade that a credit agency gives you based on information from landlords, utility companies, and lenders about how you pay your bills and how you repay the money you borrow. To have a good credit rating, you must pay your bills on time.

Hillside Apartments
3700 East 25th Avenue, Oakdale, CA 95361

Dear Tenants:

The maintenance staff at Hillside Apartments works hard to keep things running smoothly. You can depend on us whenever you have a problem. Please do everything you can to help us keep Hillside Apartments clean and safe.

Keep the hallways and all common areas clear. Store your bicycles and other personal possessions in your storage area in the basement. Don't leave trash in the hallway. Throw it in the dumpster nearest to you. There are dumpsters behind Buildings A, C, and E, and there's a recycling collection site next to each dumpster. Use the green recycling bins that we provide to recycle newspaper, glass, cardboard, and metal cans. Be sure to rinse out all glass and cans before you recycle them. Recycling in Oakdale is mandatory. It's the law. We're pleased to report that we have reduced waste by 10% since the recycling program began. That's 10% less garbage for our landfill.

For everyone's safety, call us to report any broken smoke detectors or other fire hazards as soon as you discover them. We will respond immediately.

The pest control company comes the second Monday of each month. Call the rental office if you need this service. You will have to empty all your kitchen cabinets in preparation.

Please do not call us with routine maintenance requests. Fill out a maintenance request form instead. In our experience, this is a much more reliable system. We will try to get back to you as soon as possible. Call us at (310) 457-8923 only if we haven't contacted you within 24 hours.

Our tenants' most common maintenance problem is a jammed garbage disposal. To avoid this, always turn on the water when you operate your disposal. Don't throw bones or fruit with hard pits in the center down the disposal. Don't put large amounts of garbage down the disposal all at once.

If you have an emergency maintenance request, the emergency maintenance number is (310) 278-1489. You can call at any time. Please do not use the emergency number for routine requests.

Sincerely,
Oscar Molina
Building Manager

1. Tenants should ____.
- A. store bicycles in the hallway
- B. throw metal cans into the dumpster
- C. put their trash in the hallway
- D. call when a smoke detector is broken

2. Tenants should put old newspapers in the ____.
- A. dumpster
- B. landfill
- C. recycling bin
- D. garbage disposal

3. The pest control company ____.
- A. empties kitchen cabinets
- B. comes once a month
- C. comes twice a month
- D. comes every other Monday

4. Tenants should fill out a maintenance request form when ____.
- A. they have cockroaches in their apartment
- B. a smoke detector doesn't work
- C. their garbage disposal is broken
- D. there's no hot water in their apartment

5. Tenants should NOT ____.
- A. throw peaches down the disposal
- B. rinse out cans before they recycle them
- C. use storage areas for personal possessions
- D. turn on the water when they use the disposal

6. Tenants should call (310) 278-1489 when ____.
- A. the paint in their apartment is peeling
- B. they can't find a maintenance request form
- C. their kitchen faucet is leaking
- D. their toilet doesn't work

Look at the yellow pages listings and answer the questions.

PAINTERS

see also Handymen, Home Improvement Services

D & K Painting —*See our ad previous page*
586 N 32 Mid 205 468–3498

Mike's Painting
Serving Marbury for Over 25 Years
www.mikepaint.com 334 457–2479

HARMONY PAINTERS —*See our ad this page*
1238 Main Mal 334 781–5908

RAMIREZ PAINTING INC.—*See our ad this page*
675 River May 205 672–3349

PEST CONTROL SPECIALISTS

Bugs–Away Pest Control
277 Summer Mal 334 468–1633

Modern Pest Services
1029 Market Mil 205 842–2567

PHARMACIES

Wall's Pharmacy
926 Tyler Mil 205 572–9050

PIZZA

ABC Pizza
10 Market May 205 672–4902

PLUMBING CONTRACTORS

AAA Plumbing Services
777 Harrison Mal 205 842–3310

CARTER'S PLUMBING AND HEATING —*See our ad on page 454*
1300 Franklin Mid 205 842–8061

JEFF'S PLUMBING AND HEATING INC. —*See our ad this page*
212 South Mil 205 468–2855

Harmony Painters
1238 Main Street, Malvern
Interior and Exterior
Smoke, Fire, and Water Damage Repair
Ask about our 5-year guarantee **334 781–5908**

Ramirez Painting Inc.
675 River Street, Maytown
Family-Owned Business
After-Hour Scheduling
205 672–3349
Receive 10% off labor when you mention this ad

Jeff's Plumbing and Heating Inc.
212 South Street, Millport
All Your Plumbing Needs
Tubs and Toilets
Faucets and Sinks
Water Heaters
Garbage Disposals
24-Hour Emergency Service
205 468–2855
SENIOR DISCOUNTS

1. You live in Maytown. The paint in your apartment is peeling. You should call _____.
   A. 334 781-5908
   B. 205 672-3349
   C. 334 457-2479
   D. 205 468-3498

2. You live in Midfield. Your water heater isn't working. You should call _____.
   A. 205 468-3498
   B. 205 842-3310
   C. 205 468-2855
   D. 205 842-8061

3. You need to paint the outside of your house. It's a big job, and you want a guarantee that the paint won't peel. You should call _____.
   A. 334 781-5908
   B. 205 672-3349
   C. 334 457-2479
   D. 205 468-3498

4. You live in Malvern. Your garbage disposal isn't working. You should call _____.
   A. 205 468-2855
   B. 205 842-8061
   C. 205 842-3310
   D. 334 468-1633

5. You live in Millport. There are roaches in your kitchen. You should call _____.
   A. 334 468-1633
   B. 205 842-2567
   C. 205 468-2855
   D. 205 572-9050

6. It's midnight. A pipe in your bathroom just broke, and water is leaking all over the floor. You should call _____.
   A. 205 842-3310
   B. 205 842-8061
   C. 334 781-5908
   D. 205 468-2855

ASSESSMENT

• Check-up test • Self-evaluation checklists

Choose the correct answer.

1. Officer Martinez has been ____ traffic all morning.
   A. taking C. directing
   B. disturbing D. standing

2. Do you hear something? I think the telephone is ____.
   A. talking C. running
   B. ringing D. barking

3. The students in Ms. Jackson's class are doing a chemistry ____.
   A. audience C. experience
   B. system D. experiment

4. I've worked here for a long time. I think it's time to ask my boss for a ____.
   A. raise C. resume
   B. job D. salary

5. Dr. Martinetti has ____ several babies at the Westside Hospital today.
   A. given C. delivered
   B. decided D. assembled

6. Call the landlord. The paint on the walls in our living room is ____.
   A. leaking C. picking
   B. peeling D. mending

7. Tenants should fill out ____.
   A. the rental office
   B. their trash
   C. all glass and cans
   D. a maintenance request form

8. There are roaches in my basement. I need to call ____.
   A. Ajax Plumbing Service
   B. Harrison Heating Inc.
   C. United Pest Control
   D. Rocha Painting Inc.

Look at Beverly Wong's electric bill and choose the correct answer.

Western Power & Light

Account Number
444-229-8832

Beverly Wong
228 Ocean Ave
San Diego, CA 92101

Customer Assistance:
1-800-555-1212
Billing Date: **5/15/11**
Payment Due: **6/10/11**
Next Meter Read: **6/14/11**

Billing Summary

Amount of Previous Statement **4/15/11**	87.45
Payment Received – **4/09/11 Thank You**	65.00
Balance Before Current Charges	22.45
Current Charges	86.99
Your Total Balance Due	**$ 109.44**

9. Beverly has to pay her electric bill on or before ____.
   A. May 15, 2011 C. June 14, 2011
   B. June 10, 2011 D. April 15, 2011

10. She has to pay ____ for the electricity she used during this billing period.
    A. $86.99 C. $109.44
    B. $87.45 D. $22.45

SKILLS CHECK ☑

Words:

☐ account number
☐ adjustments
☐ balance
☐ bill
☐ billing date
☐ billing period
☐ credit rating
☐ current charges
☐ due
☐ payment
☐ payment received
☐ late payment charge
☐ statement
☐ total amount
☐ common area
☐ dumpster
☐ fire hazard
☐ hallway
☐ lease
☐ maintenance
☐ mandatory
☐ recycling bin
☐ recycling collection site
☐ request form
☐ smoke detector
☐ storage area
☐ trash

I can ask & answer:

☐ How long have you been *waiting*?
☐ Have you been *waiting* for a long time?
☐ I've been *waiting* for *two hours*/since *10:00*.
☐ I've been *writing letters* since *9:00 A.M.*
☐ I've already *written twenty letters*.
☐ Have you ever *been in the hospital*?
☐ How long have you been living in *Easton*?
☐ Where else have you lived?
☐ How long have you been *studying English*?

I can express surprise:

☐ You're kidding!/No kidding!/You've got to be kidding!/ I can't believe it!/That's incredible!/ That's unbelievable!/That's amazing!

I can write about:

☐ places I have lived, worked, and gone to school

I can:

☐ inquire about lease information
☐ describe apartment building rules
☐ interpret utility bills
☐ interpret rules for housing maintenance and repairs
☐ interpret yellow pages listings

7

Gerunds
Infinitives
Review: Present Perfect and Present Perfect Continuous Tenses

- Discussing Recreation Preferences
- Discussing Things You Dislike Doing
- Habits
- Describing Talents and Skills
- Telling About Important Decisions
- Requests at Work
- Thanking Someone
- Borrow and Lending
- Workplace Notes and Messages
- "Small Talk" at Work

Vocabulary Preview

1. enjoy / like
2. hate / can't stand
3. avoid
4. begin / start
5. continue / keep on
6. quit / stop
7. consider / think about
8. decide
9. learn
10. practice

My Favorite Way to Relax

to watch	watching
to dance	dancing
to swim	swimming

A. Do you **like to watch TV**?

B. Yes. I **enjoy watching TV** very much. **Watching TV** is my favorite way to relax.

1. *you*
paint

2. *Beverly*
knit

3. *Kevin*
swim

4. *your parents*
play golf

5. *you and your friends*
dance

6. *you*
listen to music

7. *Hector*
go to the movies

8. *Valerie*
browse the web

9.

READING

ENJOYING LIFE

Howard enjoys reading. He likes to read in the park. He likes to read in the library. He even likes to read in the bathtub! As you can see, reading is a very important part of Howard's life.

Patty enjoys singing. She likes to sing in school. She likes to sing in church. She even likes to sing in the shower! As you can see, singing is a very important part of Patty's life.

Brenda enjoys watching TV. She likes to watch TV in the living room. She likes to watch TV in bed. She even likes to watch TV in department stores! As you can see, watching TV is a very important part of Brenda's life.

Tom enjoys talking about politics. He likes to talk about politics with his friends. He likes to talk about politics with his parents. He even likes to talk about politics with his barber! As you can see, talking about politics is a very important part of Tom's life.

✓ READING *CHECK-UP*

Q & A

The people in the story are introducing themselves to you at a party. Using this model, create dialogs based on the story.

A. Hello. My name is *Howard*.
B. Nice to meet you. My name is ______.
Are you enjoying the party?
A. Not really. To tell you the truth, I'd rather be *reading*.
B. Oh? Do you like to *read*?
A. Oh, yes. I enjoy *reading* very much.
B. I like to *read*, too. In fact, *reading* is my favorite way to relax.
A. Mine, too. Tell me, what do you like to *read*?
B. I like to *read books about famous people*. How about you?
A. I enjoy *reading short stories*.
B. Well, please excuse me. I have to go now. It was nice meeting you.
A. Nice meeting you, too.

She Hates to Drive Downtown

{ **like to** work / **like** work**ing** } { **hate to** work / **hate** work**ing** } { —— / **avoid** work**ing** }

A. Does Helen **like** { **to drive** / **driving** } downtown?

B. No. She **hates** { **to drive** / **driving** }* downtown.

She **avoids driving** downtown whenever she can.

* Or: can't stand { to drive / driving }

1. *Albert*
travel by plane

2. *you*
go to the mall

3. *your parents*
eat at fast-food restaurants

4. *Carmen*
sit in the sun

5. *you and your friends*
talk about politics

6. *Kathy*
use her cell phone

7. *you*
wear a suit and tie

8. *the president*
talk to reporters

9.

How About You?

What do you enjoy doing?
What do you avoid doing whenever you can?

READING

BAD HABITS

Jill's co-workers always tell her to stop eating junk food. They think that eating junk food is unhealthy. Jill knows that, but she still keeps on eating junk food. She wants to stop, but she can't. Eating junk food is a habit she just can't break.

Vincent's friends always tell him to stop gossiping. They think that gossiping isn't nice. Vincent knows that, but he still keeps on gossiping. He wants to stop, but he can't. Gossiping is a habit he just can't break.

Jennifer's parents always tell her to stop interrupting people while they're talking. They think that interrupting people is very rude. Jennifer knows that, but she still keeps on interrupting people. She wants to stop, but she can't. Interrupting people is a habit she just can't break.

Walter's wife always tells him to stop talking about business all the time. She thinks that talking about business all the time is boring. Walter knows that, but he still keeps on talking about business. He wants to stop, but he can't. Talking about business is a habit he just can't break.

✔ READING *CHECK-UP*

Q & A

You're talking with the people in the story about their bad habits. Using this model, create dialogs based on the story.

A. *Jill?*
B. Yes?
A. You know . . . I don't mean to be critical, but I really think you should stop *eating junk food.*
B. Oh?
A. Yes. *Eating junk food is unhealthy.* Don't you think so?
B. You're right. The truth is . . . I want to stop, but I can't. *Eating junk food* is a habit I just can't break.

How About You?

Do you have any habits you "just can't break"? Tell about them.

How Did You Learn to Swim So Well?

start to swim **start** swimming	**learn to** swim ——	—— **practice** swimming

A. How did you **learn to swim** so well?

B. Well, I **started** { **to swim** / **swimming** } when I was young, and I've been **swimming** ever since.

A. I envy you. I've never **swum** before.

B. I'll be glad to teach you how.

A. Thank you. But isn't **swimming** very difficult?

B. Not at all. After you **practice swimming** a few times, you'll probably **swim** as well as I do.

A. How did you learn to __________ so well?

B. Well, I started { to __________ / __________ing } when I was young,

and I've been __________ing ever since.

A. I envy you. I've never __________ before.

B. I'll be glad to teach you how.

A. Thank you. But isn't __________ing very difficult?

B. Not at all. After you practice __________ing a few times, you'll probably __________ as well as I do.

1. *draw*

2. *box*

3. *surf*

4. *figure skate*

5. *tap dance*

6.

How to Say It!

Expressing Appreciation

Practice the conversations in this lesson again. Express appreciation in different ways.

Guess What I've Decided to Do!

decide to buy	—	—
—	consider buying	think about buying

A. Guess what I've decided to do!

B. What?

A. I've **decided to get married**.

B. That's wonderful! How long have you been **thinking about getting married**?

A. For a long time, actually. I **considered getting married** a few years ago, but never did.

B. Well, I think you're making the right decision. **Getting married** is a great idea.

A. Guess what I've decided to do!

B. What?

A. I've decided to ____________.

B. That's wonderful! How long have you been thinking about ____________ing?

A. For a long time, actually. I considered ____________ing a few years ago, but never did.

B. Well, I think you're making the right decision. ____________ing is a great idea.

1. *get a dog*

2. *buy a new car*

3. *move to New York*

4. *go on a diet*

5. *go back to college*

6. *start my own business*

7. *retire*

8. *become a vegetarian*

9.

I've Made a Decision

begin = start	keep on = continue	quit = stop
begin to eat **begin** eating	—— **keep on** eating	—— **quit** eating
start to eat **start** eating	**continue to** eat **continue** eating	—— **stop** eating

A. I've made a decision.

B. What is it?

A. I've decided to **quit eating** junk food.

B. That's great! Have you ever tried to **stop eating** junk food before?

A. Yes. Many times. But every time I've **stopped eating** it, I've **begun*** { **to eat** / **eating** } it again after a few days.

B. Well, I hope you're successful this time.

A. I hope so, too. After all, I can't **keep on eating** junk food for the rest of my life.

* begin – began – begun

A. I've made a decision.

B. What is it?

A. I've decided to quit* __________ing.

B. That's great! Have you ever tried to stop* __________ing before?

A. Yes. Many times. But every time I've stopped* __________ing,

I've begun* { to __________ / __________ing } again after a few days.

B. Well, I hope you're successful this time.

A. I hope so, too. After all, I can't keep on* __________ing for the rest of my life.

* quit = stop
begin = start
keep on = continue

1. *bite my nails*

2. *tease my little sister*

3. *worry about my health*

4. *argue with my neighbors*

5. *complain about my son-in-law*

6.

READING

IMPORTANT DECISIONS

Jim had to make an important decision recently. He made an appointment for an interview at the Tektron Internet Company, and he had to decide what to wear. First, he considered wearing a sweater to the interview. Then, he thought about wearing a sports jacket. Finally, he decided to wear a suit and tie. Jim thinks he made the right decision. He's glad he didn't wear a sweater or sports jacket. He feels that wearing a suit and tie was the best thing to do.

Emily had to make an important decision recently. Her landlord sold her apartment building, and she had to decide where to move. First, she considered moving to another apartment. Then, she thought about buying a small house. Finally, she decided to move home with her parents for a while. Emily thinks she made the right decision. She's glad she didn't move to another apartment or buy a small house. She thinks that moving home with her parents for a while was the right thing to do.

Nick had to make an important decision recently. He got out of the army, and he had to decide what to do next with his life. First, he considered working in his family's grocery store. Then, he thought about taking a job in a restaurant. Finally, he decided to enroll in college and study engineering. Nick thinks he made the right decision. He's glad he didn't work in his family's grocery store or take a job in a restaurant. He feels that enrolling in college and studying engineering was the smartest thing to do.

Maria had to make an important decision recently. She lost her job as a bookkeeper because her company went out of business, and she had to decide what to do. First, she considered looking for another job as a bookkeeper. Then, she thought about working as a secretary for a while. Finally, she decided to enroll in technical school and study network programming. Maria thinks she made the right decision. She's glad she didn't look for another job as a bookkeeper or work as a secretary for a while. She thinks that enrolling in technical school and studying network programming was the best thing to do.

✓ READING *CHECK-UP*

TRUE, FALSE, OR MAYBE?

Answer True, False, or Maybe (if the answer isn't in the story).

1. Jim considered wearing a sweater to the interview.
2. He got the job at the Tektron Internet Company.
3. Emily decided not to move to another apartment.
4. Emily never considered buying a small house.
5. Emily's parents think that moving home was the right thing for her to do.
6. Nick's family is in the restaurant business.
7. Nick first became interested in engineering while he was in the army.
8. Maria wasn't a very good bookkeeper.
9. After Maria lost her job, she worked as a secretary for a while.
10. Maria feels she made the right decision.

LISTENING

Listen and choose the correct answer.

1. a. She enjoys going to the mall.
   b. She hates going to the mall.
2. a. He sold his car.
   b. He's going to sell his car.
3. a. He bites his nails.
   b. He stopped biting his nails.
4. a. She likes traveling by plane.
   b. She can't stand traveling by plane.
5. a. They're going to move to Florida.
   b. They might move to Florida.
6. a. He's married.
   b. He isn't married.
7. a. She's going to keep on practicing.
   b. She isn't going to continue practicing.
8. a. He interrupts people.
   b. He doesn't interrupt people any more.

PRONUNCIATION Reduced *to*

Listen. Then say it.

I like to watch TV.

She hates to drive downtown.

How did you learn to draw?

I started to skate last year.

Say it. Then listen.

We decided to move.

He can't stand to wear a tie.

They've already begun to eat.

I continue to worry about my health.

Write in your journal about an important decision you had to make.

I had to make an important decision recently.

______________________________,

and I had to decide what to do. First, I considered

__________. *Then, I thought about* __________.

Finally, I decided to ______________ *because*

______________________________.

GRAMMAR FOCUS

Verb + Infinitive

decide learn	to ____

Verb + Gerund

avoid consider enjoy keep on practice quit stop think about	____ing

Verb + Infinitive/Gerund

begin can't stand continue hate like start	to ____ ____ing

Gerund as Subject

Watching TV is my favorite way to relax.

Gerund as Object

I'm thinking about **getting married**.

Choose the correct word.

1. I enjoy (to listen listening) to music.
2. My daughter practices (to skate skating) every weekend.
3. We've decided (to move moving) to Florida.
4. I usually avoid (to talk talking) about politics.
5. I really want to quit (to bite biting) my nails.
6. You can't keep on (to worry worrying) all the time.
7. Where did you learn (to draw drawing) so well?
8. I know I have to stop (to eat eating) junk food.

1 CONVERSATION Requests at Work

Practice the conversations with a classmate.

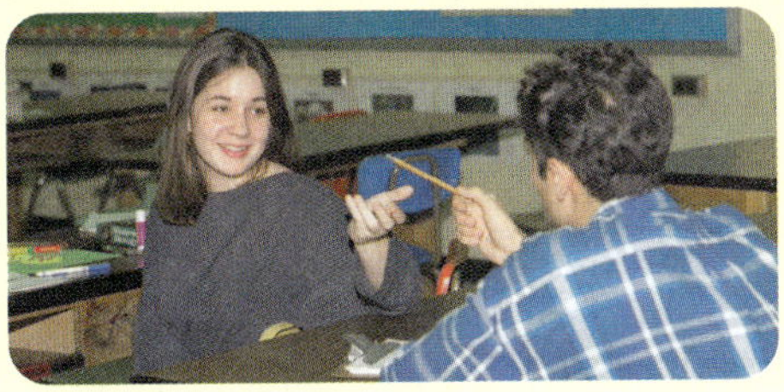

A. Would you please lend me your pencil?

B. Sure. I'll be happy to.

A. Thank you for lending me your pencil.

B. You're welcome.

Now work with other classmates. Practice making requests and thanking co-workers.

A. Would you please _________?	**A.** Thank you for _________ing.
B. Sure. I'll be happy to.	**B.** You're welcome.

1. clean table six

2. copy this report

3. set up the tables and chairs

4. hang the new coats on the racks

5. change the oil in the Ford

6. take the lunch trays to the fifth floor

2 TEAMWORK Asking to Borrow Something

Work with other classmates.
Practice both conversations.
Ask to borrow different items.

A. Would you please lend me _________?

B. Sure. I'll be happy to.

A. Thank you.

A. Could I possibly borrow _________?

B. Sure.

A. Thanks.

GWL

Emily,

Would you be able to help me with the PowerPoint presentation I have to give next month? I've given a lot of presentations, but I haven't used PowerPoint before. I know exactly what I want to say and what pictures I want to show. I attended last month's computer training sessions, but I'm still having trouble making charts with PowerPoint, and I don't know how to add pictures to my presentation. I'd really appreciate your help. Would you have some time to meet with me this week?

Thanks,
Joe

SHS SPRINGFIELD HIGH SCHOOL

Roberto,

Thank you for staying late last week and helping to mail our school's annual fund-raising letter. You were an important part of the "assembly line" of employees who helped with this. We mailed 2,000 letters last week—500 more than last year!

We have already received more than $1,000 from students who read the letter. This is just the beginning! It looks like we'll finally be able to buy a new copy machine this year.

Thanks again for all your help.
Carol

From: George_Jensen@skillcorp.com
To: Linda_Chang@skillcorp.com
Subject: Request for day off

Ms. Chang,

Could I possibly take the day off next Wednesday, November 2? I'm asking because I have to take my daughter to a doctor's appointment in the morning and a dentist's appointment in the afternoon. I tried to schedule the appointments for an afternoon when I don't work, but these were the only times available. If the appointment at the dentist is quick, I might be able to come in for an hour of work at the end of the day. I've been making excellent progress on all my work, including the monthly report. I'm sure I'll be able to complete it by November 7. I'll come in and work on it this weekend if necessary.

Thanks,
George Jensen

1. Joe does NOT know _____.

A. how to give presentations
B. what pictures to use in his presentation
C. how to make charts with PowerPoint
D. what to say in his presentation

2. We can infer that _____.

A. Joe doesn't use a computer at work
B. everybody attended the training sessions
C. Joe's presentation is about power
D. PowerPoint is a computer program for presentations

3. Carol is thanking Roberto because he _____.

A. assembled electronic equipment
B. put letters into envelopes
C. gave money for a new copy machine
D. wrote a letter

4. We can infer from Carol's note that _____.

A. a fund-raising letter asks for money
B. Roberto works in a factory
C. they mailed 2,500 letters last year
D. more than 1,000 students have already read the letter

5. George wants to take time off _____.

A. to make progress on all his work
B. to work on the monthly report
C. to work on the weekend
D. to take his daughter to the doctor and dentist

6. George made appointments for November 2nd because _____.

A. he doesn't usually work that afternoon
B. his report is due on November 7th
C. that's when the doctor and dentist can see his daughter
D. the appointment at the dentist will be quick

Read the article and answer the questions.

Small Talk

"How was your weekend?" "What are you going to do on your day off?" "Did you see the game on TV last night?" "Isn't the weather beautiful today?" These questions, and the answers to these questions, are examples of "small talk"—the short, friendly conversations that people have with friends and co-workers.

Some people avoid making small talk at work. They think they shouldn't chat about topics that aren't important on the job, or they believe their supervisors and co-workers will think they aren't serious about their work. Some people just don't enjoy making conversation about themselves.

But small talk is important! Knowing how to make small talk is a skill that can help you in your job. By making conversation, you show that you are friendly and interested in your co-workers. You become a better *team player*. If you don't make small talk, other workers might feel uncomfortable around you and think you're rude or unfriendly. Peter Harper, Director of Human Resources at the Apex Company, says, "We always look for friendly employees who know how to communicate with each other and with our customers."

Here are some tips for successful small talk. Talk about safe topics such as the weather, sports, hobbies, movies, TV programs, and celebrities (movie stars, singers, and other famous people). You can share some information about your family such as birthdays, anniversaries, and other family events, but don't share very personal information about family problems. You can talk about the news, but avoid conversations about politics. Other topics to avoid are money, religion, and illness. Don't ask personal questions such as "How old are you?" or "What's your salary?" And don't gossip. Co-workers won't want to talk with you if they think you will talk to other people about them.

Listening is an important part of small talk. Listen carefully to what the other person is saying and ask questions. Don't just talk about yourself. Show that you are interested in the other person. And remember to smile! Making conversation takes practice. The more you do it, the better you'll be at making small talk!

1. If you make small talk at work, ____.
A. your supervisor will think you're serious
B. your supervisor will be uncomfortable
C. your co-workers will think you're friendly
D. your co-workers will think you're rude

2. When you make small talk, don't ____.
A. talk about sports
B. talk about family problems
C. talk about movies and TV shows
D. smile

3. It's okay to ask, ____
A. "What's your salary?"
B. "How much do you weigh?"
C. "Who's your favorite actor?"
D. "How old are you going to be?"

4. ____ is a safe topic to talk about.
A. The weather
B. Religion
C. Money
D. Politics

5. In paragraph 2, *chat* means ____.
A. to gossip
B. to have serious conversations
C. to have long conversations
D. to make small talk

6. In paragraph 3, a *team player* refers to ____.
A. a supervisor at work
B. a person who works well with co-workers
C. a celebrity player on a sports team
D. a person who likes sports

TEAMWORK With a classmate, make a list of other topics for small talk. Then share with your classmates. As a class, vote for the best topics.

ASSESSMENT

• Check-up test • Self-evaluation checklists

Choose the correct answer.

1. I enjoy ____ the web.
   - A. traveling
   - B. browsing
   - C. watching
   - D. following

2. It's impolite to ____ people while they're speaking.
   - A. consider
   - B. complain
   - C. interrupt
   - D. quit

3. I've been thinking about ____ my own business.
   - A. starting
   - B. going back
   - C. keeping on
   - D. liking

4. I'm considering ____ in a technical school.
   - A. going
   - B. deciding
   - C. practicing
   - D. enrolling

5. I just made an important ____. I'm going to retire this year.
   - A. reason
   - B. advice
   - C. decision
   - D. idea

6. Would you please ____ your pencil?
   - A. lend you
   - B. lend me
   - C. borrow you
   - D. borrow me

7. I attended a training ____ at my company last week.
   - A. session
   - B. section
   - C. system
   - D. line

8. I've been making good ____ on all my work.
   - A. presentation
   - B. appointments
   - C. schedule
   - D. progress

9. I enjoy ____ with my colleagues during breaks at work.
   - A. arriving
   - B. changing
   - C. chatting
   - D. listening

10. ____ is a safe topic for small talk at work.
   - A. Politics
   - B. The weather
   - C. Your salary
   - D. Gossip about co-workers

SKILLS CHECK

Words:

- ☐ begin/start
- ☐ can't stand/hate
- ☐ consider/think about
- ☐ continue/keep on
- ☐ enjoy/like
- ☐ quit/stop

- ☐ avoid
- ☐ borrow
- ☐ decide
- ☐ learn
- ☐ lend
- ☐ practice

I can ask & answer:

- ☐ Do you like to *swim*?
- ☐ Do you like *swimming*?
  - I enjoy *swimming* very much.
  - *Swimming* is my favorite way to relax.
  - I avoid *swimming* whenever I can.
- ☐ How did you learn to *draw* so well?
  - I started *drawing* when I was young.
- ☐ How long have you been thinking about *moving*?
  - I considered *moving* a few years ago.
- ☐ Would you please lend me your *pencil*?
- ☐ Could I possibly borrow your *pencil*?

I can express appreciation:

- ☐ Thank you.
- ☐ I appreciate that.
- ☐ That's very kind of you.
- ☐ That's very nice of you.

I can:

- ☐ make and respond to requests at work
- ☐ ask to borrow something
- ☐ interpret workplace notes and messages
- ☐ make small talk at work and understand its importance

I can write about:

- ☐ an important decision I had to make

8

Past Perfect Tense
Past Perfect Continuous Tense

- Discussing Things People Had Done
- Discussing Preparations for Events
- Describing Consequences of Being Late
- Discussing Feelings
- Describing Accomplishments
- Scheduling Medical Appointments
- Medical Appointment Cards
- Medical History Forms
- Preventive Care Recommendations
- Public Health Information
- Nutrition: The Food Pyramid
- Reading a Health Textbook Lesson

Vocabulary Preview

1. discuss
2. fly a kite
3. go canoeing
4. go window-shopping
5. pack
6. purchase
7. realize
8. shine
9. water
10. wrestle
11. forget
12. remember
13. memorize
14. rehearse
15. perform

They Didn't Want to

I He She It We You They	had eaten.

A. Why didn't Mr. and Mrs. Henderson **see** a movie last weekend?

B. They didn't want to. They **had seen** a movie the weekend before.

1. Why didn't your parents eat out yesterday evening?

2. Why didn't Barry go canoeing last Saturday?

3. Why didn't Martha make eggs for breakfast yesterday morning?

4. Why didn't you have pizza for dinner last night?

5. Why didn't you and your friends drive to the beach last Sunday?

6. Why didn't Paul wear his polka dot shirt to work yesterday?

7. Why didn't Susan take a psychology course last semester?

8. Why didn't your neighbors give a party last month?

9. Why didn't Mozart write an opera last week?

10. Why didn't you go window-shopping last Saturday afternoon?

11. Why didn't Monica fly her kite yesterday?

12. Why didn't you and your family discuss politics at the dinner table yesterday evening?

13. Why didn't George do card tricks for his friends last weekend?

14.

READING

THE MOST IMPORTANT THING

Roger thought he was all prepared for his dinner party last night. He had sent invitations to his boss and all the people at the office. He had looked through several cookbooks and had found some very interesting recipes. He had even gone all the way downtown to buy imported fruit, vegetables, and cheese, which he needed for his dinner. However, as soon as Roger's doorbell rang and his guests arrived, he realized that he had forgotten to turn on the oven. Roger felt very foolish. He couldn't believe what he had done. He thought he was all prepared for his dinner party, but he had forgotten to do the most important thing.

Mr. and Mrs. Jenkins thought they were all prepared for their vacation. They had packed their suitcases several days ahead of time. They had gone to the bank and purchased traveler's checks. They had even asked their next-door neighbor to water their plants, feed their dog, and shovel their driveway if it snowed. However, as soon as Mr. and Mrs. Jenkins arrived at the airport, they realized that they had forgotten to bring their plane tickets with them, and there wasn't enough time to go back home and get them. Mr. and Mrs. Jenkins were heartbroken. They couldn't believe what they had done. They thought they were all prepared for their vacation, but they had forgotten to do the most important thing.

Harold thought he was all prepared for his job interview yesterday. He had gone to his barber and gotten a very short haircut. He had bought a new shirt, put on his best tie, and shined his shoes. He had even borrowed his brother's new suit. However, as soon as Harold began the job interview, he realized that he had forgotten to bring along his resume. Harold was furious with himself. He thought he was all prepared for his job interview, but he had forgotten to do the most important thing.

Janet thought she was all prepared for the school play. She had memorized the script several weeks in advance. She had practiced her songs and dances until she knew them perfectly. She had even stayed up all night the night before and rehearsed the play by herself from beginning to end. However, as soon as the curtain went up and the play began, Janet realized that she had forgotten to put on her costume. Janet was really embarrassed. She couldn't believe what she had done. She thought she was all prepared for the play, but she had forgotten to do the most important thing.

✓ READING *CHECK-UP*

TRUE, FALSE, OR MAYBE?

Answer True, False, or Maybe (if the answer isn't in the story).

1. Roger had remembered to buy the ingredients he needed.
2. Roger hadn't remembered to cook the food.
3. Roger's guests couldn't believe what he had done.
4. Mr. and Mrs. Jenkins had forgotten to buy their plane tickets.
5. When Mr. and Mrs. Jenkins realized what had happened, they felt very sad and upset.
6. Harold thinks it's important to bring a resume to a job interview.
7. Harold doesn't have a suit.
8. Janet hadn't seen the script until the night before the play.
9. Before the play began, Janet hadn't realized that she had forgotten to put on her costume.

WHICH IS CORRECT?

1. Before Barbara went on her vacation, she went to the bank and bought (tickets traveler's checks).
2. Peter wanted his boss to come over for dinner, but he forgot to send him (a resume an invitation).
3. Sheila (borrowed bought) her roommate's laptop for a few days.
4. Our grandchildren were (heartbroken foolish) when our dog ran away.
5. At the supermarket next to the United Nations, (imported important) people buy (imported important) food.

How About You?

Have you ever thought you were all prepared for something, but you realized you had forgotten to do something important?

What were you preparing for?

What had you done?

What had you forgotten to do?

They Didn't Get There on Time

A. Did you get to the **concert** on time?

B. No, I didn't. By the time I got to the **concert**, it had already **begun**.

1. *post office*
   closed

2. *plane*
   take off

3. *movie*
   start

4. *train*
   leave

5. *lecture*
   end

6. *meeting*
   finish

7. *library*
   close

8. *boat*
   sail away

9. *parade*
   go by

He Hadn't Gone Fishing in a Long Time

I He She It We You They	hadn't eaten. (had not)

A. Did Grandpa enjoy **going fishing** last weekend?

B. Yes, he did. He hadn't **gone fishing** in a long time.

1. Did Natalie enjoy swimming in the ocean last weekend?

2. Did you enjoy seeing a movie yesterday evening?

3. Did Mr. and Mrs. Ramirez enjoy taking a walk along the beach yesterday?

4. Did you and your friends enjoy eating at Burger Queen yesterday?

5. Did Henry enjoy singing with the choir last Sunday?

6. Did you enjoy having strawberry shortcake for dessert last night?

7. Did Jim and Tess enjoy riding on a roller coaster this afternoon?

8. Did Kevin enjoy playing "hide and seek" with his children last night?

9. Did Mrs. Kramer enjoy reading her old love letters last weekend?

READING

DAYS GONE BY

Michael took a very special trip last month. He went back to Fullerton, his home town. Michael's visit to Fullerton was very special to him. He was born there, he grew up there, but he hadn't been back there since he finished high school.

He went to places he hadn't gone to in years. He walked through the park in the center of town and remembered the days he had walked through the same park with his first girlfriend. He passed by the empty field where he and his friends had played baseball every day after school. And he stood for a while in front of the movie theater and thought about all the Saturday afternoons he had spent there sitting in the balcony, watching his favorite movie heroes and eating popcorn.

He did things he hadn't done in a long time. He had some homemade ice cream at the ice cream shop, he rode on the merry-go-round in the park, and he went fishing at the lake on the outskirts of town. For a while, he felt like a kid again. He hadn't had homemade ice cream, ridden on a merry-go-round, or gone fishing since he was a young boy.

He also saw people he hadn't seen in years. He visited several of his old neighbors who had never moved out of the neighborhood. He said hello to the owners of the candy store near his house. And he even bumped into Mrs. Riley, his tenth-grade science teacher.

During his visit to his home town, Michael remembered places he hadn't gone to, things he hadn't done, and people he hadn't seen since his childhood. Michael's trip back to Fullerton was a very nostalgic experience for him. Going back to Fullerton brought back many memories of days gone by.

✓ READING *CHECK-UP*

TRUE, FALSE, OR MAYBE?

Answer True, False, or Maybe (if the answer isn't in the story).

1. Michael moved back to Fullerton last month.
2. He hadn't seen Fullerton in years.
3. When Michael passed by the field last month, children were playing baseball.
4. Michael enjoyed going to the movies when he was young.
5. The ice cream shop was near Michael's home in Fullerton.
6. Michael rode on the merry-go-round when he was a young boy.
7. Some of Michael's old neighbors still live in the same neighborhood.
8. Mrs. Riley still teaches science.

WHICH IS CORRECT?

1. I always enjoy eating Aunt Betty's (home town   homemade) food.
2. The new shopping mall is located in the (outskirts   outside) of our city.
3. She recently visited the town where she had (spent   grown up) her childhood.
4. I bumped (through   into) an old friend on the street the other day.
5. They hadn't been (back   by) to their old neighborhood in several years.
6. Seeing my old college friends was a (nauseous   nostalgic) experience for me.

LISTENING

Listen and choose the correct answer.

1. a. Yes. They've never eaten there.
   b. Yes. They had never eaten there.
2. a. I had already seen it.
   b. I've already seen it.
3. a. No. It had already started.
   b. No. It has already started.
4. a. But I had already done it.
   b. But I've already done it.
5. a. She had memorized all the important names and dates.
   b. She's going to study very hard.
6. a. Have you ever stayed there before?
   b. Had you ever stayed there before?

THINK ABOUT IT! *Feelings and Experiences*

Think about times you have had these feelings. Share your experiences with other students.

Have You Heard About Harry?

A. Have you heard about Harry?

B. No, I haven't. What happened?

A. He broke his leg last week.

B. That's terrible! How did he do THAT?

A. He was roller-skating . . . and he had never roller-skated before.

B. Poor Harry! I hope he feels better soon.

A. Have you heard about ____________?

B. No, I haven't. What happened?

A. (He/She) ____________ last week.

B. That's terrible! How did (he/she) do THAT?

A. (He/She) was ____________ing . . . and (he/she) had never _________ before.

B. Poor ____________! I hope (he/she) feels better soon.

1. *twist his ankle*
fly a kite

2. *injure her knee*
ski

3. *burn himself*
bake brownies

4. *sprain her wrist*
play squash

5. *get a black eye*
box

6. *hurt her arm*
wrestle

7. *lose his voice*
sing opera

8. *dislocate her shoulder*
do gymnastics

9. *get hurt in an accident*
ride a motorcycle

10. *sprain his back*
do the tango

11. *break his front teeth*
chew on a steak bone

12.

How to Say It!

Sharing News About Someone

A. { Have you heard about / Have you heard the news about / Have you heard what happened to } *Harry?*

B. No, I haven't. What happened?

Practice the conversations in this lesson again. Begin your conversations in different ways.

It's Really a Shame

I He She It We You They	had been eating.

A. I heard that Arnold failed his driver's test last week. Is it true?

B. Yes, it is . . . and it's really a shame. He had been practicing for a long time.

A. I heard that _______________ last week. Is it true?

B. Yes, it is . . . and it's really a shame. (He/She/They) had been _________ing for a long time.

I heard that . . .

1. Fred lost his job at the factory
work there

2. Larry and Jane broke up
go together

3. Mona had to cancel her trip to France
plan it

4. Pam and Bob canceled their wedding
plan to get married

5. Mr. and Mrs. Williams moved
live in this neighborhood

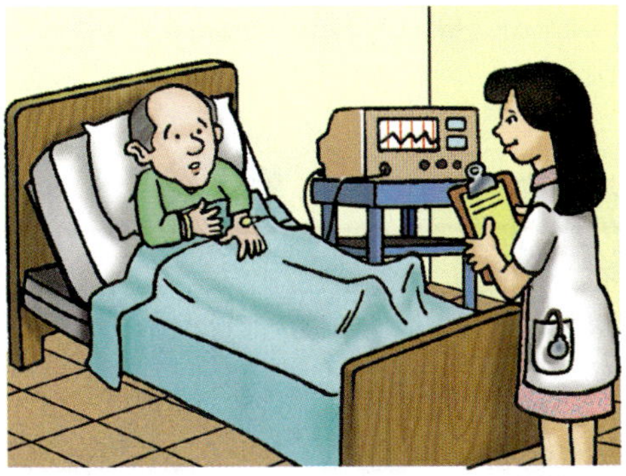

6. Walter had another heart attack
feel better

7. Alex did poorly on his science exam
study for it

8. Penny twisted her ankle and couldn't run in the marathon
train for it

9. Your daughter got sick and couldn't perform in her piano recital
rehearse for it

10. Herbert caught a cold and couldn't go camping
look forward to it

READING

THEIR PLANS "FELL THROUGH"

Patty had planned to have a party last weekend. She had been getting ready for the party for a long time. She had invited all of her friends and several co-workers, she had cooked lots of food, and she had cleaned her apartment from top to bottom. But at the last minute, she got sick and had to cancel the party. Poor Patty! She was really disappointed.

Michael had planned to ask his boss for a raise last week. He had been preparing to ask his boss for a raise for a long time. He had come to work early for several weeks, he had worked late at the office every night, and he had even bought a new suit to wear to the appointment with his boss. Unfortunately, before Michael could even ask for a raise, his boss fired him.

John and Julia had planned to get married last month. They had been planning their wedding for more than a year, and all of their friends and relatives had been looking forward to the ceremony. Julia had bought a beautiful wedding gown, John had rented a fancy tuxedo, and they had sent invitations to 150 people. But at the last minute, John "got cold feet"* and they had to cancel the wedding.

* got scared

IN YOUR OWN WORDS

For Writing and Discussion

Tell about plans you had that "fell through."

What had you planned to do?
How long had you been planning to do it?
What had you done beforehand?
What went wrong? What happened?
Were you upset? disappointed?

ON YOUR OWN *Accomplishments*

When Stella Karp won the marathon last week, nobody was surprised. She had been getting up early and jogging every morning. She had been eating health foods and taking vitamins for several months. And she had been swimming fifty laps every day after work. Stella Karp really deserved to win the marathon. After all, she had been preparing for it for a long time.

When my friend Stuart finally passed his driver's test the other day, nobody was surprised. He had been taking lessons at the driving school for several months. He had been practicing driving with his father for the past several weeks. And he had been studying the "rules of the road" since he was a little boy. My friend Stuart really deserved to pass his driver's test. After all, he had been preparing for it for a long time.

When Sally Compton got a promotion last week, nobody was surprised. She had been working overtime every day for several months. She had been studying computer programming in the evening. And she had even been taking extra work home on the weekends. Sally Compton really deserved to get a promotion. After all, she had been working hard to earn it for a long time.

We all feel proud when we accomplish something that we have prepared for. Tell other students about an accomplishment you're proud of.

Write in your journal about something you accomplished: What did you accomplish? How long had you been preparing for it? How had you been preparing?

PRONUNCIATION Reduced *had*

Listen. Then say it.

She had seen a movie the day before.

We had never roller-skated before.

It had already begun.

Patty had planned to have a party.

Say it. Then listen.

He had gone fishing the week before.

We had been studying for several hours.

I had forgotten to do it.

Tom had been practicing for a long time.

GRAMMAR FOCUS

Past Perfect Tense

I He She It We You They	had eaten.

I He She It We You They	hadn't eaten.

Past Perfect Continuous Tense

I He She It We You They	had been eating.

Complete the conversations. Use the correct forms of these verbs in your answers.

forget go have live plan play ride see take off work

1. A. Why didn't you see a movie last weekend?
   B. I didn't want to. _____ _____ _________ a movie the weekend before.
2. A. Why was your brother upset during his job interview yesterday?
   B. _____ _____ _________ to bring along his resume.
3. A. Did your daughter enjoy having chocolate cake for dessert last night?
   B. Yes, she did. _____ _______ _________ chocolate cake for dessert in a long time.
4. A. Did you get to the airport on time?
   B. No, I didn't. By the time I got to the airport, the plane _____ already _________.
5. A. Why didn't your friends go sailing with us last Sunday?
   B. They didn't want to. _____ _____ _________ sailing the weekend before.
6. A. How did Roberta hurt herself?
   B. She was _____ a motorcycle, and _____ _____ never _________ a motorcycle before.
7. A. Did you hear that Gregory and Isabelle canceled their wedding?
   B. No, I didn't. What a shame! _____ _____ _____ _________ it for a long time.
8. A. Is it true that Bruno lost his job at the factory?
   B. Yes, it is . . . and it's really a shame. _____ _____ _____ _________ there for many years.
9. A. Did you and your friends enjoy playing basketball yesterday?
   B. Yes, we did. _____ _______ _________ basketball in a long time.
10. A. Did you hear that Mrs. Ramirez moved last weekend?
    B. Yes, I did. I'm really surprised. _____ _____ _____ _________ here for more than thirty years.

1 CONVERSATION Making, Confirming, Rescheduling, & Canceling Appointments

Practice conversations with your classmates. For each conversation, use the information on any of these medical appointment cards or your own information.

Making an Appointment

A. Hello. This is __(first & last name)__. I'd like to make an appointment.

B. All right. Can you come in on __(day)__ __(date)__ at __(time)__?

A. __(day)__ __(date)__ at __(time)__? Yes. That would be fine. Thank you.

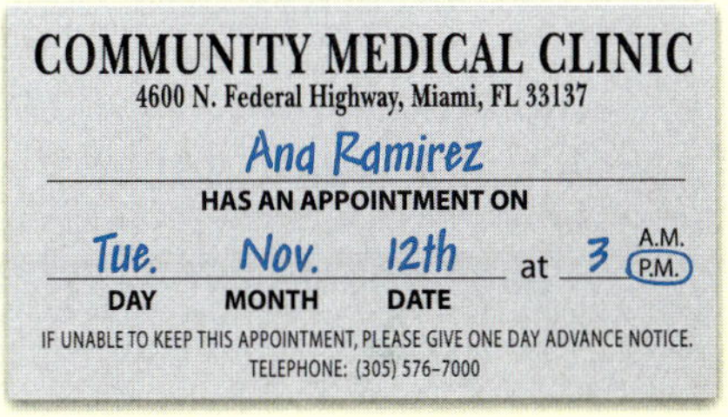

COMMUNITY MEDICAL CLINIC
4600 N. Federal Highway, Miami, FL 33137
Ana Ramirez
HAS AN APPOINTMENT ON
Tue. Nov. 12th at 3 A.M. (P.M.)
DAY MONTH DATE
IF UNABLE TO KEEP THIS APPOINTMENT, PLEASE GIVE ONE DAY ADVANCE NOTICE.
TELEPHONE: (305) 576-7000

Confirming an Appointment

A. Hello. This is __(first & last name)__. I'm calling to confirm my appointment on __(day)__ __(date)__ at __(time)__.

B. Let me check. Yes, you have an appointment on __(day)__ __(date)__ at __(time)__. We'll see you then.

A. Thank you.

APPOINTMENT
FOR Abdul Asmal
ON Mon. Feb. 4 AT 11:30 (A.M.) P.M.
DAY MONTH DATE
GLENDALE HEALTH CENTER
501 North Glendale Avenue
Glendale, CA 91206
(818) 500-8762
IF UNABLE TO KEEP THIS APPOINTMENT, KINDLY GIVE 24 HOURS NOTICE.

Rescheduling an Appointment

A. Hello. This is __(first & last name)__. I need to reschedule an appointment.

B. When are you scheduled to come in?

A. On __(day)__ __(date)__ at __(time)__.

B. Okay. We have an opening on __(day)__ __(date)__ at __(time)__. Is that a convenient time?

A. Yes. Thank you.

M Clara Wong
HAS AN APPOINTMENT ON
☐ MON ☐ TUE ☐ WED ☐ THU ☑ FRI ☐ SAT
OCT 24 AT 1:15 A.M. (P.M.)
MONTH DATE
SUNNYSIDE HEALTH CENTER
9314 Cullen Blvd. TEL (713) 732-5000
Houston, TX 77051
PATIENTS WILL BE CHARGED FOR APPOINTMENTS NOT CANCELED AT LEAST 24 HOURS IN ADVANCE.

Canceling an Appointment

A. Hello. This is __(first & last name)__. I need to cancel an appointment.

B. What's the date and time of the appointment?

A. __(day)__ __(date)__ at __(time)__.

B. Would you like to reschedule that appointment?

A. Not at this time. Thanks very much.

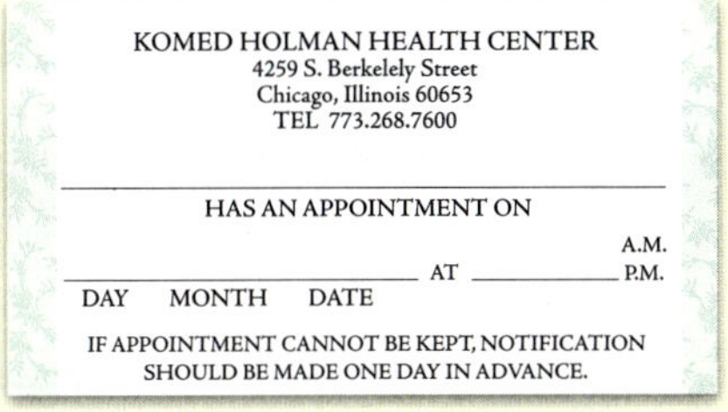

KOMED HOLMAN HEALTH CENTER
4259 S. Berkelely Street
Chicago, Illinois 60653
TEL 773.268.7600
HAS AN APPOINTMENT ON
DAY MONTH DATE AT A.M. P.M.
IF APPOINTMENT CANNOT BE KEPT, NOTIFICATION SHOULD BE MADE ONE DAY IN ADVANCE.

2 COMMUNITY CONNECTIONS Medical Care

Where can people go for free or inexpensive medical care in your community? Are there public health clinics or other medical offices? Is it difficult to get medical services? Discuss as a class.

MEDICAL HISTORY

Name Lena Kosta Date of Birth 5/15/60

List the medications you are now taking. Include non-prescription drugs and vitamins.
insulin, aspirin, multivitamins, calcium

List any allergies you have to drugs, food, or other items.
strawberries, cats, dogs, dust, bee stings

List any operations you have had, including the year. broken leg (2003), gall bladder (2007)

Please check if you have had any of the following health problems.

✓	chicken pox	✓	diabetes	___	depression
✓	measles	___	tuberculosis	___	frequent earaches
✓	mumps	___	cancer	✓	severe headaches
___	asthma	___	AIDS	___	back problems
___	heart disease	___	kidney disease	___	frequent colds
✓	high blood pressure	___	liver disease (hepatitis)	___	stomach problems
___	pneumonia	___	influenza	___	loss of appetite

FAMILY HISTORY

Please check if anyone in your family (parents, siblings, grandparents, children) has had any of the following illnesses.

___	asthma	✓	diabetes	___	AIDS
✓	heart disease	___	tuberculosis	___	kidney disease
✓	high blood pressure	___	cancer	___	liver disease

RECORD OF IMMUNIZATIONS

Please check if you had any of the following vaccinations or tests, and fill in the year of the most recent ones.

	Year
___ measles	
___ mumps	
___ chicken pox	
✓ tetanus	2008

	Year
✓ tuberculosis test	2001
___ hepatitis B	
✓ influenza	2008
___ pneumonia	

LEGACY HEALTH PLAN

Preventive Care Guidelines for Staying Healthy

Legacy Health Plan recommends the following examinations and screening tests to keep our adult members healthy. Talk with your doctor about these recommendations.

What to do:	How often:		
	Ages 18–39	Ages 40–49	Ages 50 & older
Have a physical examination	Every 1–3 years	Every year	Every year
Check your blood pressure	Every 1–2 years	Every year	Every year
Have an eye examination	Every 1–2 years	Every year	Every year
Have a hearing test	Every 10 years	Every 10 years	Every 10 years
See a dentist	1–2 times a year	1–2 times a year	1–2 times a year
Get a tetanus shot	Every 10 years	Every 10 years	Every 10 years
Have a skin examination	Every 3 years	Every year	Every year
Have a cholesterol blood test	Every 5 years	Every 5 years	Every 5 years
Have a flu shot	If doctor advises	If doctor advises	Every year
Have a pneumonia vaccination	If doctor advises	If doctor advises	Once after age 65
Have a colonoscopy to check for colon cancer	If doctor advises	If doctor advises	Every 10 years

Answer these questions about the medical history form and the preventive care guidelines.

1. What allergies does Lena have?
2. What prescription and non-prescription drugs does she take?
3. Has she had any operations? When, and what for?
4. What childhood diseases has she had?
5. What other medical problems does she have?
6. What illnesses have people in her family had?
7. When did Lena have her most recent flu shot?
8. When did she have her most recent tetanus shot?
9. According to the clinic guidelines, when should she get her next tetanus shot?
10. How often should adults between the ages of 18 and 39 have an eye examination?
11. How often should adults have a cholesterol blood test?
12. At what age should adults start having a yearly flu shot?
13. How often should adults have a dental examination?
14. How often should adults have a hearing test?
15. How often should a senior citizen have a colonoscopy?
16. When should an adult below the age of fifty get a pneumonia vaccination?

COMMUNITY CONNECTIONS You can sometimes get free medical screening tests at street festivals, community fairs, and other events. Drug stores and supermarkets sometimes offer these tests. It's a cheap and easy way to check your blood pressure, your cholesterol, your risk of heart disease, and other aspects of your health. Where can you get free tests in your area? Discuss as a class.

NORTHDALE PUBLIC HEALTH DEPARTMENT
Guide to Services

The Northdale health clinics and Northdale City Hospital provide outstanding health care to all city residents at a cost everyone can afford. Fees are on a sliding scale. The amount you pay is based on how much you earn. Northdale City Hospital is a full-service hospital with 350 beds, a family clinic, and 24-hour emergency care. The emergency room is for serious problems that put your life in danger. Do NOT call 911 or go to the emergency room with routine health problems such as an earache or a bad cough. If you do not speak English well, ask for an interpreter. Translation in 25 languages is available by phone or in person 24 hours a day.

At the Northdale Hospital Family Clinic, adults and children receive a full range of medical services including eye care. The Carter Clinic at 179 Pine Street provides medical care for children up to the age of seventeen. This is a drop-in clinic. No appointment is necessary. The multilingual staff speaks Spanish, Mandarin, and Vietnamese.

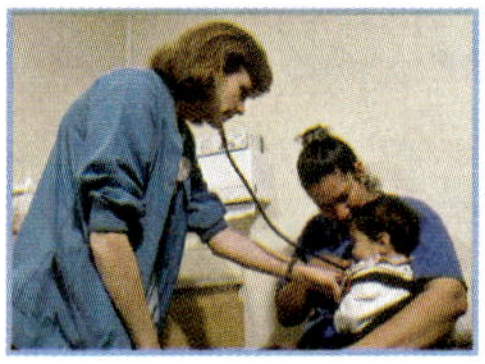

At the High School Health Center, students get free medical services that include physical exams and immunizations.

Immunizations protect your child from serious diseases such as measles and hepatitis B. All children entering kindergarten are required to already have the following vaccinations:

- Hepatitis B—3 doses
- Polio—4 doses
- Measles, mumps, rubella—2 doses
- Chicken pox—one dose
- Diphtheria, tetanus, pertussis*—5 doses

**pertussis is also called whooping cough*

Make sure your child's vaccinations are up-to-date. The following chart shows the immunization schedule that doctors recommend.

Immunization	At What Ages?
hepatitis B	birth, 1–4 months, and 6–18 months
DTaP (diphtheria, tetanus, pertussis)	2 months, 4 months, 6 months, 15–18 months, and 4–6 years
polio	2 months, 4 months, 6–18 months, and 4–6 years
MMR (measles, mumps, rubella)	12–15 months and 4–6 years
chicken pox (varicella)	12–18 months and 4–6 years
influenza	from 6 months to 5 years, every fall

1. *Fees are on a sliding scale* means _____.
- A. the more you earn, the less you pay
- B. everyone pays the same amount
- C. the more you earn, the more you pay
- D. the more you weigh, the more you pay

2. When you have a bad cough, _____.
- A. call 911
- B. call the Northdale Hospital Family Clinic
- C. get a diphtheria, tetanus, pertussis shot
- D. go to the emergency room

3. When you can't meet with an interpreter at Northdale City Hospital, _____.
- A. your family members will have to translate
- B. a nurse will translate
- C. you have to go to the Carter Clinic
- D. you can talk to an interpreter on the phone

4. A *drop-in clinic* is a clinic that _____.
- A. sees patients without appointments
- B. is for children only
- C. is multilingual
- D. is open 24 hours a day

5. Medical services are free at the _____.
- A. Northdale City Hospital
- B. Northdale Hospital Family Clinic
- C. High School Health Center
- D. Carter Clinic

6. Four-month old children should get a _____.
- A. flu shot
- B. chicken pox vaccination
- C. measles, mumps, rubella vaccination
- D. diphtheria, tetanus, pertussis vaccination

Healthy Eating and a Balanced Diet

The food pyramid can help us understand how to choose the foods we need to stay healthy. The six colored stripes in the pyramid represent the five different food groups plus oils. The pyramid shows us that we should eat foods from all of these groups every day. The person on the staircase shows us that it's also important to exercise every day.

U.S. Department of Agriculture www.mypyramid.gov

Each stripe on the pyramid is wide at the bottom and narrow at the top because within each food group some foods are healthier than others. The healthiest foods with the most nutrients belong at the bottom of each stripe. We should eat more of these foods.

The grain group (the orange stripe) consists of foods made from wheat, like bread and spaghetti, or from rice or corn. Some of these foods, such as whole wheat bread and brown rice, are whole grains. They have important vitamins, minerals, and fiber. Fiber helps keep blood cholesterol low and prevent heart disease. Most of the grains we eat should be whole grains. The orange stripe is the widest stripe on the pyramid. We should choose more food from this group than from the others.

The vegetable group (the green stripe) includes dark green vegetables, orange vegetables, and starchy vegetables such as corn and potatoes. It's important to eat vegetables from all three of these groups each week, but we should eat dark green and orange vegetables more often than starchy vegetables because they contain more nutrients and fewer calories. The fruit group (the red stripe) includes fruit and 100% fruit juice. However, most 100% fruit juice does not have fiber. Therefore, it's healthier to eat fruit than to drink fruit juice. The green stripe is wider than the red stripe. The average adult should eat 2 1/2 cups of vegetables and 2 cups of fruit a day.

The narrow yellow stripe is for oils. The oil in butter and margarine is unhealthy. On the other hand, the oil from fish, nuts, and vegetables is good for your heart.

The milk and dairy group (the blue stripe) includes foods that are high in calcium, a mineral that builds strong bones. Milk products such as yogurt and cheese are part of this group, but cream, butter, and cream cheese are not because they have little or no calcium. This is a wide stripe. Adults need three cups of dairy products each day. The meat and bean group (the purple stripe) includes meat, chicken, fish, dry beans, eggs, and nuts. These foods are a source of protein. The purple stripe isn't as wide as the orange, green, red, and blue ones. The average adult needs less protein than fruit, vegetables, grains, or dairy food. To keep blood cholesterol low and protect against heart disease, it's important to choose low-fat or fat-free dairy products and proteins.

DID YOU UNDERSTAND?

1. What food group does each stripe represent?
2. What does the yellow stripe represent?
3. Why is the orange stripe the widest?
4. Why is the blue stripe wide?
5. Why is the purple stripe narrower than the others?
6. Why are the stripes wider at the bottom?

APPLYING YOUR KNOWLEDGE

1. What vegetables do you eat?
2. How much fruit do you eat in a day?
3. What grains do you eat?
4. What protein foods do you eat?
5. What foods should you eat more of?
6. What foods should you eat less of?

ASSESSMENT

• Check-up test • Self-evaluation checklists

Choose the correct answer.

1. We need to ____ traveler's checks before our trip.

A. rehearse
B. purchase
C. perform
D. send

2. I enjoy ____ politics with my friends.

A. discussing
B. realizing
C. believing
D. memorizing

3. By the time I got to the airport, my plane had ____.

A. sailed away
B. gone by
C. taken off
D. started

4. I ____ my wrist while I was playing tennis.

A. packed
B. sprained
C. passed by
D. bumped into

5. Sally and Sam broke up and ____ their wedding.

A. called
B. closed
C. dislocated
D. canceled

6. I'm calling to ____ my appointment with Dr. Tanaka on Tuesday at 10:30.

A. have
B. need
C. confirm
D. check

7. The nurse gave me ____ for tetanus.

A. an immunization
B. insulin
C. an allergy
D. influenza

8. Do you have a family history of ____?

A. vaccinations
B. bee stings
C. high blood pressure
D. skin examinations

9. Fees at this clinic are on a ____ scale.

A. drop in
B. sliding
C. full-service
D. multilingual

10. Eating a lot of whole grains and following a low-fat diet will protect you against ____.

A. the food pyramid
B. food groups
C. nutrients and calories
D. heart disease

SKILLS CHECK

Words:

- ☐ allergy
- ☐ disease
- ☐ drop-in clinic
- ☐ fee
- ☐ illness
- ☐ immunization
- ☐ interpreter
- ☐ medical care
- ☐ medical services
- ☐ multilingual staff
- ☐ non-prescription drug
- ☐ routine health problem
- ☐ sliding scale
- ☐ vaccination
- ☐ blood cholesterol
- ☐ bones
- ☐ calcium
- ☐ calories
- ☐ fat-free
- ☐ fiber
- ☐ food group
- ☐ food pyramid
- ☐ low-fat
- ☐ minerals
- ☐ nutrients
- ☐ oils
- ☐ protein
- ☐ vitamins
- ☐ whole grains

I can say:

- ☐ I had *skied* the *day* before.
- ☐ By the time I got there, *it* had already *begun*.
- ☐ I hadn't *gone fishing* in a long time.
- ☐ I was *skiing* . . . and I had never *skied* before.
- ☐ I had been *working there* for a long time.

I can share news:

- ☐ Have you heard about/Have you heard the news about/Have you heard what happened to *Harry*?

I can:

- ☐ make, confirm, reschedule, and cancel medical appointments
- ☐ interpret medical appointment cards
- ☐ identify medical care facilities in my community
- ☐ complete a medical history form
- ☐ interpret preventive care guidelines
- ☐ interpret community health care information
- ☐ interpret food pyramid nutrition guidelines

I can write about:

- ☐ something I accomplished

SIDE by SIDE Gazette

Volume 3 Number 3

The Jamaican Bobsled Team

Amazing athletes from a Caribbean island

An unusual group of athletes arrived in Calgary, Canada for the 1988 Winter Olympic Games—the Jamaican Bobsled Team. Many people were surprised. How could the Caribbean island of Jamaica have a bobsled team? Jamaica doesn't have any snow!

The Jamaican athletes had never competed in the Winter Olympics before. In fact, most of them hadn't ever been on a bobsled or seen snow before they began to prepare for the Olympics. But by the time the team members arrived in Calgary, they had trained hard for their first Olympic event. They had been running and weight training in Jamaica. Then they had gone to a training center in Lake Placid, New York. Unfortunately, they had poor equipment, and their bobsled crashed a lot during training.

They didn't do well in the Olympics. Most people were sure they had seen the Jamaican Bobsled Team for the first and last time! But the team didn't give up. They had lost, but they had been in the Olympics, and they wanted to go back and compete again.

The team went to a special training center in Germany. They trained there four to eight hours a day. By the time these athletes arrived at the 1994 Olympic Winter Games in Norway, they had become a much stronger bobsled team. They had practiced for years. They were also very famous because a movie about the team, *Cool Runnings*, had been in theaters around the world the year before.

At the 1994 games, the team came in 14th in the four-person bobsled event, and they placed 10th in the two-person event. The team had done the impossible! They had competed well in the Olympics, and they had won the hearts of fans around the world.

The movie *Cool Runnings* tells the story of a Jamaican bobsled team at the Olympics. The movie is part fact and part fiction. The popular movie soundtrack has reggae music by famous Jamaican musicians.

The first modern Olympics were in Athens, Greece in 1896. Now there are Summer Olympics and Winter Olympics every four years. Athletes represent their countries in different events. Summer Olympic events include track, gymnastics, and swimming. Winter Olympic events include skiing, skating, and the bobsled competition.

AROUND THE WORLD

Children and Sports Training

In different countries around the world, children begin training at an early age to compete in different popular sports.

hockey in Canada

baseball in Japan

soccer in Brazil

gymnastics in Russia

basketball in the United States

distance running in Kenya

What sports are popular in your country? At what age do children start training to compete in these sports?

Interview

A Side by Side Gazette reporter interviewed Olga Petrova last week. Olga had just won the Women's Regional Figure Skating Competition.

Q: Olga, I'm sure you're very happy about today's competition.

A: Oh, yes. I'm very happy. You know, I had been preparing for this day for a long time.

Q: How had you been preparing?

A: In the months before the competition, I had been training with my coach ten hours a day. I had been getting up early, and I had been practicing my routines over and over again.

Q: When did you first know you wanted to compete as a skater?

A: I began to skate back in Russia when I was four years old. By the time I was seven, I had already skated in many competitions, and I had won several medals. We moved here when I was ten, and I began to take lessons at a skating program in our city. By the time I was eleven, I had finished all the levels of this program. My parents found a professional coach, Mr. Gary Abrams, and I've been training with him ever since.

Q: Now that you have won this regional competition, what's next?

A: The National Competition. It's in three months. I have to work very hard to prepare for that. My dream is to be in the Olympics next winter. I must do very well in the Nationals.

Q: Good luck, Olga! We'll see you in the Olympics!

A: Oh, I hope so.

FACT FILE

Countries in the Olympics

Only 14 countries competed in the first modern Olympics in 1896. Over the years, the number of participating countries has grown. Does your country compete in the summer or winter games? In which events does your country do well?

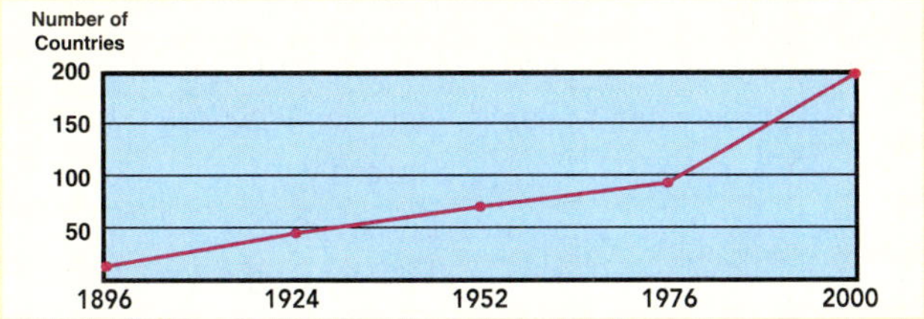

LISTENING

Olympic Game Highlights

b	1	a.	figure skating
___	2	b.	basketball
___	3	c.	running
___	4	d.	gymnastics
___	5	e.	swimming

FUN with IDIOMS

Do You Know These Expressions?

c	1. Break a leg!		a.	Don't be sad!
___	2. Hold your tongue!		b.	Try hard!
___	3. Keep your chin up!		c.	Good luck!
___	4. Keep your eye on the ball!		d.	Pay attention!
___	5. Put your best foot forward!		e.	Don't bother me!
___	6. Get off my back!		f.	Be quiet!

We've Got Mail!

Dear Side by Side,

I have a question about gerunds and infinitives after verbs. I'm very confused. I know that after some verbs, I must use a gerund, such as "practice swimming" and "consider buying." After other verbs, I must use an infinitive, such as "learn to swim" and "decide to buy." And finally, I know that after some verbs, I can use either a gerund or an infinitive, such as "like to swim" and "like swimming." Are there any rules that will tell me what to do with different verbs?

Sincerely,
"Worrying About the Rules"

Dear "Worrying About the Rules,"

You seem to understand how to use gerunds and infinitives. Unfortunately, we're sorry to tell you that there aren't any rules about what to do with different verbs. You just have to learn about each verb. Keep on practicing gerunds and infinitives, and stop worrying about the rules! Using these verbs is a lot better than thinking about them too much! Good luck!

Sincerely,
Side by Side

Dear Side by Side,

We've been studying the present perfect and present perfect continuous tenses in our class for the past several weeks. I think I finally understand this grammar, but now we have begun learning the past perfect tense, and to tell the truth, I don't understand when to use it. Can you help?

Sincerely,
"Life Was Perfect Before the Past Perfect"

Dear "Life Was Perfect,"

We understand your problem because we use both the present perfect and past perfect tenses to talk about things that happened in the past. Here's the difference. We use the present perfect tense to talk about things that happened before now. For example:

I don't want to see that movie today.
I have already seen it.

We use the past perfect tense to talk about things that happened before another time in the past. For example:

I didn't want to see that movie yesterday.
I had already seen it.

We're glad you have learned the present perfect tense, and we're sure you'll do well with the past perfect!

Best wishes,
Side by Side

Global Exchange

Stamp4: Have I told you about my hobby? I've been collecting stamps since I was a little kid. I began to collect stamps when I was eight years old. At that time, my mother worked at an international bank. Every Friday, she brought home stamps from all the letters she had received during that week. I also had many penpals in different countries, and we wrote letters to each other very often. By the time I was twelve, I had collected more than 1000 stamps from 50 different countries! I've continued collecting stamps, but now it's more difficult. My mother retired from her job, and my penpals send me e-mail messages instead of letters. (The Internet has been very bad for my stamp collection!) Tell me, do you have a hobby? What do you enjoy doing in your free time? How long have you been doing that? Write and tell me about it.

Send a message to a keypal. Tell about your favorite hobby.

What Are They Saying?

9

Two-Word Verbs: Separable
Inseparable

- Discussing Future Events
- Remembering and Forgetting
- Discussing Obligations
- Asking for and Giving Advice
- School Assignments
- Making Plans by Telephone
- Shopping for Clothing
- Identifying Bargains
- Returning and Exchanging Defective Items
- Advertisements
- Store Coupons

VOCABULARY PREVIEW

1. cross out
2. fill out
3. hand in
4. hang up
5. hook up
6. pick out
7. put away
8. put on
9. take down
10. take off
11. throw away
12. try on
13. turn on
14. turn off
15. wake up

Sometime Next Week

bring back the TV	**bring** it **back**
call up Sally	**call** her **up**
throw out the newspapers	**throw** them **out**

A. When is the repairman going to **bring back** our TV?

B. He's going to **bring** it **back** sometime next week.

1. When are you going to **call up** your uncle in Ohio?

2. When is Ted going to **throw out** his old newspapers?

3. When is your daughter going to **fill out** her college application forms?

4. When is Jeff going to **pick up** his clothes at the cleaner's?

5. When is Vicky going to **take back** her library books?

6. When are you going to **hook up** your new computer?

7. When is Howard going to **hang up** his new portrait?

8. When is Gloria going to **take down** her Christmas decorations?

9. When is Mr. Grumpkin going to **turn on** the heat in the building?

Oh, No! I Forgot!

put on your boots / put your boots **on** — **put** them **on**

A. Did you remember to {**turn off** the oven / **turn** the oven **off**}?

B. Oh, no! I forgot! I'll **turn** it **off** right away.

1. *take back videos*

2. *fill out the accident report*

3. *turn on the alarm*

4. *put away your toys*

5. *hand in your English homework*

6. *wake up the kids*

7. *put on your raincoat*

8. *take off your boots*

9. *take out the garbage*

How to Say It!

Remembering & Forgetting

A. Did you remember to *turn off the oven*?

B. Oh, no! {I forgot! / I forgot all about it! / I completely forgot! / It slipped my mind! / It completely slipped my mind!}

Practice the conversations in this lesson again. Tell that you forgot in different ways.

READING

A BUSY SATURDAY

Everybody in the Peterson family is very busy today. It's Saturday, and they all have to do the things they didn't do during the week.

Mr. Peterson has to fill out his income tax form. He didn't have time to fill it out during the week.

Mrs. Peterson has to pick up her clothes at the cleaner's. She was too busy to pick them up during the week.

Their son Steve has to take his library books back. He forgot to take them back during the week.

Their other son, Michael, has to throw out all the old newspapers in the garage. He didn't have time to throw them out during the week.

Their daughter Stacey has to hook up the new modem for her computer. She was too busy to hook it up during the week.

And their other daughter, Abigail, has to put her toys away. She didn't feel like putting them away during the week.

As you can see, everybody in the Peterson family is going to be very busy today.

✓ READING *CHECK-UP*

Q & A

You're inviting somebody in the Peterson family to do something with you. Using this model, create dialogs based on the story.

A. Would you like to *play tennis* with me this morning?
B. I'd like to, but I can't. I have to *fill out my income tax form.*
A. That's too bad.
B. I know, but I've really got to do it. I *didn't have time to fill it out during the week.*
A. Well, maybe some other time.

How About You?

What do YOU have to do on your next day off from work or school?

I Don't Think So

A. Do you think I should keep these old love letters?

B. No, I don't think so. I think you should **throw** them **away**.

1. *hand in my homework*
do over

2. *use up this old milk*
throw out

3. *erase all my mistakes*
cross out

4. *leave the air conditioner on*
turn off

5. *try to remember Amy's telephone number*
write down

6. *ask the teacher the definition of this word*
look up

7. *make my decision right away*
think over

8. *keep my ex-boyfriend's ring*
give back

9. *accept this invitation to my ex-girlfriend's wedding*
turn down

READING

LUCY'S ENGLISH COMPOSITION

Lucy is very discouraged. She handed in her English composition this morning, but her English teacher gave it back to her and told her to do it over. Apparently, her English teacher didn't like the way Lucy had done it. She hadn't erased her mistakes. She had simply crossed them out. Also, she had used several words incorrectly. She hadn't looked them up in a dictionary. And finally, she hadn't written her homework on the correct paper because she had accidentally thrown her notebook away. Poor Lucy! She didn't feel like writing her English composition in the first place, and now she has to do it over!

✓ READING *CHECK-UP*

TRUE, FALSE, OR MAYBE?

Answer True, False, or Maybe (if the answer isn't in the story).

1. Lucy gave her composition to her English teacher this morning.
2. Lucy's English teacher was satisfied with Lucy's composition.
3. The teacher gave back other students' compositions.
4. Lucy had made some mistakes in her composition.
5. Lucy knew the definitions of all the words she used in her composition.
6. Lucy is going to hand in her composition again tomorrow.

WHAT'S THE WORD?

Choose the correct words to complete the sentences.

cross ___ out	do ___ over	give ___ back	hand ___ in	look ___ up	throw ___ away

1. I need the dictionary you borrowed from me. Please ______.
2. I want to check your homework. Please ______.
3. Ms. Smith, there are too many mistakes in this letter. Please ______.
4. I haven't read today's newspaper yet. Please don't ______.
5. I don't remember his phone number. I've got to ______.
6. You should erase your mistakes. Don't just ______.

COMPLETE THE LETTERS

Complete these letters with the correct form of the verbs.

call ___ up   give ___ back   think ___ over   throw ___ away   turn ___ down

Dear Alice,

I'm very discouraged. I'm having a lot of trouble with my girlfriend, and I don't know what to do. The problem is very simple. I'm in love with her, but she isn't in love with me. A few weeks ago, I gave her a ring, but she ________1 to me. During the past few months, I have written several love letters to her, but she has ________2. Recently I asked her to marry me. She ________3 for a while, and then she ________4. Now when I try to ________5, she doesn't even want to talk to me. Please help me! I don't know what to do.

"Discouraged Donald"
Denver, Colorado

hang ___ up   put ___ away   take ___ down   take ___ out   turn ___ off   turn ___ on

Dear Alice,

I'm extremely frustrated. My husband is a very difficult person. Every time I do something, he does the opposite. For example, every time I turn on the stereo system to listen to music, he ________1. Every time I turn off the air conditioner in our apartment, he ________2. Last week I bought a beautiful new painting for our bedroom. The day after I ________3, he ________4. We had a lot of old photographs on a table in our living room. I decided to ________5 in a closet, but two hours later he ________6. Please help me! I don't know what to do.

"Frustrated Fran"
Phoenix, Arizona

What should "Discouraged Donald" and "Frustrated Fran" do? Write answers to their letters.

Would You Like to Get Together Today?

take back my library books = **take** my library books **back**

- ☑ **take** my library books **back**
- ☑ **pick up** my car at the repair shop
- ☑ **drop** my sister **off** at the airport

A. Would you like to get together today?

B. I'm afraid I can't. I have to **take** my library books **back**.

A. Are you free after you **take** them **back**?

B. I'm afraid not. I also have to **pick up** my car at the repair shop.

A. Would you like to get together after you **pick** it **up**?

B. I'd really like to, but I can't. I ALSO have to **drop** my sister **off** at the airport.

A. You're really busy today! What do you have to do after you **drop** her **off**?

B. Nothing. But by then I'll probably be exhausted. Let's get together tomorrow instead.

A. Fine. I'll call you in the morning.

A. Would you like to get together today?

B. I'm afraid I can't. I have to ____________________.

A. Are you free after you ____________________?

B. I'm afraid not. I also have to ____________________.

A. Would you like to get together after you ____________________?

B. I'd really like to, but I can't. I ALSO have to ____________________.

A. You're really busy today! What do you have to do after you ____________________?

B. Nothing. But by then I'll probably be exhausted. Let's get together tomorrow instead.

A. Fine. I'll call you in the morning.

- **clean up** my living room
- **throw out** all my old newspapers
- **pick** my brother **up** at the train station

1.

- **figure out** my hospital bill
- **fill out** my insurance form
- **call** the doctor **up**

2.

- **take down** my Christmas decorations
- **hang up** my New Year's decorations
- **drop** my suit **off** at the cleaner's

3.

- **pick out** my wedding dress
- **write down** the names of all the wedding guests
- **pick** the wedding invitations **up**

4.

- **clean up** my room
- **put** my toys **away**
- **do** my math homework **over**

5.

- ____________________
- ____________________
- ____________________

6.

I Heard from Her Just Last Week

hear from Aunt Betty	**hear from** her
~~hear Aunt Betty from~~	~~hear her from~~

A. Have you **heard from** Aunt Betty recently?

B. Yes, I have. I **heard from** her just last week.

1. Have you **run into** Mr. Clark recently?

2. Have you **run out of** paper recently?

3. Has Martha **gotten over** the flu yet?

4. Has your English teacher **called on** you recently?

5. Have you and your husband **looked through** your photo album recently?

6. Has Ricky been **picking on** his little sister recently?

How About You?

Tell about some of the people in your life.

Do you have a good friend in another city? Who is he/she?

How often do you **hear from** him/her? How long have you known each other?

Who do you **get along with** very well? Why?

Who do you **take after**? How?

Who do you **look up to**? Why?

READING

A CHILD-REARING PROBLEM

Timothy and his little sister, Patty, don't get along with each other very well. In fact, they fight constantly. He picks on her when it's time for her to go to bed. She picks on him when his friends come over to play.

Timmy and Patty's parents are very concerned. They don't know what to do about their children. They have looked through several books on child rearing, but so far they can't seem to find an answer to the problem. They're hoping that eventually their children will learn to get along with each other better.

READING *CHECK-UP*

TRUE, FALSE, OR MAYBE?

Answer True, False, or Maybe (if the answer isn't in the story).

1. Patty picks on Timmy when it's time for her go to bed.
2. Timmy is Patty's older brother.
3. Timmy and Patty's parents have a child-rearing problem.
4. They can't seem to find any books about child rearing.
5. Timmy and Patty will eventually learn to get along with each other better.

CHOOSE

1. Please don't ____ your little sister.
   a. pick on
   b. get along with
2. We've been ____ these old family pictures.
   a. looking through
   b. taking after
3. My history teacher ____ me three times today.
   a. looked up to
   b. called on
4. I haven't ____ my aunt and uncle recently.
   a. gotten over
   b. heard from
5. Everybody thinks I ____ my mother.
   a. take after
   b. look through
6. I really ____ my older sister because she's so smart.
   a. run into
   b. look up to
7. I ____ my cousin Jane on Main Street yesterday.
   a. ran into
   b. heard from
8. Don't kiss me! I haven't ____ my cold yet.
   a. gotten along with
   b. gotten over

ROLE PLAY *May I Help You?*

You're looking for clothing in a department store. Complete this conversation and act it out with another student.

A. May I help you?

B. Yes, please. I'm **looking for** (a/an) __________.

A. What size do you wear?

B. { Size 32/34/36/ . . .
Small/Medium/Large/Extra Large.

A. Here. How do you like (this one/these)?

B. Hmm. I think (it's/they're) a little too __________.* Do you have any __________s that are a little __________er?*

A. Yes. We have a wide selection. Why don't you **look through** all of our __________s and **pick out** the (one/ones) you like?

B. Can I **try** (it/them) **on**?

A. Of course. You can **try** (it/them) **on** in the dressing room over there.

* fancy – plain
dark – light

[5 minutes later]

A. Well, how (does it/do they) fit?

B. I'm afraid (it's/they're) a little too __________.* Do you have any __________s that are a little __________er*?

A. Yes, we do. I think you'll like (THIS/THESE) __________. (It's/They're) a little __________er* than the one(s) you just **tried on**.

B. Will you **take** (it/them) **back** if I decide to return (it/them)?

A. Of course. No problem at all. Just **bring** (it/them) **back** within __________ days, and we'll **give** you your money **back**.

B. Fine. I think I'll take (it/them). How much (does it/do they) cost?

A. The usual price is __________ dollars. But you're in luck! We're having a sale this week, and all of our __________s are __________ percent off the regular price.

B. That's a real bargain! I'm glad I decided to buy (a/an) __________ this week. Thanks for your help.

* large – small
long – short
wide – narrow
tight – loose (baggy)

1. *suit*

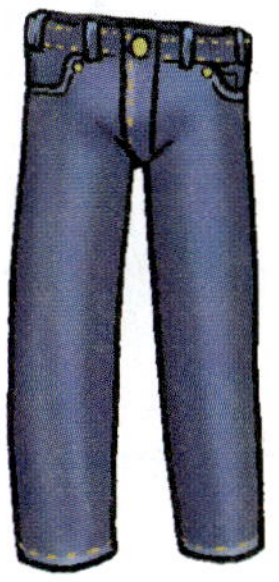

2. *jeans*

3. *sweater*

4.

How About You?

Where do you shop for clothing?
What kind of clothing do you like to wear?

Think about clothing you own:
What's your favorite clothing item?
How long have you had it?
Where did you get it?
Why is it your favorite?

READING

ON SALE

Gary went to a men's clothing store yesterday. He was looking for a new sports jacket. He looked through the entire selection of jackets and picked out a few that he really liked. First, he picked out a nice blue jacket. But when he tried it on, it was too small. Next, he picked out an attractive red jacket. But when he tried it on, it was too large. Finally, he picked out a very fancy brown jacket with gold buttons. And when he tried it on, it seemed to fit perfectly.

Then he decided to buy a pair of trousers to go with the jacket. He looked through the entire selection of trousers and picked out several pairs that he really liked. First, he picked out a light brown pair. But when he tried them on, they were too tight. Next, he tried on a dark brown pair. But when he tried them on, they were too loose. Finally, he picked out a pair of brown-and-white plaid pants. And when he tried them on, they seemed to fit perfectly.

Gary paid for his new clothing and walked home feeling very happy about the jacket and pants he had just bought. He was especially happy because the clothing was on sale, and he had paid fifty percent off the regular price. However, Gary's happiness didn't last very long. When he got home, he noticed that one arm of the jacket was longer than the other. He also realized very quickly that the zipper on the pants was broken.

The next day Gary took the clothing back to the store and tried to get a refund. However, the people at the store refused to give him his money back because the clothing was on sale and there was a sign that said "All Sales Are Final!" Gary was furious, but he knew he couldn't do anything about it. The next time he buys something on sale, he'll be more careful. And he'll be sure to read the signs!

READING *CHECK-UP*

What's the Sequence?

Put these events in the correct order, based on the story.

____ Gary picked out a few jackets he really liked.
____ Gary went back and asked for a refund.
__1__ Gary went shopping for clothes yesterday.
____ He walked home feeling very happy.
____ He walked home feeling very upset and angry.
____ The brown jacket seemed to fit perfectly.
____ The store refused to give him back his money.
____ A pair of plaid pants fit very well.
____ He paid only half of the regular price.
____ He picked out several pairs of trousers.
____ But then, Gary noticed a few problems with the jacket and the pants.

How About You?

Have you ever bought something you had to return?
What did you buy?
Where?
What was wrong with it?
What did you do?
Were you successful?

LISTENING

Listen and choose what the people are talking about.

1. a. shorts
   b. a blouse
2. a. shoes
   b. a library book
3. a. an application form
   b. a math problem
4. a. homework
   b. children
5. a. pictures
   b. pants
6. a. the flu
   b. a decision
7. a. a coat
   b. the heat
8. a. milk
   b. the garbage
9. a. a telephone number
   b. an invitation

PRONUNCIATION Linking "t" Between Vowels

Listen. Then say it.	Say it. Then listen.
Turn it on!	Fill it out!
Turn it off!	Do it over!
Clean it up!	Drop it off!
Throw it away!	Hand it in!

Write in your journal about someone you look up to—a member of your family, a person in your community, or a famous person in your country or in history. Who do you look up to? Why do you admire this person?

GRAMMAR FOCUS

Two-Word Verbs: Separable

I'm going to	**put on** my boots. **put** my boots **on**. **put** them **on**.

Two-Word Verbs: Inseparable

I	**hear from** Aunt Betty **hear from** her ~~**hear** Aunt Betty **from**~~ ~~**hear** her **from**~~	very often.

Complete the sentences.

1. A. When are you going to throw out those old magazines?
   B. I'll _____ _____ _____ this weekend.
2. A. Have you heard from your cousins in Detroit recently?
   B. Yes, I have. I _____ _____ _____ a few weeks ago.
3. A. Did you hook up your new computer?
   B. Not yet. I'm going to _____ _____ _____ tonight.
4. A. Did you fill out the insurance form?
   B. Oh, no! I forgot. I'll _____ _____ _____ right away.
5. A. Does your English teacher call on you a lot in class?
   B. Yes. She _____ _____ _____ all the time.
6. A. I hope you get over the flu soon.
   B. I'm sure I'll _____ _____ _____ in a few days.
7. A. Please take out the garbage!
   B. I _____ _____ _____ a few minutes ago.
8. A. Lilly, did you put away your toys?
   B. Yes, I did. I _____ _____ _____ a little while ago.
9. A. Have you run into your old friend Bob recently?
   B. Yes, I have. I _____ _____ _____ just the other day.
10. A. How do you get along with your neighbors?
    B. I _____ _____ _____ _____ very well.
11. A. Don't forget to take back the videos.
    B. Don't worry. I'll _____ _____ _____ today.

LIFE SKILLS

• Identifying bargains • Returning & exchanging defective items

1 CONVERSATION Identifying Sale Prices & Bargains

Look at the sale signs. Practice conversations with your classmates.

A. Excuse me. I think that price is wrong.

B. It is?

A. Yes. The sign on the rack says "_________________."

B. Okay. Let me check.

1.

2.

3.

4.

5.

THINK & SHARE Do you buy things when they're on sale? Which stores in your community have sales? How much can you save when you buy something on sale?

2 CONVERSATION Returning & Exchanging Defective Products

Practice conversations. Return these defective items to a store.

A. I'd like to return this/these _____________.

B. What's the matter with it/them?

A. ______________________________

B. Would you like to exchange it/them?

A. No, thank you. I'd like a refund, please. Here's my receipt.

1. coat
Two buttons are missing.

2. pants
The zipper is broken.

3. blouse
The sleeve is stained.

TEAMWORK Work with a classmate. Make a list of items you buy in a store and the reasons you might return them. Practice conversations about these items.

Look at the store advertisements and answer the questions.

1. The sale price for a $72 Vera West skirt is ____.

A. $8 C. $32
B. $18 D. $36

2. You get a ____ discount on $60 running shoes at Perry's.

A. 25% C. 50%
B. 40% D. 60%

3. When you buy 2 pairs of $46 jeans on sale at Watson's, the second pair costs ____.

A. $23 C. $50
B. $24 D. $92

4. You pay ____ when you buy four tee shirts on sale at Perry's.

A. $20.00 C. $40.00
B. $30.00 D. $43.96

5. During the sale at Perry's, Lexis Men's Jeans are ____ off the regular price.

A. $16 C. $40
B. $24 D. 24%

6. On September 22, a dress shirt at Watson's costs ____ than a dress shirt at Perry's.

A. $5.99 less C. $16 less
B. $25.99 more D. $16 more

TEAMWORK Cut out some newspaper ads for department store sales. Bring the ads to class and work with a classmate. Compare the products on sale at these stores. Which sale is better? Why? Share your ads and opinions with the class.

Look at the coupons and answer the questions.

1. You save $1.00 when you buy ____ with a coupon.
   A. a quart of yogurt
   B. 2 pints of ice cream
   C. a can of coffee
   D. 3 cans of tomatoes

2. A can of Farini Tomatoes costs $1.50. With a coupon you pay ____ for 3 cans.
   A. 75¢
   B. $3.00
   C. $3.50
   D. $3.75

3. A can of Crandall Soup costs $1.65. If you buy ten cans with a coupon, you pay ____.
   A. $5.50
   B. $8.90
   C. $15.40
   D. $15.50

4. You bought a jar of Pollyanna Jam with a coupon and paid $1.85. The original price was ____.
   A. $1.50
   B. $2.20
   C. $2.35
   D. $2.60

5. You can use a coupon for ____ on November 12, 2012.
   A. Crandall Soup
   B. Maxima Coffee
   C. Alan's Bread
   D. Eggtown Eggs

6. You bought two pints of Bob and Joe's Chocolate Ice Cream with a coupon and paid $5.00. The regular price for a pint is ____.
   A. $2.50
   B. $2.75
   C. $3.00
   D. $4.00

7. A 6 oz. container of Farmtown Yogurt costs 90¢. With a coupon you pay ____ for each container when you buy ten.
   A. 80¢
   B. 85¢
   C. 90¢
   D. $1.00

8. Happy Heart Cereal costs $2.79. With a coupon you can get ____ for $5.58.
   A. one box
   B. two boxes
   C. three boxes
   D. four boxes

TEAMWORK Bring food product coupons to class and work with a classmate. Compare coupons for similar products. Which coupons offer the best bargains? Share your information with the class. Then use some coupons to save money at the supermarket!

ASSESSMENT

• Check-up test • Self-evaluation checklists

Choose the correct answer.

1. Could you possibly help me ____ my new computer?

A. hear from C. hook up
B. hang up D. hand in

2. Do you have a dictionary? I need to ____ a word I don't know.

A. look through C. look up to
B. look up D. call on

3. I'm going to ____ my clothes at the cleaner's this morning.

A. pick up C. pick out
B. pick on D. put away

4. Please ____ the garbage before you leave.

A. take after C. take out
B. take back D. take off

5. I ____ an old friend while I was walking down the street today.

A. got over C. ran out of
B. got along with D. ran into

6. It's very hot today. Let's ____ the air conditioner all afternoon.

A. drop off C. do over
B. use up D. leave on

7. I don't want to exchange it. I'd like ____, please.

A. a sign C. a refund
B. a receipt D. a clearance

8. Shirts are usually $48. They're on ____ today for $28.

A. sale price C. bargain
B. sale D. discount

Look at the food coupons. Choose the correct answer.

9. A container of Fieldstone Yogurt costs $1.00. With a coupon, you pay ____ for each container when you buy ten.

A. 80¢
B. 90¢
C. 95¢
D. $1.00

10. Healthy Start Cereal costs $2.99. With a coupon, you can get ____ for $5.98.

A. one box
B. two boxes
C. three boxes
D. four boxes

SKILLS CHECK ☑

Words:

☐ bring __ back
☐ call __ up
☐ clean __ up
☐ cross __ out
☐ do __ over
☐ drop __ off
☐ figure __ out
☐ fill __ out
☐ give __ back
☐ hand __ in
☐ hang __ up
☐ hook __ up
☐ leave __ on
☐ look __ up
☐ pick __ out
☐ pick __ up
☐ put __ away
☐ put __ on
☐ take __ back
☐ take __ down
☐ take __ off
☐ take __ out
☐ think __ over
☐ throw __ away
☐ throw __ out
☐ try __ on
☐ turn __ down
☐ turn __ off
☐ turn __ on
☐ use __ up
☐ wake __ up
☐ write __ down

☐ call on
☐ come over
☐ get along with
☐ get over
☐ hear from
☐ look for
☐ look through
☐ look up to
☐ pick on
☐ run into
☐ run out of
☐ take after

☐ bargain
☐ coupon
☐ discount
☐ refund
☐ receipt
☐ sale price

I can ask & answer:

☐ When are you going to *fill out the form*?
☐ Did you remember to *turn off the oven*?
☐ Do you think I should *erase my mistakes*?
☐ Have you heard from *Betty* recently?

☐ What size do you wear?
☐ Can I try it/them on?
☐ How does it/do they fit?

I can:

☐ identify sale prices and bargains
☐ return and exchange defective products
☐ interpret ads to compare item prices and quantities
☐ interpret food product coupons

I can write about:

☐ someone I look up to

10

Connectors: And . . . Too
And . . . Either
So, But, Neither

- Coincidences
- Asking for and Giving Reasons
- Describing People's Backgrounds, Interests, and Personalities
- Looking for a Job
- Referring People to Someone Else
- Discussing Opinions
- Requesting Help at Work
- Giving and Following a Sequence of Instructions
- Operating Equipment
- Career Advancement
- Continuing Education
- Developing a Personal Education Plan

Vocabulary Preview

1. allergic
2. athletic
3. frightened
4. strict
5. lenient
6. alarm clock
7. army
8. lightning
9. parking space
10. want ad
11. enroll
12. hide
13. kiss
14. walk *my* dog
15. work out

What a Coincidence!

I'm hungry.	I am, too. / So am I.	I have a car.	I do, too. / So do I.
I can swim.	I can, too. / So can I.	I worked yesterday.	I did, too. / So did I.
I've seen that movie.	I have, too. / So have I.		

A. I'm allergic to cats.

B. What a coincidence!
I am, too. / So am I.

1. I'm a vegetarian.

2. I like peppermint ice cream.

3. I can speak four languages fluently.

4. I just got a raise.

5. I'll be on a business trip next week.

6. I've been feeling tired lately.

7. I have to work late at the office tonight.

8. I forgot my umbrella this morning.

9.

What a Coincidence!

I'm not hungry.	I'm not either. / Neither am I.	I don't have a car.	I don't either. / Neither do I.
I can't swim.	I can't either. / Neither can I.	I didn't work yesterday.	I didn't either. / Neither did I.
I haven't seen that movie.	I haven't either. / Neither have I.		

A. I'm not a very good dancer.

B. What a coincidence!
{ I'm not either. / Neither am I. }

1. I don't like macaroni and cheese.

2. I didn't see the stop sign.

3. I can't skate very well.

4. I haven't seen a movie in a long time.

5. I wasn't very athletic when I was younger.

6. I won't be able to go bowling next Saturday.

7. I don't have a date for the prom.

8. I've never kissed anyone before.

9.

And They Do, Too

I'm tired, { and he is, too. / and so is he. }	They sing, { and she does, too. / and so does she. }
He'll be busy, { and she will, too. / and so will she. }	She studied, { and I did, too. / and so did I. }
She's been sick, { and he has, too. / and so has he. }	

A. Why can't you or the children help me with the dishes?

B. I have to study, { **and they do, too.** / **and so do they.** }

1. Why weren't you and Bob at the meeting this morning?
I missed the bus, _____.

2. Why are you and Vanessa so nervous today?
I have two final exams tomorrow, _____.

3. What are you and your brother going to do when you grow up?
I'm going to start an Internet company, _____.

4. Where were you and your wife when the accident happened?
I was standing on the corner, _____.

5. How do you know Mr. and Mrs. Crandall?
They walk their dog in the park, ____.

6. Why can't you or your roommates come to my party?
I'll be out of town, ____.

7. Why haven't you and your brother been in school for the past few days?
I've been sick, ____.

8. Could you or your friend help me take these packages upstairs?
I'll be glad to help you, ____.

9. How did you meet your wife?
I was working out at the health club, ____.

10. What are you two arguing about?
He wants this parking space, ____.

11. Why don't you or your neighbors complain about this leak?
I've already spoken to the landlord, ____.

12. How did you and your husband like the play?
I fell asleep during the first act, ____.

13. Why are you and your cats hiding under the bed?
I'm afraid of thunder and lightning, ____.

14.

"MADE FOR EACH OTHER"

Louise and Brian are very compatible people. They have a lot in common. For example, they have similar backgrounds. He grew up in a small town in the South, and so did she. She's the oldest of four children, and he is, too. His parents own their own business, and so do hers.

They also have similar academic interests. She's majoring in chemistry, and he is, too. He has taken every course in mathematics offered by their college, and so has she. She enjoys working with computers, and he does, too.

In addition, Louise and Brian like the same sports. He goes swimming several times a week, and so does she. She can play tennis very well, and so can he. His favorite winter sport is ice skating, and hers is, too.

Louise and Brian also have the same cultural interests. She has been to most of the art museums in New York City, and so has he. He's a member of the college theater group, and she is, too. She has a complete collection of Beethoven's symphonies, and so does he.

In addition, they have similar personalities. She has always been very shy, and he has, too. He tends to be very quiet, and so does she. She's often nervous when she's in large groups of people, and he is, too.

Finally, they have very similar outlooks on life. She has been a vegetarian for years, and so has he. He supports equal rights for women and minorities, and so does she. She's opposed to the use of nuclear energy, and he is, too.

As you can see, Louise and Brian are very compatible people. In fact, everybody says they were "made for each other."

READING *CHECK-UP*

TRUE, FALSE, OR MAYBE?

Answer True, False, or Maybe (if the answer isn't in the story).

1. Louise spent her childhood in the South.
2. Brian has older brothers and sisters.
3. Louise and Brian are both students in college.
4. They both ski very well.
5. They haven't been to all the art museums in New York City.
6. They both like to be in large groups of people.
7. They both feel that people shouldn't eat vegetables.

LISTENING

Listen and choose what the people are talking about.

1. a. personality
   b. background
2. a. sports
   b. cultural interests
3. a. academic interests
   b. outlook on life
4. a. personality
   b. background
5. a. sports
   b. academic interests
6. a. cultural interests
   b. outlook on life

And She Hasn't Either

I'm not tired, { and he isn't either. / and neither is he. }	They don't sing, { and she doesn't either. / and neither does she. }
He won't be busy, { and she won't either. / and neither will she. }	She didn't study, { and I didn't either. / and neither did I. }
She hasn't been sick, { and he hasn't either. / and neither has he. }	

A. Why do you and your sister look so frightened?

B. I've never been on a roller coaster before, { **and she hasn't either.** / **and neither has she.** }

1. Why haven't you and your roommate hooked up your new DVD player?
   I don't understand the instructions, ____.

2. Why didn't you or your parents answer the telephone all weekend?
   I wasn't home, ____.

3. Why did you and your wife move to the center of the city?
   She didn't like living in the suburbs, ____.

4. What do you and Greg want to talk to me about?
   I won't be able to work overtime this weekend, ____.

5. Why do you and your husband want to enroll in my dance class?
I don't know how to dance, ____.

6. Why does the school nurse want to see us?
I haven't had an eye examination, ____.

7. Why didn't you or Mom wake us up on time this morning?
I didn't hear the alarm clock, ____.

8. Why did you and your husband leave the concert so early?
I couldn't stand the loud music, ____.

9. What are you and your sister arguing about?
She doesn't want to take the garbage out, ____.

10. Why don't you and your friends want to come to the game?
They aren't very interested in football, ____.

11. Why were you and your wife so nervous during the flight?
I had never flown before today, ____.

12. Why have you and your friends stopped shopping at my store?
I can't afford your prices, ____.

13. Why don't you and your sister want me to read "Little Red Riding Hood"?
I don't like fairy tales very much, ____.

14.

READING

LAID OFF

Jack and Betty Williams are going through some difficult times. They were both laid off from their jobs last month. As the days go by, they're becoming more and more concerned about their futures, since he hasn't been able to find another job yet, and neither has she.

The layoffs weren't a surprise to Jack and Betty. After all, Jack's company hadn't been doing very well for a long time, and neither had Betty's. However, Jack had never expected both of them to be laid off at the same time, and Betty hadn't either. Ever since they have been laid off, Jack and Betty have been trying to find new jobs. Unfortunately, she hasn't been very successful, and he hasn't either.

The main reason they're having trouble finding work is that there simply aren't many jobs available right now. He can't find anything in the want ads, and neither can she. She hasn't heard about any job openings, and he hasn't either. His friends haven't been able to help at all, and neither have hers.

Another reason they're having trouble finding work is that they don't seem to have the right kind of skills and training. He doesn't know anything about computers, and she doesn't either. She can't type very well, and neither can he. He hasn't had any special vocational training, and she hasn't either.

A third reason they're having trouble finding work is that there are certain jobs they prefer not to take. He doesn't like working at night, and neither does she. She isn't willing to work on the weekends, and neither is he. He doesn't want to commute very far to work, and she doesn't either.

Despite all their problems, Jack and Betty aren't completely discouraged. She doesn't have a very pessimistic outlook on life, and neither does he. They're both hopeful that things will get better soon.

READING *CHECK-UP*

TRUE, FALSE, OR MAYBE?

Answer True, False, or Maybe (if the answer isn't in the story).

1. Betty quit her job last month.
2. Jack and Betty had been working for the same company.
3. Some of their friends have been laid off, too.
4. Typing skills are important in certain jobs.
5. Jack and Betty will find jobs soon.

You're at a job interview. Role-play with another student, using the interviewer's questions below.

Tell me about your skills.
Tell me about your educational background.
Have you had any special vocational training?
Are you willing to work at night or on the weekend?
When can you start?

You Should Ask Them

I don't sing, **but** my sister does.	He can play chess, **but** I can't.
She didn't know the answer, **but** I did.	We're ready, **but** they aren't.

A. Can you baby-sit for us tomorrow night?

B. No, I can't, but my SISTER can. You should ask HER.

1. Have you heard the weather forecast?
my father

2. Do you have a hammer?
my upstairs neighbors

3. Are you interested in seeing a movie tonight?
Maria

4. Did you write down the homework assignment?
Jack

5. Have you by any chance found a brown-and-white dog?
the woman across the street

6. Were you paying attention when the salesman explained how to assemble this?
the children

How to Say It!

Offering a Suggestion

Practice the conversations in this lesson again. Offer suggestions in different ways.

READING

"TOUCHY SUBJECTS"

Larry and his parents always disagree when they talk about politics. Larry is very liberal, but his parents aren't. They're very conservative. Larry thinks the president is doing a very poor job, but his parents don't. They think the president is doing a fine job. Also, Larry doesn't think the government should spend a lot of money on defense, but his parents do. They think the country needs a strong army. You can see why Larry and his parents always disagree when they talk about politics. Politics is a very "touchy subject" with them.

The Greens and their next-door neighbors, the Harrisons, always disagree when they talk about child rearing. The Greens are very lenient with their children, but the Harrisons aren't. They're very strict. The Greens let their children watch television whenever they want, but the Harrisons don't. They let their children watch television for only an hour a day. Also, the Harrisons have always taught their children to sit quietly and behave well at the dinner table, but the Greens haven't. They have always allowed their children to do whatever they want at the dinner table. You can see why the Greens and the Harrisons always disagree when they talk about child rearing. Child rearing is a very "touchy subject" with them.

READING *CHECK-UP*

TRUE, FALSE, OR MAYBE?

Answer True, False, or Maybe (if the answer isn't in the story).

1. Larry and his parents never agree when they talk about politics.
2. Larry probably supports equal rights for women and minorities.
3. The Harrisons' children watch television more often than the Greens' children.
4. The Greens' children probably go to bed later than the Harrisons' children.
5. Since the Greens and the Harrisons disagree, they never talk about child rearing.

How About You?

Do you and someone you know always disagree about a "touchy subject"? Who is this person? What do you disagree about? In what ways do you disagree?

ON YOUR OWN *Same and Different*

In many ways, my sister and I are exactly the same.
I'm tall and thin, and she is, too.
I have brown eyes and curly black hair, and so does she.
I work in an office downtown, and she does, too.
I'm not married yet, and neither is she.
I went to college in Boston, and so did she.
I wasn't a very good student, and she wasn't either.

And in many ways, my sister and I are very different.
I like classical music, but she doesn't.
She enjoys sports, but I don't.
I've never traveled overseas, but she has.
She's never been to New York, but I have many times.
She's very outgoing and popular, but I'm not.
I'm very quiet and philosophical, but she isn't.

Yes, in many ways, my sister and I are exactly the same, and in many ways, we're very different. But most important of all, we like and respect each other. And we're friends.

Tell other students about somebody you are close to—a friend, a classmate, or someone in your family. Tell how you and this person are the same, and tell how you are different.

SIDE by SIDE JOURNAL

Write in your journal about somebody you are close to—a friend, a classmate, or someone in your family. Tell how you and this person are the same, and tell how you are different.

In many ways, __________ and I are exactly the same.

____

____

____

And in many ways, __________ and I are very different.

____

____

____

PRONUNCIATION Contrastive Stress

Listen. Then say it.

No, I can't, but my SISTER can.

No, I don't, but my NEIGHBORS do.

You should ask HER.

Why don't you ask THEM?

Say it. Then listen.

No, I haven't, but my FATHER has.

No, I wasn't, but my CHILDREN were.

You should ask HIM.

How about asking THEM?

GRAMMAR FOCUS

CONNECTORS:

TOO/SO

I'm hungry.	I am, too. / So am I.
I can swim.	I can, too. / So can I.
I've seen that movie.	I have, too. / So have I.
I have a car.	I do, too. / So do I.
I worked yesterday.	I did, too. / So did I.

EITHER/NEITHER

I'm not hungry.	I'm not either. / Neither am I.
I can't swim.	I can't either. / Neither can I.
I've haven't seen that movie.	I haven't either. / Neither have I.
I don't have a car.	I don't either. / Neither do I.
I didn't work.	I didn't either. / Neither did I.

BUT

I don't sing, **but** my sister does.

She didn't know the answer, **but** I did.

He can play chess, **but** I can't.

We're ready, **but** they aren't.

I'm tired,	and he is, too. / and so is he.
He'll be busy,	and she will, too. / and so will she.
She's been sick,	and he has, too. / and so has he.
They sing,	and she does, too. / and so does she.
She studied,	and I did, too. / and so did I.

I'm not tired,	and he isn't either. / and neither is he.
He won't be busy,	and she won't either. / and neither will she.
She hasn't been sick,	and he hasn't either. / and neither has he.
They don't sing,	and she doesn't either. / and neither does she.
She didn't study,	and I didn't either. / and neither did I.

Complete the sentences.

1. She just got a raise, and _____ _____ I.
2. He hasn't arrived yet, and _____ _____ they.
3. They can't lift it, and we _____ _____.
4. I have to work late, and you _____, _____.
5. She's leaving soon, and _____ _____ we.
6. He doesn't like to swim, and I _____ _____.
7. A. Are you interested in sports?
   B. No, _____ _____, but my sister _____.
8. I'm going to a meeting, and they _____, _____.
9. He hadn't been there before, and she _____ _____.
10. I won't be able to go, and _____ _____ you.
11. She types very well, and he _____, _____.
12. We've been very busy, and _____ _____ she.
13. You aren't allergic to anything, and _____ _____ I.
14. A. Do you have a ladder?
    B. No, I _____, but my neighbor _____.

1 CONVERSATION — REQUESTING HELP; SEQUENCES OF INSTRUCTIONS

Practice the conversation with a classmate.

How to make coffee:

- ☐ take out the old filter
- ☐ put in a new filter
- ☐ add the coffee
- ☐ press the ON button

A. Excuse me. Can you help me?
B. Sure. How can I help?
A. Can you show me how to make coffee?
B. Sure. I'll be happy to.
First, take out the old filter.
Then, put in a new filter.
After that, add the coffee.
And finally, press the ON button.
A. I see.
First, I take out the old filter.
Then, I put in a new filter.
After that, I add the coffee.
And finally, I press the ON button.
Is that right?
B. Yes. That's correct.
A. Thanks very much.

Look at the instructions. Practice conversations with your classmates.

1. 

How to make a copy:

- ☐ lift up the lid
- ☐ put the original document on the glass
- ☐ put down the lid
- ☐ press the START button

2. 

How to turn on the alarm system:

- ☐ close the door
- ☐ enter the code
- ☐ press ON
- ☐ leave the building within 20 seconds

A. Excuse me. Can you help me?
B. Sure. How can I help?
A. Can you show me ________?
B. Sure. I'll be happy to.
First, ________.
Then, ________.
After that, ________.
And finally, ________.
A. I see.
First, I ________.
Then, I ________.
After that, I ________.
And finally, I ________.
Is that right?
B. Yes. That's correct.
A. Thanks very much.

2 TEAMWORK — INSTRUCTIONS FOR OPERATING EQUIPMENT

Work with a classmate. Think of a procedure for operating equipment at work, at school, or at home. Write down the instructions. Then practice a conversation and present it to the class.

Read the article and answer the questions.

Getting a Promotion

You've worked in the same job at the same company for many years. Many of your co-workers have gotten promotions to better jobs with higher pay. When will it be *your* turn? What can you do to get the promotion you've been waiting for?

First, check your appearance. Do you look professional? Are the clothes you wear appropriate for work? Dress for success! Look at what the successful people in your company wear and copy them. Good grooming is also an important part of your appearance. Take care of your hair, skin, and fingernails, and make sure that your clothes are clean and ironed. You can't look professional if you aren't well groomed.

If you want to move ahead in your company, you have to get along well with your supervisor, your co-workers, and your company's customers. Smile and be friendly to everybody. Listen carefully to what they say. Ask for their opinions, and try to understand their point of view. We all see things differently. Learn to communicate clearly. When you think your co-workers have done something well, tell them. Everybody likes to receive a compliment. Offer to help others, and be sure to say thank you when someone helps you. If you make a mistake, say you're sorry. It's important to apologize.

Above all, have a positive attitude towards your work. Don't complain or gossip about other people. Work hard and enthusiastically. This will show your supervisor that you like your job and care about the company. Get to work early before your co-workers arrive. You can accomplish a lot when nobody is there to interrupt you. If you start to lose interest in your job because you've had the same responsibilities for a long time, you need to bring new energy to your work. Ask for more responsibilities. Volunteer to work on difficult projects that can teach you new skills. Be creative. Try to find new and more efficient ways to work that will save you time. *Think outside the box*. Look for new ways to solve problems. Employees who can solve problems creatively are valuable. Speak up at meetings. Your supervisor will begin to notice and appreciate you.

Think ahead and prepare for the next job you want. Find out what skills you'll need and do what you can to develop them. For example, if the job you want requires report writing, register for an evening class in business English and volunteer to work on projects that give you the opportunity to write. In addition, check to see what training programs your company offers. It's important to continue your education both on the job and on your own time outside of work. Most jobs these days require strong computer skills, so it's a good idea to take computer classes.

Your employer will use your job performance evaluation to decide if you deserve a raise or a promotion. This yearly evaluation is like a school report card. It compares you to other workers in your group. Workers with low grades can lose their jobs. On the other hand, if your evaluation shows that you have the right qualities, such as being *dependable* and *hardworking*, you can move ahead. When you meet with your supervisor to discuss your evaluation, have a positive attitude. This is your opportunity to find out what you've done well and what you can do better. Make sure you understand the evaluation. Listen carefully and ask questions so you can learn from the feedback you receive about your performance. If you don't agree with your supervisor, politely explain your point of view. Make sure your supervisor knows about everything you have accomplished during the year. And if your evaluation is good, this is an excellent time to talk about your future at the company and a promotion.

TEST YOURSELF! *Do You Deserve a Promotion?*

Give yourself one point for every Yes answer. If you have a score of 14 or higher, you probably deserve a promotion!

	Yes	No
1. Do you dress appropriately?		
2. Are you well groomed?		
3. Do you get along with your co-workers?		
4. Do you get along with customers?		
5. Are you friendly?		
6. Do you communicate clearly?		
7. Are you helpful?		
8. Do you have a positive attitude?		
9. Do you work hard?		
10. Do you get to work early?		
11. Do you ask for more responsibilities?		
12. Do you find new ways to solve problems?		
13. Do you speak up at meetings?		
14. Do you take classes to learn new skills?		
15. Are you dependable and hardworking?		
16. Do you learn from the feedback you receive?		

1. To be *well groomed* means ____.

A. to dress for success
B. to wear the right clothes
C. to be clean and neat
D. to be successful

2. When you *apologize* to someone, ____.

A. you give the person a compliment
B. you say you're sorry
C. you say thank you
D. you smile

3. When you work *enthusiastically*, people will see that ____.

A. you like your job
B. you look professional
C. you are creative
D. you communicate clearly

4. When you *think outside the box*, ____.

A. you work outside
B. you find new ways to solve problems
C. you have the same responsibilities for a long time
D. you copy successful people

5. When someone is *efficient*, he or she ____.

A. works slowly
B. works extra hours
C. uses time well at work
D. makes a lot of mistakes

6. If you want a promotion, you should NOT ____.

A. volunteer for difficult projects
B. get to work before your co-workers
C. discuss your evaluation with your boss
D. complain about your job

7. The main idea of paragraph 5 is ____.

A. it's important to learn new skills
B. it's important to volunteer
C. companies offer training programs
D. it's important to take classes after work

8. If your job performance evaluation is poor, ____.

A. don't show it to your supervisor
B. complain to your co-workers
C. ask for a promotion
D. learn from the feedback

WESTVILLE VALLEY ADULT EDUCATION COURSES—FALL TERM

BUSINESS

BUS 101 Business Procedures—M, W, F
Become familiar with the procedures in a business office. Topics include filing, telephone skills, receiving and sending mail, organizing meetings and conferences, scheduling appointments, making travel reservations, and time management.

BUS 103 Customer Service—Tu, Th
In this course students will discuss and analyze common customer complaints and develop ways to deliver better customer service.

BUS 105 Business Writing—M, W
In the business world, time is money. Learn to write clear and concise business letters, memos, and reports.

BUS 106 Public Speaking—W, F
This course helps students develop the ability to speak confidently in a variety of public speaking situations. Participants will prepare and present a speech each week.

BUS 201 Bookkeeping—M, Tu, W, Th, F
This course prepares students for the national Certified Bookkeeper examination. Topics include payroll (paying wages, reporting taxes) and inventory.

BUS 205 Entrepreneurship—W, F
Learn how to start and operate your own business. Each student will develop a business plan.

COMPUTERS

COM 101 Microsoft Word I—Tu, Th
Students will learn to create documents with today's most popular word processing software.

COM 102 Microsoft Outlook—F
Learn to use Microsoft Outlook to send, receive, and organize electronic mail.

COM 103 Introduction to the Internet—M, F
Learn how to search the World Wide Web to find information online. Students will get hands-on experience when they research a topic that interests them.

COM 106 Excel Spreadsheets—Tu, Th
You don't have to be good with numbers to balance a checkbook or calculate how you spend your money each month. Learn how to enter the information and let Excel software do the math for you. This course covers the basics of spreadsheets. Students will learn how to create worksheets and charts.

COM 201 Microsoft Word II—W, Th, F
Use the advanced features of Word to create documents with charts. Students will also learn to create newsletters and flyers.

COM 203 PowerPoint Presentations—M, F
Learn to create professional-looking presentations that include graphs, charts, and pictures using PowerPoint. Prerequisite: Students must have keyboarding skills to take this course.

CULINARY ARTS

CA 100 Food Preparation—M, Tu, W, Th, F
This course introduces students to the culinary arts profession and prepares them for an entry-level position as a Food and Beverage Specialist in a hotel, hospital, or restaurant kitchen. Participants will learn kitchen procedures and how to follow basic recipes.

CA 104 Food Sanitation—W, F
Learn how to prepare food safely. This course teaches health regulations and procedures and the reasons for them.

HEALTH SCIENCE

HS 101 CPR (Cardiopulmonary Resuscitation)—M
This course covers emergency procedures to follow when someone has stopped breathing or the heart has stopped beating. Red Cross certification.

HS 102 Basic Emergency Care—Tu, W
Learn how to prevent accidents and give first aid. Students learn to recognize and respond to emergencies including shock, breathing emergencies, poison, cuts, and burns.

Look at the adult education course catalog and answer the questions.

1. The ____ course helps students learn how to start a business.
   A. Business Procedures
   B. Bookkeeping
   C. Entrepreneurship
   D. Business Writing

2. Business Procedures prepares students for a job as a ____.
   A. manager
   B. bookkeeper
   C. programmer
   D. secretary

3. Students learn research skills in course number ____.
   A. COM 102
   B. COM 103
   C. COM 106
   D. COM 203

4. In Business Writing, students do NOT learn to write ____.
   A. reports
   B. letters
   C. resumes
   D. memos

5. We can infer that a concise business letter ____.
   A. is short
   B. has many long words
   C. is hard to understand
   D. is long

6. Students have to be able to type on a computer before they can take ____.
   A. Microsoft Word I
   B. Microsoft Outlook
   C. Introduction to the Internet
   D. PowerPoint Presentations

7. After students complete ____, they will be ready to take a national exam.
   A. HS 102
   B. BUS 201
   C. CA 100
   D. CA 104

8. Microsoft Outlook is software for ____.
   A. word-processing
   B. spreadsheets
   C. e-mail
   D. presentations

9. Culinary Arts 100 does NOT prepare students for a job in ____.
   A. a hospital
   B. an office
   C. a restaurant
   D. a hotel

10. Students learn how to take care of bad burns when they take ____.
   A. CA 104
   B. CA 100
   C. HS 101
   D. HS 102

YOUR EDUCATION PLAN

What classes do you plan to take in the future? When and where will you take these classes? Fill in the chart.

MY EDUCATION PLAN		
WHAT I PLAN TO STUDY	WHEN	WHERE

CLASS DISCUSSION Where in your community can you learn about different careers? Where can you go for help with career planning? Where can you take courses to learn new skills? Discuss as a class.

ASSESSMENT

• Check-up test • Self-evaluation checklists

Choose the correct answer.

1. This table is very expensive. I don't think we can ____ it.
A. allow
B. afford
C. spend
D. support

2. Marco plays soccer very well. He's very ____.
A. athletic
B. available
C. compatible
D. lenient

3. I'm very ____ about the environment.
A. opposed
B. allergic
C. concerned
D. similar

4. My sister likes science, and so do I. We have the same academic ____.
A. instructions
B. decisions
C. collections
D. interests

5. It's important to ____ when the teacher is talking.
A. explain
B. respect
C. pay attention
D. express

6. You and I have very similar ____ on life.
A. outlooks
B. personalities
C. backgrounds
D. reasons

7. I always try to have a positive ____ towards my work.
A. appearance
B. attitude
C. quality
D. grooming

8. Be creative. Try to look for new ways to ____ problems.
A. accomplish
B. volunteer
C. develop
D. solve

9. In this course, you will become familiar with common ____ in a business office.
A. inventory
B. procedures
C. information
D. service

10. I'm learning to use PowerPoint to ____ professional-looking graphs and charts.
A. prevent
B. search
C. create
D. balance

SKILLS CHECK

Words:

- ☐ appropriate
- ☐ creative
- ☐ dependable
- ☐ efficient
- ☐ hardworking
- ☐ professional
- ☐ valuable
- ☐ well groomed

- ☐ appearance
- ☐ attitude
- ☐ co-worker
- ☐ energy
- ☐ feedback
- ☐ grooming

- ☐ job performance evaluation
- ☐ opportunity
- ☐ performance
- ☐ point of view
- ☐ positive attitude
- ☐ project
- ☐ promotion
- ☐ qualities
- ☐ responsibility
- ☐ training program

- ☐ accomplish
- ☐ apologize
- ☐ appreciate

- ☐ care about
- ☐ communicate
- ☐ compare
- ☐ develop
- ☐ *dress for success*
- ☐ find out
- ☐ move ahead
- ☐ register
- ☐ solve problems
- ☐ speak up
- ☐ think ahead
- ☐ *think outside the box*
- ☐ volunteer

I can say:

- ☐ I'm a *vegetarian*.
  I am, too./So am I.
- ☐ I'm not *a good dancer*.
  I'm not either./
  Neither am I.
- ☐ I don't *have a dog*,
  but *my neighbor* does.

- ☐ Can you show me *how to make coffee*?
  First, ______.
  Then, ______.
  After that, ______.
  And finally, ______.

I can offer a suggestion:

- ☐ You should *ask* HER.
- ☐ Why don't you *ask* HER?
- ☐ How about *asking* HER?

I can:

- ☐ request help at work
- ☐ give & follow a sequence of instructions
- ☐ identify important factors for career advancement
- ☐ interpret an adult education course catalog
- ☐ complete an education plan

I can write about:

- ☐ somebody I am close to

Feature Article
Fact File
Around the World
Interview
We've Got Mail!

SIDE by SIDE Gazette

Global Exchange
Listening
Fun with Idioms
What Are They Saying?

Volume 3 Number 4

From Matchmakers to Dating Services

Traditions, customs, modern life, and the ways people meet

Marriage traditions and customs are very different around the world. In many cultures, young people meet at school, at work, or in other places; they decide to go out together; they fall in love; and they get married. In other cultures, parents or other family members arrange a match between two young people.

In India, for example, a father traditionally finds his daughter a husband. The father might ask friends or relatives to recommend a possible husband, and he might put an ad in the newspaper. The father looks for someone with a good education, occupation, and salary. When he finds a possible match, he sends his daughter's horoscope to the boy's family. An astrologer reads the horoscope and decides if there is a good astrological match between the young man and woman. If the astrologer approves, the families then discuss the marriage arrangements.

In many cultures around the world, families use a matchmaker to bring young people together and arrange marriages. This is especially common in rural areas of many countries. Families pay the matchmaker to find a partner for their child. Sometimes, the matchmaker also helps families with the "business" part of a marriage agreement. For example, a family may give or receive animals, products, or other valuable things as part of the marriage arrangement. In some cultures, parents even arrange marriages between children before they are born.

An astrologer approved the marriage of these newlyweds from India. The astrologer examined their horoscopes to decide if the date and time of their births were a good match.

These traditions and customs are changing in many places, especially in the modern cities of the world. Young people want the freedom to choose their own partners. Many, however, actually use modern-day versions of the traditional matchmaking services! For example, some people put personal ads in newspapers or magazines. In these ads, people describe themselves and tell what kind of person they're looking for. Others use dating services—companies that bring people together. Most dating services ask people to submit a photograph and fill out a long questionnaire about their background and interests. Some dating services even make videos of their customers. People who use a dating service can usually browse through the company's information to find a possible partner.

FACT FILE

When People Get Married

People around the world get married at different ages. At what age do men and women usually get married in different countries you know?

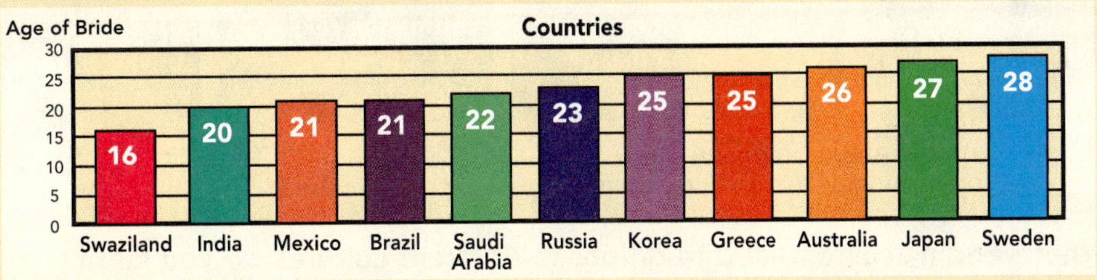

AROUND THE WORLD

Wedding Customs and Traditions

a wedding ceremony in the United States

a Hindu ceremony

a wedding in the Slovak Republic

a ceremony in a Korean village

Wedding customs and traditions are very different around the world. In many cultures, weddings happen in churches or other places of worship. In other cultures, people get married outdoors, in their homes, in special reception halls for family celebrations, or in other places. The bride and the groom usually wear clothing that is traditional for weddings in their culture. The type of clothing and the colors are very different around the world. Brides often wear a veil or a crown on their heads. Some weddings are private—just for family members and friends. Other weddings are public. Everybody in the neighborhood or the entire town might attend the celebration. Some weddings are short, and other weddings can last for hours, days, or even a week!

a traditional Romanian dance

musicians leading a wedding procession

Music and dancing are an important part of wedding celebrations in different cultures. There are often special dances for the bride and groom, their parents, and other family members. Musicians might play special wedding music during the ceremony, at the celebration after the ceremony, or even in the street!

confetti

flower petals

rice

In some cultures, people like to throw things at weddings! Before or after the ceremony, it is often traditional for guests to shower the bride and groom with something to wish them good luck.

Guests have pinned money on this bride and groom in Cyprus.

a wedding couple in Colombia lighting candles during the ceremony

cutting the cake at a U.S. wedding celebration

a Japanese bride arriving at her wedding by boat

a bride in the U.S. throwing a bouquet of flowers (According to tradition, the person who catches it will get married next.)

Many cultures around the world have special wedding customs. These traditions often involve candles, flowers, special foods, money, and the ways that couples get to their wedding ceremonies.

What wedding customs and traditions in different cultures do you know?

Interview

A Side by Side Gazette reporter spoke with several young couples.

Q: "How did you meet?"

A: We met in college.

A: We met at work.

A: We met at a bookstore.

A: We were high school "sweethearts."

A: We met on a "blind date" that our friends arranged.

A: We met through a dating service.

A: Our parents arranged our marriage through a matchmaker.

FUN with IDIOMS

Do You Know These Expressions?

_____ 1. He's nuts about me.

_____ 2. She gave me the cold shoulder.

_____ 3. I fell for him the moment I met him.

_____ 4. We had planned to go on a date, but she stood me up.

a. I liked him right away.

b. He likes me a lot.

c. She didn't meet me.

d. She didn't pay attention to me.

We've Got Mail!

Dear Side by Side,

I'm trying to figure out two-word verbs. Is there a rule that will tell me which two-word verbs are separable and which are inseparable? I hope to hear you from soon.

Sincerely,
"Looking for an Answer"

Dear "Looking for an Answer,"

We're sorry to tell you that there isn't a rule for this. You need to learn about each verb separately. Here's a suggestion. On a piece of paper, make two lists. Write down separable two-word verbs in one list and inseparable two-word verbs in the other. Then look up the words on your lists when you can't remember them.

By the way, we've circled some words in the last sentence of your letter because "hear from" is an inseparable two-word verb. The correct way to say this is "I hope to hear from you soon." Thanks for writing, and good luck with two-word verbs!

Sincerely,
Side by Side

Dear Side by Side,

I think two-word verbs are very difficult. The verb in a two-word verb has one meaning, but the whole two-word verb often has a different meaning. For example, "I turned on the light," but "I turned down the invitation"; "I take out the garbage," but "I take after my father." In my language, we have different words for all these expressions. Why does English use the same words over and over again?

Sincerely,
"Turned Off by Two-Word Verbs"

Dear "Turned Off,"

We're sorry to hear you're unhappy. Two-word verbs are very common in everyday English. We actually have special words for many of these meanings, but these words are more formal. For example, you can say, "I declined the invitation" and "I resemble my father." Most English speakers, however, prefer to use informal language, so they use lots of two-word verbs. With time, we're sure you'll get over this problem with two-word verbs. Thanks for your question.

Sincerely,
Side by Side

Global Exchange

PedroJ: Let me tell you about my best friend. His name is Marco. People think we're brothers because we look alike. He's short and thin, and so am I. I have curly brown hair, and he does, too. We also have similar backgrounds. He's originally from Peru, and I am, too. He moved to this country when he was a little boy, and so did I. His parents work in factories, and so do mine. Marco and I have very different interests. He enjoys playing sports, but I don't. I play a musical instrument, but he doesn't. I've been in several plays in school, but he hasn't. How about you? Tell me about your best friend.

Tell a keypal about your best friend.

LISTENING

"Telephone Tag" True or False?

____ 1 Mary likes jazz, and Jim does, too.

____ 2 Mary likes to play tennis, and so does Jim.

____ 3 Jim wants to go to the ballet, but Mary doesn't.

____ 4 Jim hasn't seen the movie, and neither has Mary.

____ 5 Jim doesn't like Italian food, but Mary does.

What Are They Saying?

Listening Scripts

Unit 1 – Page 6

Listen and choose the correct answer.

1. What are you doing?
2. Do you watch the news very often?
3. Are you a good swimmer?
4. What's Cathy reading?
5. Who cooks in your family?
6. Do they like to skate?
7. Does your sister want to be a ballet dancer?
8. Do you and your friends play basketball very often?
9. Are your parents good dancers?
10. What does Peter want to be when he grows up?

Unit 2 – Page 17

Listen and choose the correct answer.

1. Did you do well at your job interview yesterday?
2. Were your children tired last night?
3. What was he doing when he broke his leg?
4. Did you finish your dinner last night?
5. How did your husband lose his wallet?
6. What was your supervisor doing?
7. Did you do well on the exam?
8. What happened while you were preparing lunch?

Unit 3 – Page 24

Listen to the conversation and choose the answer that is true.

1. A. Are you going to wear your brown suit today?
   B. No, I don't think so. I wore my brown suit yesterday. I'm going to wear my gray suit.
2. A. Let's make beef stew for dinner!
   B. But we had that last week. Let's make spaghetti and meatballs instead.
   A. Okay.
3. A. Do you want to watch the game show on Channel 5 or the news program on Channel 9?
   B. Let's watch the news program.
4. A. What's the matter with it?
   B. The brakes don't work, and it doesn't start very well in the morning.
5. A. What are you going to do tomorrow?
   B. I'm going to plant carrots, tomatoes, and lettuce.
6. A. This computer is very powerful, but it's too expensive.
   B. You're right.

Side by Side Gazette – Page 35

Listen to the messages on Dave's machine. Match the messages.

You have five messages.

Message Number One: "Hi, Dave. It's Sarah. Thanks for the invitation, but I can't come to your party tomorrow. I'll be taking my uncle to the hospital. Maybe next time." *[beep]*

Message Number Two: "Hello, Dave. It's Bob. I'm sorry that my wife and I won't be able to come to your party tomorrow. We'll be attending a wedding out of town. I hope it's a great party. Have fun!" *[beep]*

Message Number Three: "Dave? It's Paula. How's it going? I got your message about the party tomorrow. Unfortunately, I won't be able to go. I'll be studying all weekend. Talk to you soon." *[beep]*

Message Number Four: "Hi, Dave. It's Joe. Thanks for the invitation to your party. I'll be visiting my parents in New York City, so I'm afraid I won't be around. I'll call you when I get back." *[beep]*

Message Number Five: "Hello, Dave? It's Carla. Thanks for the invitation to your party. I don't have anything to do tomorrow night, so I'll definitely be there. I'm really looking forward to it. See you tomorrow." *[beep]*

Unit 4 – Page 49

1. *Linda is on vacation in San Francisco. This is her list of things to do. Check the things on the list Linda has already done.*

   Linda has already seen the Golden Gate Bridge. She hasn't visited Golden Gate Park yet. She took a tour of Alcatraz Prison yesterday. She's going to go to Chinatown tomorrow. She hasn't ridden a cable car yet. She's eaten at Fisherman's Wharf, but she hasn't had time to buy souvenirs.

2. *Alan is a secretary in a very busy office. This is his list of things to do before 5 P.M. on Friday. Check the things on the list Alan has already done.*

   Alan has already called Mrs. Porter. He has to type the letter to the Mervis Company. He hasn't taken the mail to the post office yet. He's gone to the bank. He hasn't sent an e-mail to the company's office in Denver, and he's going to speak to the boss about his salary next week.

3. *It's Saturday, and Judy and Paul Johnson are doing lots of things around the house. This is the list of things they have to do today. Check the things on the list they've already done.*

   Judy and Paul haven't done the laundry. They have to wash the kitchen windows. They've paid the bills. They haven't given the dog a bath. They'll clean the garage later. They couldn't fix the bathroom sink or repair the fence, but they vacuumed the living room rug.

Unit 5 – Page 60

Listen to the conversation and choose the answer that is true.

1. A. How long have you had a backache?
   B. For three days.
2. A. Has your father always been an engineer?
   B. No, he hasn't.
3. A. How long has your knee been swollen?
   B. For a week.
4. A. How long have you known how to ski?
   B. Since I was a teenager.
5. A. Did you live in Tokyo for a long time?
   B. Yes. Five years.
6. A. How long has Roger been interested in Egyptian history?
   B. Since he lived in Cairo.
7. A. Is Amy still in the hospital?
   B. Oh. I forgot to tell you. She's been home for two days.
8. A. Have you played hockey for a long time?
   B. Yes. I've played hockey since I moved to Toronto three years ago.

Side by Side Gazette – Page 67

Listen to the voice-mail messages between Gloria Rivera and her office assistant, Sam. Has Sam done the things on Ms. Rivera's list? Check Yes or No.

You have one message. Tuesday, 8:15 A.M.

Hello, Sam? This is Ms. Rivera. I'll be out of the office all day today. I'm not feeling well. Here's a list of things you'll need to do while I'm not here. First, please write a note to Mrs. Wilson and tell her I'm sick. Then, please call Mr. Chen and change the time of our appointment. Also, send an e-mail to everybody in the office, and tell them about next week's meeting. Don't forget to speak to the custodian about my broken desk lamp. I hope he can fix it. Hmm. Let's see. I know there are a few more things. Oh, yes. Please make a list of all the employees and give it to Ms. Baxter. She asked me for the list last week. Okay, Sam. I think that's everything. Oh . . . one more thing. Please take the package on my desk to the post office if you have time. And that's it. Thanks, Sam. I'll see you tomorrow morning.

You have reached the voice mailbox of Gloria Rivera. Please leave a message after the tone.

Ms. Rivera? This is Sam. I'm sorry you aren't feeling well. I hope you feel better tomorrow. I'm calling to tell you what I've done today, and what I haven't done yet. It's been very busy here, so I haven't had time to do everything. I wrote a note to Mrs. Wilson. I called Mr. Chen and changed the time of your appointment. I also sent the e-mail about next week's meeting. I haven't spoken to the custodian. He's been sick all week. I made a list of all the employees, but I haven't given it to Ms. Baxter yet. I'll give it to her early tomorrow morning. Finally, I haven't taken the package to the post office yet. I haven't had time. I'm going to take it to the post office on my way home. Again, I hope you're feeling better. I'll see you in the morning.

Unit 6 – Page 79

Which Word Do You Hear?

Listen and choose the correct answer.

1. He's gone to the bank.
2. I've never written so many letters in one day before.
3. She's been seeing patients all day.
4. What courses have you taken this year?
5. Is Beverly giving blood?
6. Ben has driven all night.

Who Is Speaking?

Listen and decide who is speaking.

1. What a day! All the tenants have been complaining that nothing is working.
2. I'm very tired. I've given six lessons today.
3. Thank you! You've been a wonderful audience!
4. I'm really tired. I've been watching them all day.
5. I'm very tired. I've been looking at paychecks since early this morning.
6. It's been a long day. I've been selling tickets since ten A.M.

Unit 7 – Page 93

Listen and choose the correct answer.

1. **A.** I avoid going to the mall whenever I can.
   B. Me, too.
2. **A.** I've decided to sell my car.
   B. Your beautiful car?
3. **A.** Please try to quit biting your nails.
   B. Okay. Mom.
4. **A.** Do you enjoy traveling by plane?
   B. Very much.
5. **A.** We're thinking about moving to Florida.
   B. Oh. That's interesting.
6. **A.** I've been considering getting married for a long time.
   B. Oh, really? I didn't know that.
7. **A.** Don't stop practicing.
   B. Okay.
8. **A.** Interrupting people is a habit I just can't break.
   B. That's too bad.

Unit 8 – Page 103

Listen and choose the correct answer.

1. Did your parents enjoy eating at Joe's Restaurant last night?
2. Why don't you want to see the new James Bond movie with us next weekend?
3. Did you get to the play on time last night?
4. Michael, please go upstairs and do your homework.
5. Why did Carmen do so well on the history test?
6. We really enjoyed our vacation at the Ritz Hotel.

Side by Side Gazette – Page 113

Listen to the Olympic Game highlights. Match the highlight and the sport.

And now, sports fans, let's finish today's program with highlights of the Olympic Games. Here are five of my favorite moments in the most recent summer and winter games:

There are three seconds left in the game. Number 38 gets ready to shoot again. His team needs this point to win the game. He shoots, and it's in the basket! [*Buzzer*] That's it! The game is over! And the United States wins 99 to 98. The U.S. gets the gold medal!

Kirshner is still in front. But wait! Look at Tanaka in the next lane! What speed! Look at him move through the water! Tanaka is even with Kirshner. Now Tanaka is ahead! And Tanaka wins the event! Japan wins the gold medal, Germany gets the silver, and Hungary gets the bronze.

Natasha knows she must do this floor routine perfectly to win the gold medal. She had problems today when she fell off the balance beam, and that's usually her best event. She's doing very well. What a strong and graceful athlete! And here's the most difficult part of her routine. Beautiful! But, oh . . . she falls! Natasha has fallen at the very end of her routine. What a shame! There will be no gold for Natasha this year.

What a race! Anderson is still in first place and Sanchez is right behind him in second place. Look at Sanchez run! He's moving ahead of Anderson. The lead has changed! Sanchez is now in front! He crosses the finish line! Sanchez wins with a time of two hours, ten minutes, and eleven seconds. So Mexico wins the gold, Canada gets the silver, and France gets the bronze.

And Tamara leaves the ice after a beautiful long program! I think that's one of the best programs I've ever seen at the Olympics. She moved so gracefully to the music. Let's see what the judges think. Look at these marks! Five-point-eight, five-point-nine, five-point-nine, five-point-eight, five-point-seven, five-point-nine, five-point-nine, six-point-oh, five-point-eight. Excellent scores! Tamara wins the gold medal! Look at all the flowers people are throwing on the ice! I'm sure this is the happiest day of Tamara's life!

Unit 9 – Page 129

Listen and choose what the people are talking about.

1. A. Where can I try them on?
   B. The dressing room is over there.
2. A. Now remember, you can't bring them back!
   B. I understand.
3. A. Have you filled it out yet?
   B. No. I'm having some trouble. Can you help me?
4. A. Please drop them off at the school by eight o'clock.
   B. By eight o'clock? Okay.
5. A. Where should I hang them?
   B. What about over the fireplace?
6. A. Have you thought it over?
   B. Yes, I have.
7. A. It's cold in here.
   B. You're right. I'll turn it on.
8. A. Should we use it up?
   B. No. Let's throw it out.
9. A. What are you going to do?
   B. I'm going to turn it down.

Unit 10 – Page 137

Listen and choose what the people are talking about.

1. A. To tell the truth, I'm a little shy.
   B. What a coincidence! I am, too.
2. A. I enjoy going to plays and concerts.
   B. We're very compatible. So do I.
3. A. I'm enjoying this course.
   B. I am, too.
4. A. I'm from Minnesota.
   B. That's interesting. So am I.
5. A. I go swimming three times a week.
   B. What a coincidence! I do, too.
6. A. I'm opposed to using animals in scientific experiments.
   B. I am, too.

Side by Side Gazette – Page 148

Listen to the messages on Mary and Jim's answering machines. Answer true or false.

[Monday, 6:15 P.M.]

Hi, Mary. It's Jim. Are you by any chance interested in going to a jazz concert this Friday night? Please call me and let me know. Talk to you later.

[Monday, 9:13 P.M.]

Hi, Jim. It's Mary. I'm returning your call. Thanks for the invitation. I know you like jazz, and I do, too. And I'd really like to go to the concert with you, but I have to work this Friday night. Do you want to play tennis on Saturday afternoon? Let me know. 'Bye.

[Tuesday, 3:40 P.M.]

Hi, Mary. It's Jim. I'm sorry I missed your call last night. I was at the laundromat, and I got home very late. I'm free on Saturday, but unfortunately, I really don't like to play tennis. Actually, I'm a very bad tennis player. Do you want to go to the ballet with me on Saturday night? Let me know, and I'll order tickets. Talk to you soon.

[Wednesday, 5:50 P.M.]

Hi, Jim. It's Mary. I got your message. Believe it or not, I've already gone to the ballet this week. I went with my sister last night. I have an idea! Let's see the new Steven Steelberg movie. I hear that it's great. Call and let me know.

[Thursday, 6:30 P.M.]

Hi, Mary. It's Jim. Sorry I missed your call again. I guess we're playing "telephone tag!" The movie sounds great. I haven't seen it yet. Do you want to have dinner before the movie? There's a wonderful new Italian restaurant downtown. Let me know. 'Bye.

[Friday, 5:17 P.M.]

Hi, Jim. Guess who! You won't believe it! I just found out that I have to work this Saturday night. It's a shame because I really wanted to see that movie. I'm not busy on Sunday. Are you free on Sunday afternoon? Let me know. By the way, I don't really like Italian food very much. There's a very good Greek restaurant in my neighborhood. Maybe we can have dinner there after the movie. What do you think? Talk to you later.

Vocabulary List

Numbers indicate the pages on which the words first appear.

Actions and Activities

Irregular Verbs

be	was/were	been
become	became	become
begin	began	begun
bite	bit	bitten
blow	blew	blown
break	broke	broken
bring	brought	brought
build	built	built
buy	bought	bought
catch	caught	caught
choose	chose	chosen
come	came	come
cost	cost	cost
cut	cut	cut
do	did	done
draw	drew	drawn
drink	drank	drunk
drive	drove	driven
eat	ate	eaten
fall	fell	fallen
feed	fed	fed
feel	felt	felt
fight	fought	fought
find	found	found
fit	fit	fit
fly	flew	flown
forget	forgot	forgotten
forgive	forgave	forgiven
freeze	froze	frozen
get	got	gotten
give	gave	given
go	went	gone
grow	grew	grown
hang	hung	hung
have	had	had
hear	heard	heard
hide	hid	hidden
hit	hit	hit
hold	held	held
hurt	hurt	hurt
keep	kept	kept
know	knew	known
lead	led	led
leave	left	left
lend	lent	lent
let	let	let
light	lit	lit
lose	lost	lost
make	made	made
mean	meant	meant
meet	met	met
put	put	put
quit	quit	quit
read	read	read
ride	rode	ridden
ring	rang	rung
run	ran	run
say	said	said
see	saw	seen
sell	sold	sold
send	sent	sent
set	set	set
sew	sewed	sewed/sewn
shake	shook	shaken
shrink	shrank	shrunk
sing	sang	sung
sit	sat	sat
sleep	slept	slept
speak	spoke	spoken
spend	spent	spent
stand	stood	stood
steal	stole	stolen
sweep	swept	swept
swim	swam	swum
take	took	taken
teach	taught	taught
tell	told	told
think	thought	thought
throw	threw	thrown
understand	understood	understood
wake	woke	woken
wear	wore	worn
win	won	won
wind	wound	wound
write	wrote	written

Skill Index

Grammar Index

Topic Index

PACIFIC
MOUNTAIN
CENTRAL
EASTERN
PACIFIC OCEAN
ATLANTIC OCEAN
Gulf of Mexico
Hawaii
Honolulu
Alaska
Juneau
Washington
Olympia
Oregon
Salem
California
Sacramento
Nevada
Carson City
Idaho
Boise
Montana
Helena
Wyoming
Cheyenne
Utah
Salt Lake City
Arizona
Phoenix
Colorado
Denver
New Mexico
Santa Fe
North Dakota
Bismarck
South Dakota
Pierre
Nebraska
Lincoln
Kansas
Topeka
Oklahoma
Oklahoma City
Texas
Austin
Minnesota
St. Paul
Iowa
Des Moines
Missouri
Jefferson City
Arkansas
Little Rock
Louisiana
Baton Rouge
Wisconsin
Madison
Illinois
Springfield
Michigan
Lansing
Indiana
Indianapolis
Ohio
Columbus
Kentucky
Frankfort
Tennessee
Nashville
Mississippi
Jackson
Alabama
Montgomery
Georgia
Atlanta
Florida
Tallahassee
South Carolina
Columbia
North Carolina
Raleigh
Virginia
Richmond
West Virginia
Charleston
WASHINGTON DC
Maryland
Annapolis
Delaware
Dover
Pennsylvania
Harrisburg
New Jersey
Trenton
New York
Albany
Connecticut
Hartford
Rhode Island
Providence
Massachusetts
Boston
Vermont
Montpelier
New Hampshire
Concord
Maine
Augusta
500 KM
500 Miles
100 Miles
100 Km
N
S
E
W